# Action Research:
# An Educational Leader's
# Guide to School Improvement

# Action Research:
# An Educational Leader's
# Guide to School Improvement

by Jeffrey Glanz
Kean University

Christopher-Gordon Publishers, Inc.
Norwood, Massachusetts

# Credits

Every effort has been made to contact copyright holders for permission to reproduce borrowed material where necessary. We apologize for any oversights and would be happy to rectify them in future printings.

Excerpt from *School Administrator's Public Speaking Portfolio* by Susan Mamchak and Steven Mamchak. Copyright © 1983. Reprinted with permission of the Center for Applied Research in Education/Prentice-Hall.

Excerpt from *Tracking Your School's Success, A Guide to Sensible Evaluation*, "Hints for Creating Useful Reports," reprinted with permission of Corwin Press, Sage Publications.

Olivero, J. (1982). "Principals and Their Inservice Needs." *Educational Leadership 43*, (5):343–344. Reprinted with permission of the Association for Supervision and Curriculum Development. Copyright © 1982 by ASCD. All rights reserved.

Excerpt from page 162 of Crowl. *Fundamentals of Educational Research*, 2nd Edition used with permission of the McGraw-Hill Companies.

Christopher-Gordon Publishers, Inc.
1502 Providence Highway, Suite 12
Norwood, MA 02062
(781) 762-5577
(800) 934-8322

Printed in the United States of America

10 9 8 7 6 5 4 3 2                          03 02 01 00 99

Library of Congress Catalog Card Number: 97-78323
ISBN: 0-926842-75-7

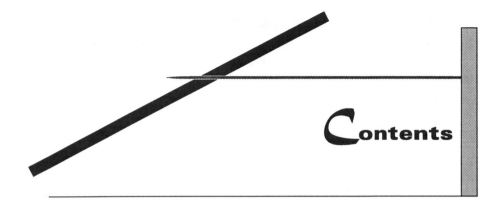

# Contents

## Chapter 1

### An Introduction to Action Research: It's Not All That Complicated .. 1

## Chapter 2

**Teaching and Doing Action Research Through General Semantics . 35**

## Chapter 3

**Cut to the Chase: Getting Started by Choosing Sound Quantitative and Qualitative Research Approaches, Methods, and Designs . 49**

# List of Figures

# List of Tables

---
# List of Illustrations
---

---
# List of Worksheets
---

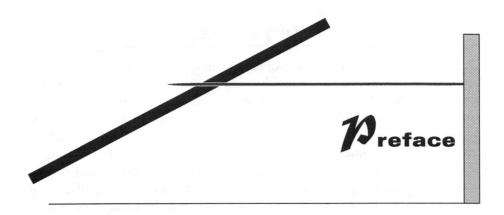

# Preface

*"The reason everyone goes into education is to have a powerful influence on the educational lives of students. Action research helps reinforce and cement the belief that together (teachers and administrators) can make a difference."*

*(Glickman, 1995)*

## Brief Description

This book is intended as a practical guide to conducting action research in schools. Although it offers neither a cookbook nor a quick-fix approach, this book does outline the process of designing and reporting an action research project. Useful as a classroom text and self-teaching tool, *Action Research: An Educational Leader's Guide to School Improvement* is a comprehensive training manual. It can be used by practitioners in the field, by graduate students enrolled in leadership and/or master's thesis courses, or by anyone interested in learning how to conduct action research projects.

The underlying assumption of this work is that research is not a domain that belongs only to academics, but is a powerful approach that can be used by practitioners to contribute to school renewal and instructional improvement. Rather than being merely a philosophical treatise or theoretical analysis, *Action Research* provides you with concrete strategies and techniques for conducting action research in schools.

# Uniqueness

*Action Research* differs dramatically from other works on the subject. In this book, action research is more broadly conceived than it is in previous works on the subject. Many works on the subject describe the process simply as one in which a problem is identified by the practitioner, some questions are framed, data are collected from some sources, conclusions are drawn, and some action is then taken. Although the basic steps in action research are included, this latter approach to action research simplifies the process to the point that it renders the project insignificant or as capable of making only minimal contributions at best. Action research, as described and explained in this book, places more faith in practitioners as professional educators, who can be trained and expected to utilize elaborate, thoughtful, and significant approaches to solving problems in school settings. Hence, in *Action Research* attention is devoted to specific strategies and techniques that have traditionally only been reserved for the more advanced practice of educational research.

Action research, then, is not merely a type of research reserved for individuals with little, if any, formal training in educational research. Rather, action research is a viable tool used by professional and skilled educators who incorporate a wide variety of methodologies, designs, and approaches when conducting research. This underlying assumption makes this book unique, compared with other works on the subject.

Moreover, as will be reinforced later, action research is *not* a separate method of research (along with **descriptive, historical, correlational**, and **evaluative research**). Rather, it is a type of research that may utilize and incorporate many different methods of research. Hence, this book is also unique because it considers action research a process that may include various methods to suit its purpose(s).

# Audience

*Action Research* is designed primarily for three groups of practitioners:

1. graduate students, usually teachers, enrolled in a research seminar or course as part of a program leading to a master's degree in administration/supervision and/or state/city certification as a school administrator/supervisor;

2. practicing administrators and supervisors such as principals, vice-principals, department chairpeople, curriculum directors, and supervisors of instruction; and

3. teachers in leadership positions. (Walling, 1994)

Three other groups may find this book useful:

1. teachers who just want more information about action research;

2. parents involved in collaborative research projects in site-based managed schools; and

3. staff developers who conduct workshops on action research.

---

# Rationale

---

Many fine textbooks present a general overview of educational research. Most of these books, however, go far beyond what practitioners (e.g., teachers, school administrators, or supervisors) may need to know in conducting on-site research. Having taught research techniques to teachers as well as supervisor-trainees for many years, I have found that students do not need or would rarely use many of the research techniques described in more traditional textbooks. Statistical procedures such as factor, multivariate, discriminant, path, and meta-analyses have marginal value, at best, for the teacher-practitioner or the practicing school administrator. Students have frequently asked for a text that encapsulates the essence of research in a straightforward and understandable way, emphasizing strategies and techniques of research that have practical value. *Action Research* is an attempt to fill this perceived need.

Although discussion of advanced statistical analyses goes beyond the purview of this text, action research can and does utilize both **qualitative** *and* **quantitative** approaches. I will argue that although action research is a process that can be simply applied to improve schools, it is by no means a simple approach to research. Action research, as described in this volume, can involve some rather sophisticated methods and approaches to research. This latter point is often neglected or underemphasized by many individuals who write about and advocate action research.

*Action Research*, however, is not designed to treat all the fundamental research strategies and techniques that, for example, students who are writing doctoral dissertations may require. The student interested in a more comprehensive text on research can consult Charles (1995), Crowl (1996), Gay (1996), McMillan and Schumacher (1997), Tuckman (1994), and Wiersma (1995), among others. This book is designed to introduce those research strategies that are likely to be used by practicing supervisors and teachers in their attempt to improve school practices on a daily basis. As such, this book might also be a valuable guidebook for conducting action research at the graduate master's and doctoral levels.

The field of action research, specifically, has a number of useful introductory books that give the reader a general overview (see, e.g., McLean, 1995; McNiff, 1991; Sager, 1992; Stringer, 1996). Although a scarcity of books exists that deal specifically with action research, many of the works that have been published on action research are not very user-friendly, do not provide enough techniques, are often too technical and brief, and are not geared at all to practicing school administrators. The value of this book is that specific, easy-to-use techniques and strategies are discussed so that practitioners in the supervision field can apply action research for school improvement more judiciously and comprehensively.

# Assumptions

*Action Research: An Educational Leader's Guide to School Improvement* was written with the following assumptions in mind:

1.  Most students reading this textbook have had little, if any, exposure to research methodology and **design.**

2.  School administrators, supervisors, and teachers do not have enough time to engage in lengthy, complicated research. As such, they need to be acquainted with practical and useful research techniques and strategies in order to gather sufficient data before making decisions.

3.  Many textbooks on educational research are far too technical to have much practical value for administrators, supervisors, and teachers.

4.  School administrators, supervisors, and teachers need training in conducting action research.

5.  Action research is an invaluable tool for simultaneously improving instruction at the classroom level and rejuvenating the overall health of the school organization.

# Goals

After completing *Action Research*, you should be familiar with the basic elements of **research design** as well as equipped with a number of effective research and evaluative strategies. You will better understand the importance of research, feel more confident about implementing an action research project, and realize how applying these strategies and techniques can help you become a better decision-maker and problem-solver. The organizational health of your school depends, to a large extent, on the degree to which you are committed to an inquiry-oriented approach toward instructional excellence. In sum, the three main goals of this book are to:

1. familiarize you with the steps necessary to carry out action research and **evaluation** in educational settings;

2. provide you with a method for making intelligent and informed decisions about educational problems or concerns; and

3. encourage you to appreciate the art of disciplined inquiry.

# Organization and Content

*Action Research* is meant to be interactive in the sense that you are encouraged to complete the sample *review exercises* provided in each chapter in order to reinforce newly learned concepts. A general pretest (which can serve as a posttest as well) is presented in Appendix A. I suggest you assess your knowledge of research by taking this test before starting Chapter 1. Please note that you are *not* expected to know many of the answers to the questions on this pretest. The pretest serves to assess your knowledge of some areas of research. After completing the book, you will certainly have an increased knowledge of research. Don't get frustrated when taking the pretest; just try to do your best.

I have tried to make this book as user-friendly as possible. Examples are drawn from everyday school experiences and situations that those concerned with supervision and teaching are likely to encounter. Exercises are provided, in most chapters, to help you think of meaningful ways to use and apply research in your position as a supervisor or teacher. The book will serve as a reference guide and handy manual as you continue to undertake a research-oriented approach to school improvement.

I start with a basic introduction to research in the opening chapter, "An Introduction to Action Research: It's Not All That Complicated." This chapter takes you through some concepts and principles of research, in general, and then explains the meaning and value of action research. General steps are provided for conducting action research and exercises are introduced to help you think through some of the ways action research may be incorporated. The chapter suggests that action research is a viable, useful, and relatively easy-to-use means of promoting school improvement, as well as an approach that can certainly enhance your personal professional development.

In Chapter 2, "Teaching and Doing Action Research Through General Semantics," I introduce a multidimensional model that is integral to understanding and planning any sort of action research project. Drawing briefly from general semantics (the study of the relationship among language, thought, and human behavior) the chapter challenges you to gain a varied perspective when confronting an educational problem. This multidimensional view limits potential bias because a multitude of data sources are utilized. The concept of **triangulation** is introduced as a powerful tool for conducting research.

Chapter 3, "Cut to the Chase: Getting Started by Choosing Sound Quantitative and Qualitative Research Approaches, Methods, and Designs," discusses the first steps action researchers must take. The chapter opens by suggesting that both quantitative and qualitative approaches are desirable. Once an approach or approaches have been identified, selection of a suitable method and type of research is considered. Then the importance of designing the research to suit the area of investigation is emphasized. You will also be introduced to some basic principles and elements of research that form the foundation for being able to select an appropriate research strategy. You will read about situations in which educational leaders make decisions and solve problems as they refine their **research designs.** You will learn several practical research designs that can be used by practitioners in almost any school setting.

In Chapter 4, "Easy Steps to Program Development and Evaluation Research," I discuss the most common form of action research for educational leaders. Developing programs and evaluating their effectiveness assume great importance among educational leaders. The chapter includes a discussion of eight steps in program development and five steps in program evaluation, as well as examples and applications.

In Chapter 5, "Data Collection Techniques That Work," I discuss various methods for collecting data that can be readily used by practitioners. Various **data collection** instruments for conducting both quantitative and qualitative research are explained in depth.

Chapter 6, "How to Analyze Data Easily," explains what to do once all the data have been collected. Various methods for analyzing data are presented, and basic statistical and qualitative procedures are discussed.

Chapter 7, "Putting It All Together: What Does It All Mean?", discusses concrete ways of interpreting and reporting findings generated from action research projects. Suggested guidelines for writing reports are also offered.

The final chapter, "Action Research in Action," discusses ways to implement action research in your school by providing concrete strategies and argues that action research, as a form of inquiry, would be most welcome in a school or a district that is framed as a learning community. Action research case studies are provided for analysis and discussion.

The Epilogue summarizes the action research approach advocated in this book, provides seven final suggestions or caveats for conducting action research, and briefly discusses some ethical issues related to conducting action research.

A Glossary of key terms that are used throughout the text is provided. Although many terms are explained in the text where they occur, some terms are discussed anew and at length in the Glossary. Use the Glossary interactively as you read the text. (*Note*: Words throughout this textbook that are printed in **bold** are defined in the Glossary.) Annotated references of selected key works are then provided as a guide for further reading. Appendixes are particularly useful in that they include materials that will not only supplement and reinforce your newfound knowledge, but provide information necessary to conduct and report action research.

I hope you will find the research techniques described in this book useful. As you seek better ways to improve your school, you will appreciate action research as a user-friendly process for making more intelligent decisions about various educational problems. Follow the guidelines suggested in this book, especially the ones outlined in the Epilogue. Feel free to share your experiences and seek advice. If you would like to continue dialogue about school improvement through action research and/or offer suggestions for future editions of this book, please e-mail me at jglanz@turbo.kean.edu. I wish you continued success in all your professional and personal endeavors.

# References

[Note that references with an asterisk are annotated later in the book.]

Charles, C. M. (1995). *Introduction to educational research*. New York: Longman.

Crowl, T. K. (1996). *Fundamentals of educational research* (2nd ed.). Madison, WI: WCB Brown & Benchmark Publishers.

Gay, L. R. (1996). *Educational research: Competencies for analysis and application* (5th ed.). Englewood Cliffs, NJ: Prentice Hall.

*Glickman, C. D. (1995). Action research: Inquiry, reflection, and decision-making. (Video). ASCD.

*McLean, J. E. (1995). *Improving education through action research: A guide for administrators and teachers*. Thousand Oaks, CA: Corwin Press.

McMillan, J. H., & Schumacher, S. (1997). *Research in education: A conceptual introduction*. New York: Longman.

*McNiff, J. (1991). *Action research: Principles and practice*. London: Routledge.

*Sager, R. (1992). *How to conduct collaborative action research*. Alexandria, VA: Association for Supervision and Curriculum Development.

*Stringer, E. T. (1996). *Action research: A handbook for practitioners*. Thousand Oaks, CA: Sage Publications.

Tuckman, B. (1988). *Conducting educational research*. New York: Harcourt.

Walling, D. R. (Ed.). (1994). *Teachers as leaders: Perspectives on the professional development of teachers*. Bloomington, IN: Phi Delta Kappa Educational Foundation.

Wiersma, W. (1995). *Research methods in education: An introduction*. Boston: Allyn and Bacon.

# $\mathcal{A}$cknowledgments

I wish to acknowledge my students at Kean University and the College of Staten Island, CUNY, who have helped me develop this volume into a useful and practical guide to action research. Special acknowledgment is offered to Kean University's Released Time for Research Committee who have supported my research efforts.

I wish to acknowledge the following individuals who have particularly inspired or assisted me in completing this project: Osborne Abbey, Virginia Burrows, Arkady Dudko, Nathan Fisher, Barry Friedman, Aida Garcia, Dorothy Hennings, Linda Bowman-Hopson, Jamie Horowitz, Kim Lindgren, Barry Persky, Wendy Poole, Gilda Spiotta, Susan Sullivan, Myra Weiger, Gerald Weiss, and my wife, Lisa, for her continuous moral and spiritual support. Any misrepresentations and inaccuracies are, of course, my sole responsibility.

# An Introduction to Action Research: It's Not All That Complicated

### Chapter 1

*"Although action research is not a quick fix for all school problems, it represents a process that . . . can focus the brain-power of the entire instructional staff on maximizing learning."*

(McLean, 1995, p. 5)

## Research Has a Bad Rap

Mentioning *research* to almost anyone conjures up images of some scientist conducting experiments in a distant and secluded laboratory. Mention *educational research* and reactions may include recollections of one's master's thesis project, or less complimentary thoughts of some eccentric professor engaging in some inane study unrelated to practice. To many educators—teachers and supervisors alike—the value of research is marginal at best. Educators who work in public and private schools remain unconvinced of the efficacy of most of what gets published in professional and scholarly journals in the field of education. Debating the efficacy and relevance of much of this type of educational research is not my intended purpose, although I could cite some strong reasons for its value and utility for practicing school people. It seems to me that the inclination to avoid research, of any sort, is shortsighted, provincial, and possibly deleterious. A fundamental premise of this book is that proper utilization of research is not only beneficial, but necessary and urgent in order to renew our schools as well as empower both teachers and supervisors.

1

# What Is Research?

The word *research* is derived, etymologically, from the French word, *rechercher*, meaning to travel through or to survey. As such, research can be thought of as some sort of investigation "to discover or establish facts and relationships" (Charles, 1995, p. 5). Research, at its most basic level, however, is a process of gathering information. All of us have conducted research in many ways. As teachers we found ways of gathering information in order to assess our students' achievement and social development. Observing Sarah interact in a cooperative learning group, for instance, gave us much information about the degree to which she cooperated with her peers. As educational leaders, we may informally observe a teacher working with a group of students during a reading lesson. As we observe, we collect information. We may note, for instance, that the teacher is asking her male students more thought-provoking questions than she is asking the female students. We also may note that she allows more wait-time for boys than for girls. As we continue to observe, we begin to better understand the nature of the interaction between this teacher and her students.

Research, in a sense, is also a way of knowing. At times we come to know something intuitively. Educational leaders, as specially trained observers, are often able to *see* aspects of a particular situation that is unbeknownst to the "unenlightened eye" (Eisner, 1991). They can *gather information*, at times, instinctively. Relying, however, on instinct alone is certainly insufficient as a way to fully appreciate the complexity involved in a teaching/learning situation. I'm reminded of the impressionistic and imprecise methods employed by supervisors of the past century. James M. Greenwood (1891), a prominent city school superintendent from Kansas, for example, described the skilled supervisor as someone who could simply walk into a classroom and "judge from a compound sensation of the disease at work among the inmates" (p. 227). Not a very appealing metaphor, wouldn't you agree?

Although there are different ways of knowing, research is essentially a more disciplined, scientific, if you will, approach. Although I hesitate to use the word *scientific* so early in this book for fear that the word may conjure up some unpleasant memories or negative associations, research, nevertheless, is a systematic approach of applying the **scientific method** to study a given educational problem. As we apply the scientific method, in part, by noting a problem, posing relevant questions, and gathering and analyzing information related to the questions, we begin to get a more accurate understanding of a specific situation.

*Situation:* Dr. Bea Williams, middle school principal, institutes a pilot literature-based reading program in selected classes in grades six through eight. After a six-month period, the principal wishes to assess the impact of this literature-based program on reading comprehension achievement.

*Analysis:* Dr. Williams essentially wants to know whether or not this new program is successfully meeting the academic needs of students. She may "know" that the impact of the program is a positive one by:

(a) informally observing classes and speaking with one or two teachers;

(b) being informed by others of the program's success;

(c) surmising that the program is very successful;

(d) logically deducing that since instances of reports of misbehavior have declined dramatically since the implementation of the program, it is likely that students are learning; or

(e) assessing posttest scores on a reading comprehension examination of two comparable classes per grade, one of which was exposed to literature-based reading and the other taught by traditional basal readers.

Obviously, a research-oriented approach would favor the latter more "scientific" method. We may very well be suspicious of an approach that seems to rely on informal, haphazard, and, perhaps biased, observations. Conclusions drawn from observations only based on information derived by others, and/or observations based on intuition or presumed logical reasoning may be equally suspicious.

Research, as disciplined inquiry, can contribute enormously to the work of educational leaders. Research is not some esoteric activity reserved for Ph.D.'s and research scientists. Research is something we all can do to help us understand, if not solve, some of the urgent issues we confront on a daily basis in schools. To do so thoughtfully, comprehensively, and intelligently is what research is all about.

# Ignorance about the Utility of Research

Many teachers, administrators, and other educational leaders have not been adequately prepared to understand how research can positively affect their work. More disturbing, from my experience I have concluded and I suspect others will concur that many educational leaders eschew research as being impractical and simply "not worth the effort." This apparent dichotomy between research and practice is troublesome and unfortunate. As a former practicing school administrator, supervisor, and teacher, I can personally attest to the lack of interest in or ignorance about educational research among many practitioners. Yet, I have seen significant numbers of educational leaders who successfully incorporated research as a viable means for promoting effective schooling and enhancing student achievement.

# Research as a Professional Responsibility

An essential characteristic of any profession is the possession of expertise by its members. In order to question and evaluate effectively, the professional educational leader must have knowledge of research methodology. The leader is confronted by a plethora of problems on a daily basis that demand careful consideration and analysis. The decision-making ability of an educational leader is greatly hindered without the scrutiny of **evaluation** and research. As educational expert, s/he is required to test the validity of various proposals. S/he, in other words, is a **hypothesis** maker and tester. The leader is not a neutral technician who merely dictates policies without conducting appropriate follow-ups. S/he is an educational expert who possesses professional knowledge and technical skills that enable her/him to analyze and solve problems with insight and imagination.

Unfortunately, as mentioned above, many educators avoid research, condemning it as having dubious practical value. To these individuals, research is nothing more than theoretical formulations having little, if any, impact on schools. As James Olivero (1982) states in *Educational Leadership*, "unfortunately, practitioners frequently believe researchers are so protected from the hassles of everyday life that the ivory-tower types can't possibly understand the real world" (p. 343). This dichotomy between theory and practice has long been a chief complaint of many practitioners. The educational leader, however, is in a pivotal position in schools to bridge the gap between theory and practice by demonstrating the importance of research in the day-to-day operation of a school (Kagan, 1995). Research *is* a major professional responsibility of any educational leader.

*Situation:* Mr. Charles Daley, an elementary school principal in a midwestern urban setting, has been informed by two of his more experienced faculty that they would like to initiate a team teaching project. Inspired, in large measure, by an Association for Supervision and Curriculum Development (ASCD) conference from which they both recently returned, these two veteran teachers seem, to Mr. Daley, more enthusiastic than they've been in years. Concerned, attentive, and somewhat curious about their enthusiasm, Mr. Daley begins a computer search to collect information on team teaching. Using the Educational Resources Information Center (ERIC) CD-ROM database and a World Wide Web search on Yahoo, Mr. Daley begins to collect the latest research on team teaching. In a relatively short time, he has amassed an extensive number of articles published on the topic and has gathered information about schools that have experimented with team teaching for years. Mr. Daley forwards this information to his teachers and offers his continued support.

Mr. Daley's interest in assisting his teachers by doing some preliminary research on team teaching demonstrates his sense of professionalism in two ways: (1) his willingness to encourage his faculty by collecting some basic research on a topic that interests them is admirable and is likely to promote a learning community; and (2) although Mr. Daley's efforts are very basic in terms of what can eventually be accomplished through action research, his initial efforts demonstrate not only his knowledge of data collecting, but his commitment to a spirit of inquiry.

## Some Reasons Why Educational Leaders Might Avoid Research

*Lack of Time*—Educational leaders are confronted daily with a plethora of demanding tasks. The increasingly complex nature of the educational leader's job may indeed seem overwhelming (Whitaker, 1995). Principals and other educational leaders often complain of time management issues. Yet, despite the apparent tensions and pressures that are characteristic of the principalship, for instance, lack of time to attend to necessary tasks and responsibilities may, in fact, be remedied with effective time management strategies. Educational leaders would benefit from time management workshops to enable them to better cope with their ever-increasing responsibilities. Simply, however, to say that one has no time to undertake research is not a viable, nor acceptable, response. I have personally worked with many principals and other educational leaders who have utilized research to improve and renew their schools. If they were able to find time to undertake action research, you certainly can, but only if you believe such an undertaking is important.

*Impractical*—As alluded to earlier, many individuals assume that research is reserved for the research scientist or college professor, but is not feasible for the practitioner. For these individuals, *research* is narrowly defined. Different types of research, in fact, exist. Although some types of research are best reserved for specially trained individuals, other forms of research, such as action research, are indeed viable. A growing literature base (e.g., Stringer, 1996) as well as documented experiences of many practitioners (e.g., Palanki & Burch, 1995) attest to the practicality and usefulness of action research.

*Ignorance*—Many educational leaders simply lack knowledge on how best to conduct and utilize research. They have not been formally trained in research strategies and methods that are appropriate and viable in schools. Consequently, many educational leaders often fear or eschew research. *Action Research* is an attempt to provide technical knowledge and requisite skills so that you will feel more knowledgeable and comfortable in employing research strategies in your daily practice.

## A Paradigm for Research

While textbook authors of educational research have categorized types, methods, and forms of research differently (Best & Kahn, 1993), I have found the paradigm in Figure 1.1 a useful means to give my students an overall understanding of how action research is situated in a broader context as well as highlight specific methods and research techniques that may be valuable to an action researcher.

## An Overview of Research in Education

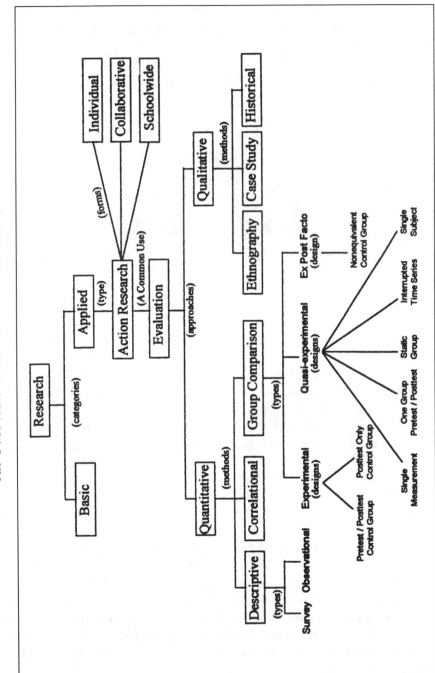

Figure 1.1

Earlier in this chapter, I introduced the paradigm, in part, by defining **research** as disciplined inquiry that utilizes a systematic approach by applying the **scientific method** to study educational problems. There are two *categories* of research: *basic* and *applied* (see Figures 1.1 and 1.2). They differ from one another in purpose, not necessarily in complexity or value.

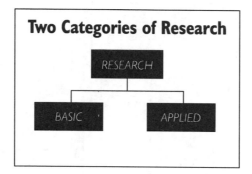

**Figure 1.2**

*Basic* (also called pure or fundamental research) involves experiments that attempt to extend our knowledge in a given discipline or field of study. The goal of basic research is to develop **theory** through broad generalizations. Basic research has no immediate practical value, but is essential in furthering our understanding of important phenomena. Theories of learning, for example, are generated from basic research.

*Applied* research is conducted chiefly in order to improve practice by solving some sort of specific problem. Attempts at applying learning theory to solve practical problems that teachers face in the classroom are examples of this category of research (see, e.g., Hunter, 1967).

*Action* research is one *type* of applied research (see Figures 1.1 and 1.3). Administrators and supervisors (and other educational leaders) conduct action research in order to address a specific problem by using the principles and methodologies of research. Although action research utilizes less rigorous **designs** and methodologies than other forms of applied research, its benefits are enormous not only for the professional development of those educational leaders who use action research, but for the school as a whole.

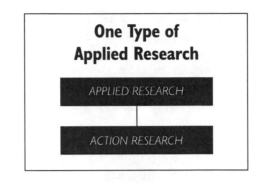

**Figure 1.3**

Three forms of action research allow educators to investigate areas of concern in their classrooms and schools: individual, collaborative, and schoolwide (see Figures 1.1 and 1.4) (Calhoun, 1993). Individual teachers and supervisors may conduct a research project that focuses on a specific class, program, or activity. The educator may define an area of investigation and then seek a solution or may simply collect data to determine a course of action. All action research projects, indeed, begin with an individual educator who has the necessary knowledge, skills, and desire to carry out such an enterprise.

**Collaborative action research** is a *form* of action research (see Figures 1.1 and 1.4) that is taken on by a group or team of individuals that can, for instance, focus on one classroom or several classrooms. A collaborative

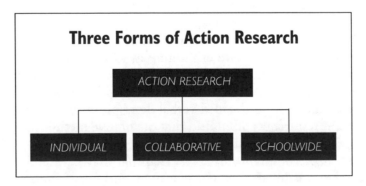

**Figure 1.4**

action research team may also conduct a districtwide investigation (Oja & Smulyan, 1989). Schoolwide action research, a third form of action research, is undertaken by a community of practitioners including teachers, parents, students, and administrators to address schoolwide issues and solve common problems (see, e.g., Calhoun, 1994; Calhoun, Allen, Halliburton, & Jones, 1996; *Equity and Choice*, 1993; McNiff, 1991; Sagor, 1992; Stringer, 1996).

The distinction between collaborative and schoolwide research may be subtle and even arbitrary. Certainly a school faculty committee that involves parents and students, for instance, is collaborative in nature. Regardless of the differences between the two forms of action research, this volume essentially deals with individual action research projects. Although collaborate and schoolwide action research are essential for school renewal (Glickman, 1993), this book will address the basics of how individual supervisors and other educational leaders may conduct action research. This approach is justified by the belief that before teams of committed professionals can deal with complex schoolwide problems, training in action research should be provided for dealing with classroom or gradewide projects. Action research projects are more likely to be encouraged and supported by educational leaders who have experienced firsthand the benefits of this type of research on a small scale. Furthermore, such training empowers administrators and teachers to conduct action research themselves without reliance on "outside" experts.

Action research, just as is true of educational research in general, may utilize two *approaches* to inquiry: quantitative and qualitative (see Figure 1.1). Although action research is generally thought of as only entailing qualitative approaches, I stated earlier that sound action research may, indeed, benefit from a varied approach to disciplined inquiry that includes *both* qualitative and quantitative approaches.

Three *methods* of **qualitative research**, among others, that may be useful to the action researcher are **ethnography, case study**, and **historical inquiry** (see Figures 1.1 and 1.5). Qualitative approaches do not, of course, utilize statistical or mathematical expressions, as will be explained in Chapter 3. Rather, they rely on detailed verbal descriptions of phenomena observed. Action researchers often find that qualitative methods can be very easily adopted in school settings.

Three *methods* of **quantitative research** that may be useful to the action researcher are **descriptive, correlational**, and **group comparison** research (see Figures 1.1 and 1.6). **Descriptive research** can be broken down

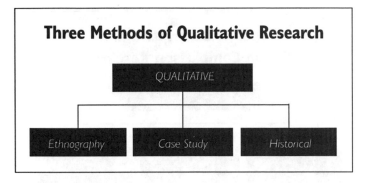

**Figure 1.5**

further into two *types*: **survey** and observational research (see Figures 1.1 and 1.7). **Correlational research** has no subdivisions, whereas **group comparison research** can be divided into three *types*: **experimental, quasi-experimental,** and **ex post facto research** (see Figures 1.1 and 1.7). Specific **research designs** are employed to conduct experimental, quasi-experimental, and ex post facto research.

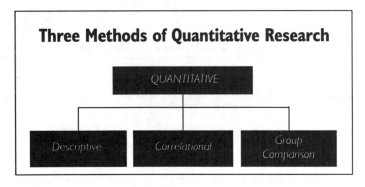

**Figure 1.6**

As each *approach, method, type,* and *design* of research is explained in the text, Figure 1.1 and the other figures should be referred to in order to help place the concept within context. Key terms are explained in the Glossary; however, most terms are treated more fully where they naturally occur in the text.

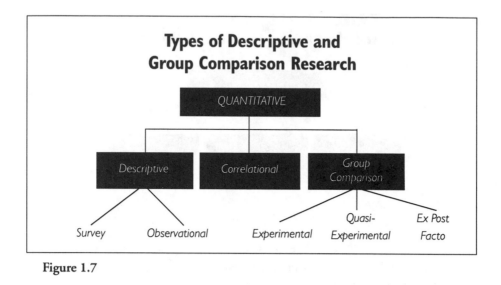

**Figure 1.7**

---

# Evaluation Research: The Most Common Use of Action Research for Educational Leaders

---

*"Effective school principals must be evaluation-oriented leaders, and they need substantial competence in measurement and other aspects of evaluation."*

*(Stufflebeam, 1996)*

Some authors include **evaluation research** as a separate category of research (McMillan & Schumacher, 1989). In this volume, however, evaluation research is considered as one possible use of action research. A goal of evaluation research is to assess the quality of a particular practice or program in a school. Evaluation research is very much involved in addressing a specific problem. From my experience, educational leaders as action researchers undertake evaluative studies quite often. Thus, evaluation research is considered the most common use of action research (see Figure 1.1). Educational leaders are likely to engage in evaluation research since, for the most part, they are involved in assessing a variety of educational concerns such as special programs, methods of teaching, or instructional materials.

## What Is Evaluation Research?

**Evaluation research** is the gathering of data in order to make a decision. Administrators and other educational leaders need to make many decisions on a daily basis. Unfortunately, many of these decisions are often made hurriedly and without the scrutiny of thoughtful, scientific investigation. What seems to be most expedient at the time is often the most important criterion for determining, for example, the fate of a new music program. Based on my experiences in schools, I have found that when educational leaders are trained in sound research methodology, decisions are made more intelligently and equitably. To determine the "fate of the new music program," the educational leader would collect appropriate data from a number of sources before making the final decision to disband, modify, or even continue the music program. The value of **evaluation research** is its ability to help leaders make informed educational decisions.

Parenthetically, evaluation research may also be undertaken for the purpose of identifying problems. This strategy is usually undertaken during a needs assessment phase during which potential problems and issues are identified. Discussion of such an approach will be undertaken in Chapter 4 when discussing needs assessment in establishing a program. Furthermore, evaluation as action research may be used for benchmarking purposes by examining what other schools, for instance, are doing in regard to a particular instructional strategy. In this way, the school might better assess itself in regard to its own instructional program. While other uses of evaluation as action research are possible, this text will focus primarily on overall program evaluation because of its ubiquitous nature.

## A Typical Day in the Life of a Vice-Principal

Today was a typical day for Ms. Roberta Rodriguez, vice-principal of Boynton High School located in an affluent suburb of Chicago. In addition to preparing the day's scheduling and arranging for substitute teachers, she was involved in the all-too-mundane activities associated with her position as vice-principal in a large school of nearly 2,500 students. Today, Ms. Rodriguez:

- distributed newly obtained textbooks to the English Department;
- selected Mr. William Johnson to escort the school band to the district's Open House celebration;
- decided to call an emergency grade conference to familiarize teachers about the newly adopted core content curriculum standards;
- recommended to the School-Community Council that Ms. Sylvia Barnett be selected as Parent-of-the-Month;
- completed her evaluation report of the after-school student at-risk program;
- began a needs assessment in order to implement an interdisciplinary team teaching program;
- placed a new admission in Mr. Steve Goldman's already overcrowded home room;
- suggested that the art/science program be revised;
- scheduled time for the Chess Club to meet during period 4;
- recommended suspension for Maurice and Christopher for pulling the fire alarm at dismissal;
- interviewed a prospective teacher for a vacancy in the English Department;
- supervised first period lunch duty in the cafeteria;
- determined that Ms. Joan Smith, an untenured teacher, should not be rehired for the next semester;
- observed Ms. Phyllis Williams, a veteran teacher, during the 4th period; and
- conducted a post-conference with Ms. Williams during the 8th period.

As you can see, Ms. Rodriguez's day, like those of most other educational leaders, was not only arduous and frenetic, at times, but also filled with many situations in which decisions had to be made. Quite often educational leaders are challenged by decisions related to student discipline, administration of school policies, evaluation of teachers, graduation activities, emergency arrangements, efficacy of new curricula, implementation and evaluation of varied school programs, and much more.

Taken together, decisions educational leaders make help establish, organize, and monitor various aspects of the school organization. Leaders' effectiveness is ultimately entwined with the overall efficacy of the school organization. It is imperative, then, that decisions be made thoughtfully, yet decisively. The decisions Ms. Rodriguez made were based upon many different kinds of evidence that she collected. Why, for example, did Ms. Rodriguez suggest that the art/science program be revised? How did she know that the program was in serious trouble? Why did she decide to implement an interdisciplinary team teaching program? All of these decisions were based upon information Ms. Rodriguez had gathered. This book is about the process of gathering and using information to help make better supervisory decisions and that is what **evaluation research** is all about.

## What to Evaluate?

**Evaluation research** can be divided into three types (the 3-P's):

1. Program evaluation;
2. Procedural evaluation; and
3. Product evaluation.

Educational leaders are usually involved with making judgments about the effectiveness or desirability of various Programs. They can and should assess school goals and priorities, academic programs, extracurricular activities, school policies and rules, school climate, and special projects, among others.

An educational leader might ask questions such as these: "Does the new program work?"; "What impact does inclusion have on the attitudes of teachers?"; or "Does the whole language program affect reading achievement levels among third graders?" Program evaluation that is regular, dynamic, and ongoing contributes greatly to the overall effectiveness of the school organization. This book, although not attending to all aspects of **evaluation research**, will describe program evaluation as one facet of action research that is often neglected.

Perhaps the most common form of decision-making undertaken by educational leaders is Procedural evaluation. This second type of **evaluation research** assesses personnel such as teachers and staff. Insuring the competence of teachers is perhaps the foremost concern among educational leaders. Although personnel evaluation is important, I will not address this topic because much work has been published in this area (see, e.g., Peterson, 1995) and this form of research is not directly applicable to our discussion of action research.

Educational leaders also need to evaluate facilities and equipment, financial plans, school resources, and instructional materials on an ongoing basis. Product evaluation deserves special analysis which is, however, beyond the scope of this volume (see, e.g., DeRoche, 1987).

Before proceeding with the remainder of the chapter, complete the following exercises that help reinforce some of the ideas expressed above.

---

# Exercises

1. The process of gathering information to aid decision making is known as

    a. evaluation.

    b. research.

    c. sampling.

    d. action projects.

    e. networking.

    Answer: choice "b"

2. The greatest obstacle faced by an educational leader in undertaking evaluative research is that he/she

    a. is deluged with other administrative and instructional tasks.

    b. doesn't really care to go to the trouble of undertaking extensive research.

    c. is not knowledgeable about research in schools.

    d. is not given sufficient leeway from the building principal.

    e. has no support from the district office or central board of education.

    > Answer: choice "c" is correct because it is not that educational leaders are too busy, don't care, and/or don't have the authority or support to undertake research, but rather their lack of professional development in this area precludes involvement in action research. Once equipped with the requisite knowledge, skills, and dispositions, leaders will apply the principles of research to improve their schools.

3. What images are conjured up in your mind when you think of "research"? Share responses with classmates.

    _____

    _____

    _____

    Answers will vary

4.  Research is a professional responsibility. Rate yourself on your knowledge and comfort levels in undertaking research. A score of ten would indicate that you are "ready-to-go" and a score of zero might mean that you have much to learn. Share responses with classmates.

    _____

    _____

    _____

    Answers will vary

5.  What kinds of programs might you evaluate in your school or district?

    _____

    _____

    Answers will vary

# Evolution of Action Research

Kemmis (cited in Oja & Smulyan, 1989) outlines four phases in the history of educational research. The earliest phase of educational research is characterized by attempts to "make sense of practice by developing educational theory 'on a grand scale'" (p. vii). Developing **theory** to guide practice was a foremost concern to theorists such as John Dewey. Dissatisfied with the application of theory to practice, educators urged researchers to apply the techniques and principles of science to "examine and improve practice" directly. This second phase of research in education was direct and practical in the sense that once problems were identified solutions through the application of the **scientific method** could be attained. A third approach appeared in opposition to this technical approach, which some thought simplified educational theory and practice by trying to find ready-made solutions to complex problems. During this phase, which Kemmis calls the "pessimistic phase," tensions between practitioners and theoreticians were heightened. Research undertaken during this phase soon became seen as divorced from practice. Consequently, a fourth phase emerged, the self-reflective phase, which "recognizes practitioners' rights and skills as professionals and encouraged their involvement in the examination of practice and the clarification of theory" (p. vii). Action research emerges from this self-reflective phase of educational research.

Although first popularized in the 1940s by Kurt Lewin (Adelman, 1993), action research was first systematically applied in education by Stephen Corey, a professor at Teachers College, Columbia University. Corey encouraged teachers and supervisors to use action research to improve their own practice. Corey, a man ahead of his time, advocated that fundamental change could not occur without direct involvement of teachers and supervisors. As Corey (1953) explained,

> The studies must be undertaken by those who may have to change the way they do things . . . Our schools cannot keep up with the life they are supposed to sustain and improve unless teachers, pupils, supervisors, administrators, and school patrons continuously examine what they are doing. Singly and in groups, they must use their imaginations creatively and constructively to identify the practices that must be changed to meet the needs and demands of modern life, courageously try out those practices that give better promise, and methodically and systematically gather evidence to test their worth . . . This is the process I call action research. (p. viii)

Action research gained further legitimacy when distinguished educators such as Hilda Taba, curriculum specialist and also a professor of education at Teachers College, Columbia University, advocated action research in the late fifties. She believed that action research contributed much toward curriculum development. She saw two basic purposes for action research:

> (a) to produce evidence needed to solve practical problems; and (b) to help those who are doing the action research to acquire more adequate perspective regarding their problems, to deepen their insights as to what is involved in their task and to extend their orientation toward children—toward methods of teaching them or toward what is significant in content of learning. (Taba & Noel, 1957, p. 2)

Interest in action research waned in the 1960s because it was questioned as a viable research method by the scientific establishment. Foshay (1994) explained that the educational research establishment opposed action research, which was often reported merely in **case study** form, because "no attempt was made to see whether the examined population was representative of a larger population." Foshay continued, ". . . the data often were flawed . . . , the movement was ridiculed in the publications of the American Educational Research Association (AERA), and it did not spread" (p. 320). Yet, it emerged again in the late 1970s with the work of Lawrence Stenhouse and John Elliott in Europe (Kemmis, cited in Oja & Smulyan, 1989).

Historically, action research served as a problem-solving strategy for improving the school organization (Corey, 1953; Lewin, 1948), as a process of individual reflection on practice (Elliott, 1991), as a process to support staff development (Oja & Smulyan, 1989), as a collaborative process to support teachers' professional development (Sagor, 1992), and as a strategy to guide site-based school improvement (Glickman, 1993).

Calhoun, Allen, and Halliburton (1996) recently described the current fascination with and interest in action research. Whether undertaken by individuals or collaborative teams, "part of the promise inherent in action research is to build the capability of individuals and organizations to move beyond current cognitions and practice. Recognized in the past as a powerful tool for simultaneously improving practice and the health of the organization, such is its appeal today" (p. 5).

While few educators ever described the role of administrators or supervisors beyond overseeing or administering the action research process, thus enabling teachers to successfully complete a particular project, Taba and Corey were among the first educators to envision the supervisor as integral to the process. Taba believed that supervisors "needed to become learners along with the teachers . . . Instead of acting as experts, they had to become helpers . . ." Taba explained that supervisors needed expertise in action research not only to facilitate teachers' work, but to "act as a research technician, devising, adapting, and borrowing research techniques as needed" (Taba & Noel, 1957, p. 50). Still, the suggestion that supervisors themselves might benefit from action research without engaging teachers was unrealized. One of the major intents of this book is to suggest that supervisors can and should become involved in action research for their own professional development.

## Action Research Defined

Many practitioners will complain that much educational research has a minimal effect on practice. Teachers often identify themselves as "practitioners," and research, even in "action," sounds like some "university thing." Practitioners also assert that "research can be made to support anything" (Calhoun, Allen, Halliburton, & Jones, 1996). Breaking such stereotypical thinking based on erroneous assumptions and beliefs is difficult, although not impossible. The many attempts to involve teachers and principals in action research projects attest to its efficacy. My experience as both a teacher and assistant principal also supports the notion that research is an invaluable tool for school improvement.

Action research is a kind of research that has reemerged as a popular way of involving practitioners, both teachers and supervisors, so that they better understand their work. Although originally developed primarily for the professional development of teachers, action research has recently gained favor among administrators, supervisors, other educational leaders, and school-based managed teams including parents, community members, and even students, as a way of improving schools. Corey (1953) explained that action research is undertaken "by practitioners in order that they may improve their practices" (p. 141). Corey was the first educator to include supervisors as they "attempt to solve their practical problems by using the methods of science" (p. 141).

Therefore, action research, a *type* of applied research, is a form of research that is conducted by practitioners to improve practices in educational settings. Action research, like other types of research, utilizes an array of methodologies and approaches. Although action research is generally identified with qualitative approaches, action research, as defined in this volume, incorporates *both* qualitative and quantitative approaches (see Figure 1.8).

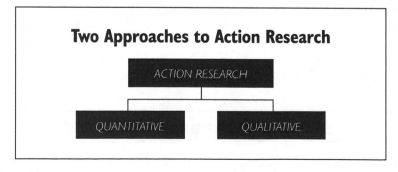

Figure 1.8

Action research differs with traditional research in three ways:

1. Action research is often less sophisticated than traditional methods that incorporate, for example, complicated statistical techniques.
2. Action research is utilized primarily by practitioners to solve specific problems.
3. Findings from action research are often not generalizable to other groups and situations.

## Benefits of Action Research

Although some educators think that research is impractical, irrelevant, and simply not feasible for practitioners given the exigencies and pressures of working in a school, research, properly used, can have immeasurable benefits, for it

- Creates a systemwide mindset for school improvement—a professional problem-solving ethos.
- Enhances decision making—greater feelings of competence in solving problems and making instructional decisions. In other words, action research provides for an intelligent way of making decisions.
- Promotes reflection and self-assessment.
- Instills a commitment to continuous improvement.
- Creates a more positive school climate in which teaching and learning are foremost concerns.
- Impacts directly on practice.
- Empowers those who participate in the process. Educational leaders who undertake action research may no longer, for instance, uncritically accept theories, innovations, and programs at face value.

Action research should *not* be viewed as just another technique or innovation in a long list of reform measures. If we've learned anything from educational history, we've learned to suspect such panaceas (see, e.g., Cuban, 1984). Although often heralded as a one-shot solution to school reform, action research, more realistically, is a viable tool used by practitioners to improve schools (Sagor, 1997).

# Action Research Is Not Complicated

Equipped with technical knowledge and requisite skills, any educational leader can easily apply research methodology to almost any situation or problem area. Admittedly, there are areas or specific research strategies that are very sophisticated and require advanced knowledge. Aren't there aspects of the operation of your automobile that are beyond your comprehension? When was the last time you were able to dismantle a carburetor or change your transmission? Yet, you still can drive a car!! So too in this case. Understanding *how* a particular statistic, for instance, is able to consider disparate test scores from two groups and treat them comparably is immaterial as long as you know that it is the correct procedure to use. Anyone can utilize research without having to understand minutia or intricacies of advanced mathematical calculations.

As this book will demonstrate, any graduate student is capable of readily applying sound research strategies to solve real problems in schools. Don't avoid research simply because it seems complicated. It's really very simple, as you'll see.

Before proceeding with the remainder of the chapter, complete the following exercises that help reinforce some of the ideas expressed above.

---

## Exercises

6.  CLASS DISCUSSION

The rift between theoretician and practitioner is ever-widening. One of the aims of *Action Research* is to indicate the necessity for the educational leader to assume leadership in bridging this gap. The educational leader is in a unique position to accomplish this by articulating the concerns of the school practitioner and applying theoretical research design to possibly alleviate existing problems.

Read the quotation below and consider the following questions:

  A. What is your reaction to the quote?

  B. What strategies might you, as an educational leader, employ to bridge the gap between theory and practice?

  C. What is the role of the educational leader in regard to interpreting and disseminating current research?

Quoted, with permission of the Association for Supervision and Curriculum Development, from Olivero, J. (1982). Principals and their inservice needs. *Educational Leadership, 39*, 343–344.

RESEARCH TO PRACTICE: Unfortunately, practitioners frequently believe researchers are so protected from the hassles of everyday life that the ivory-tower types can't possibly understand the real world. On the contrary, theoreticians are confused by and irritated with practitioners who could benefit from learning better ways to function but don't.

What is needed is an intervention to bridge this gap. Lorre Manasee, staff member at NIE, offers a realistic solution to the problem. She has initiated a plan that calls for the dissemination of research through training. The idea is to incorporate the very best of what is known about the learning process into training programs for principals and other administrators. This notion is considerably different and potentially far more effective than the typical research paper that seems to be written by one researcher—certainly not for the benefit of the site leader.

WE NEED MORE PEOPLE WHO CAN INTERPRET RESEARCH RESULTS AND THEN SHOW OTHERS HOW THE RESULTS MAKE SENSE FOR STUDENTS [emphasis mine]. This calls for some rather unique people with unique skills, capable of making the link between research and practice and translating user needs into researchable problems. They could help researchers understand teachers' (sic) lives and problems. They would need to know something about both worlds and have resources and credibility in both.

Answers will vary

7. How might the benefits of action research, noted above, actually help to improve your school/district?

_____

_____

_____

Answers will vary

# Steps in Action Research

Action research is an ongoing process of examining educational problems in school settings. For those of you interested in applying action research, there are four (4) guiding steps, as shown in Figure 1.9.

**Figure 1.9**

1. *Select a focus*—includes three steps:
   a. know what you want to investigate;
   b. develop some questions about the area you've chosen; and
   c. establish a plan to answer these questions.

   Come to an agreement on what aspect of the school program you would like to study. Ask, "What am I concerned about?" and "Why am I concerned?" Identify what is known and what needs to be known about this program or practice. Ask, "What do I know about this program?" and "What information should be known in order to improve the program?" Identify specific aspects of the program that might need scrutiny such as:

*Student Outcomes:* e.g., achievement, attitudes, etc.

*Curriculum:* e.g., effectiveness of instructional materials, alignment with state content standards, etc.

*Instruction:* e.g., teaching strategies, use of technology, etc.

*School Climate:* e.g., teacher morale, relationships between teachers and supervisors, etc.

*Parental Involvement:* e.g., participation on committees, attendance at school events, etc.

As you focus on a specific concern or problem, you need to begin to pose some questions that will serve to guide your research. If, for instance, low levels of parental involvement are a concern in your school, you might ask: "How can I document these low levels of parent involvement?"; "What impact do these low levels of participation have on students' completion of science projects?"; "Will increased levels of involvement yield higher student achievement levels?"; and "How might parental involvement in school affairs be increased?"

Developing these guiding questions will eventually lead to specifying **research questions** and/or **hypotheses**. Selecting a focus also includes developing a **research design**, which is explained in detail in Chapter 3.

2. *Collect data*—Once you have narrowed your focus, that is, have a specific area of concern, have developed some **research questions**, and know how you plan to answer them, you are now ready to gather information to answer your research questions. Let's say you're investigating the new science program adopted by the district. You've posed some research questions about achievement levels and students' attitudes toward science. You can now begin to collect data that will provide evidence for the effectiveness of this program in terms of achievement and attitudes.

You may administer teacher-made and **standardized tests**, conduct **surveys** and **interviews**, and examine **portfolios**. What other kinds of evidence could you collect to help you understand the impact of this new science program? How would you collect such evidence? Discuss these questions with a classmate.

Quite often action researchers collect data, but do not organize them so that they can be shared with others. Raw data that just "sit around" in someone's file drawer are useless. Collected data must be transformed so that they can be used. Data that are counted, displayed, and organized by classroom, grade level, and school, for example, can then be used appropriately during the data analysis and interpretive phases. In order to present action research in the most concise and useable way possible, data organization is included in the data analysis phase that is described in detail in Chapter 6.

3. *Analyze and interpret data*—Once you've collected relevant data, you need to begin the process of analysis and interpretation in order to arrive at some decision. Data analysis and interpretation of results will be major concerns of Chapters 6 and 7.

4. *Take action*—Finally, you've reached the stage at which a decision must be made. You've answered your **research questions** about the effectiveness of the new science program. At this point, three possibilities exist:

   a. continue the science program as originally established;

   b. disband the program; or

   c. modify the program in some way(s).

Action research is cyclical (see Figure 1.10). The process doesn't necessarily have to stop at any particular point. Information gained from previous research may open new avenues of research. That's why action research is ongoing. In the role of educational leader-as-action researcher, you're continually involved in assessing instruction and seeking ways of improving your school. Action research affords you the opportunity and tools necessary to accomplish these lofty goals.

# The Educational Leader as a Reflective Practitioner

"Reflection? Who has the time?", asks an assistant principal in an inner-city school in Los Angeles. "Certainly, we've learned about 'reflective practice' in graduate courses, but who has much time to really 'reflect' when you're on the job," complains a principal in a suburban school in Westchester, New York.

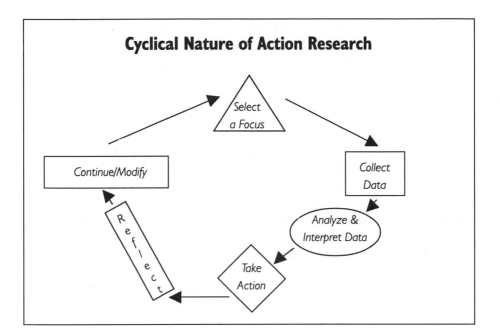

**Figure 1.10**

Anyone who has worked as an educational leader in a fairly large school setting realizes that "educational leadership is riddled (or blessed) with situations that demand quick action and almost immediate response" (Beck, 1994, p. 128). In spite of the fact that leaders often have to make quick decisions, reflection is indeed possible.

Donald Schon (1983, 1984, 1987) advocates reflection in and on the practice of educational administration and supervision. Schon maintains that " . . . the problems of real-world practice do not present themselves as problems at all but as messy, indeterminate situations" (1987, p. 4). Schon (1987) describes two types of reflective thinking: *reflection-in-action* and *reflection-on-action*. Reflection-in-action is the ability to "think on one's feet" when faced with the many surprises and challenges in our daily lives in schools. Educational leaders who are successful certainly are able to "think on their feet" as they face the multitude of crises that are all too common in almost any school. Leaders must often decide quickly when confronted by an irate parent's demand that she be allowed "to whip" her child in front of the class. Even when challenged by less inflammatory situations, leaders must act decisively. Management by crisis is, unfortunately, all too common in today's schools.

On the other hand, Schon also discusses reflection-on-action, which is most relevant to our discussion of action research. Reflection-on-action occurs when educational leaders look back upon their work and consider what practices were successful and what areas need improvement. Reflection-on-action is critical to understanding and thinking about events and phenomena as they unfold in the school. Special time must be set aside to allow for reflection-on-action.

Overwhelmed and sometimes incapable of dealing with increased demands, educational leaders think that reflection-on-action is impossible when, in fact, it is not only essential, but indeed possible (Whitaker, 1995). How then can an educational leader find the time to become a "reflective educator"? Here are some suggestions:

1. Set aside 15–30 minutes a day for reflective thinking. Build time into your schedule by informing your secretary that between 11:20 A.M. and 11:45 A.M., you are not to be disturbed, unless an emergency arises (and do give your secretary some example of "legitimate" emergencies). During this time you should close and lock your door and deliberate on the overall structure of the day or on one specific issue.

2. Some leaders prefer to "reflect" early in the morning before school begins or after school. Time for reflection should be determined by your schedule and preference. Choose a time during which you are alert and can seriously contemplate the many issues that need attention. Personally, I am a late night person and find that 1:00 A.M. suits me just fine. I am most productive when the house is quiet and I am able to think undisturbed.

3. One principal I had the opportunity to work with held a "cabinet meeting" every day, from 7:30 A.M. until around 8:30 A.M., before students arrived. Such meetings allowed supervisory personnel to "reflect" and bring up important issues for general discussion. Anyone on the faculty or staff was allowed to attend these meetings to share their concerns or simply join in on "reflecting."

One of the most important decisions an educational leader must make is whether or not to become a "reflective practitioner." A reflective leader is someone who takes the time to think about what has transpired or what steps should be taken tomorrow. A reflective leader thinks before s/he acts. S/he is proactive, not reactive. A reflective leader takes responsibility for making those tough decisions and is willing to admit error. Reflective leaders do not act impulsively or overreact to a situation. Instead, they carefully consider options and decide on a course of action.

Reflection is the heart of professional practice. Robert Starratt (1995) explains that "practitioners who analyze the uniqueness of a problem confronting them, frame the problem in ways that structure its intelligibility, think about the results of their actions, and puzzle out why things worked and why they did not tend to build up a reservoir of insights and intuitions that they can call upon as they go about their work" (p. 66).

# Reflective Practice

*"Reflective process is a powerful approach to professional development."*
*(Osterman & Kottkamp, 1993, p. 19)*

Reflective practice is a process by which educational leaders take the time to contemplate and assess the efficacy of programs, products, and personnel in order to make judgments about the appropriateness or effectiveness of these aspects so that improvements or refinements might be achieved. Research-oriented leaders have a vision that guides their work. As they plan and work to improve their schools, they collect and analyze data to better inform their decisions. Research-oriented leaders are engaged in ongoing self-study in which they assess the needs of their schools, identify problem areas, and develop strategies for becoming more effective.

Instilling habits of reflection, critical inquiry, and training in reflection is not usually part of a supervisor preparatory program. Supervisors should submit their own practice to reflective scrutiny by posing some of these questions, among others:

1. What concerns me?

2. Why am I concerned?

3. Can I confirm my perceptions?

4. What mistakes have I made?

5. If I was able to do it again, what would I do differently?

6. What are my current options?

7. What evidence can I collect to confirm my feelings?

8. Who might be willing to share their ideas with me?

9. What have been my successes?

10. How might I replicate these successes?

11. In what other ways might I improve my school?

# Chapter Summary

Action research, as disciplined inquiry, is an invaluable tool that allows educational leaders to reflect upon their practices, programs, and procedures. Many practitioners avoid research for a variety of reasons. Foremost among these reasons are that practitioners do not realize that implementing an action research project is not necessarily laborious, time-consuming, or difficult. Educational leaders who are truly concerned about improving their schools or programs will likely prioritize their responsibilities and expend appropriate energies toward undertaking some form of action research.

Although action research projects may be developed by teams of educational professionals, this book provides the impetus for individual leaders to acquire the requisite knowledge, skills, and dispositions to make action research an effective and valuable experience. This chapter has provided an overview of various categories, types, and forms of research and has argued that evaluation research, discussed at length in Chapter 4, is a primary use of action research that educational leaders are most likely to undertake on a regular basis.

Aside from providing you with a brief history, this chapter has explained the benefits of and basic steps in action research. Finally, you may better understand that reflective practice is critically important in order to make intelligent judgments about the effectiveness of various programs, procedures, and practices. Research, as a tool of an educational leader, *is* reflection in action!

Before proceeding to the next chapter, complete the following exercises:

# Exercises

8. Brainstorm some ideas for assessing a program in your school/district using the first step in action research, as described above.

   _____

   _____

   _____

   Answers will vary

9. How might you find more time for reflection-on-action? Be specific.

   _____

   _____

   _____

   Answers will vary

10. Submit your own practice to reflective thinking by answering the eleven questions noted in the section on Reflective Practice above. What other questions come to mind?

    _____

    _____

    _____

    Answers will vary

11. Which is *not* accurate regarding the four steps in action research?

    a. defining a problem can be teacher or supervisor initiated

    b. state the hypothesis

    c. in the research design you must state how the sample was formed and what statistical measures will be employed

    d. the final stage is to collect and analyze the data

    e. none of these

    Answer: choice "d"

# References

[Note that references with an asterisk are annotated later in the book.]

Adelman, C. (1993). Kurt Lewin and the origins of action research. *Educational Action Research, 1*(1), 7–24.

Beck, L. G. (1994). *Reclaiming educational administration as a caring profession.* New York: Teachers College Press.

Best, J., & Kahn, J. (1993). *Research in education* (7th ed.). Needham Heights, MA: Allyn and Bacon.

Calhoun, E. F. (1994). *How to use action research in the self-renewing school.* Alexandria, VA: Association for Supervision and Curriculum Development.

Calhoun, E. F. (1993). Action research: Three approaches. *Educational Leadership, 51,* 62–65.

Calhoun, E., & Allen, L. (in press). *The action research network: Action research on action research.* In B. Joyce & E. Calhoun (Eds.), *Learning experiences in school renewal.* Eugene, OR: Clearinghouse on Educational Management.

Calhoun, E. F., Allen, L., & Halliburton, C. (1996). *A report on the implementation of and results from schoolwide action research.* Paper presented at the annual meeting of the American Educational Research Association, New York, April.

Calhoun, E. F., Allen, L., Halliburton, C., & Jones, S. (1996). *Schoolwide action research: A study of facilitation.* Paper presented at the annual meeting of the American Educational Research Association, New York, April.

Charles, C. M. (1995). *Introduction to educational research.* New York: Longman.

*Corey, S. M. (1953). *Action research to improve school practices.* New York: Teachers College Press.

Cuban, L. (1984). *How teachers taught: Constancy and change in American classrooms, 1890–1980.* New York: Longman.

DeRoche, E. F. (1987). *An administrator's guide for evaluating programs and personnel* (2nd ed.). Boston: Allyn and Bacon.

Eisner, E. W. (1991). *The enlightened eye.* New York: Macmillan.

*Elliott, J. (1991). *Action research for educational change.* Bristol, PA: Open University Press.

*Equity and Choice.* (1993), 10(1).

Foshay, A. W. (1994). Action research: An early history in the United States. *Journal of Curriculum and Supervision, 9,* 317–325.

Glickman, C. D. (1993). *Renewing America's schools: A guide for school-based action.* San Francisco: Jossey-Bass Publishers.

Greenwood, J. M. (1891). Discussion of Gove's paper. *NEA Proceedings,* 227.

Hunter, M. (1967). *Reinforcement theory for teachers.* El Segundo, CA: TIP Publications.

Kagan, D. M. (1995). *Laura and Jim and what they taught me about the gap between educational theory and practice.* New York: State University of New York Press.

Kemmis, S. (1980). *Action research in retrospect and prospect.* Paper presented to the annual meeting of the Australian Association for Research in Education, Sydney.

Lewin, K. (1948). *Resolving social conflicts.* New York: Harper and Brothers.

*McLean, J. E. (1995). *Improving education through action research: A guide for administrators and teachers.* Thousand Oaks, CA: Corwin Press.

McMillan, J. H., & Schumacher, S. (1989). *Research in education: A conceptual introduction* (2nd ed.). Glenview, IL: Scott, Foresman.

*McNiff, J. (1991). *Action research: Principles and practice.* London: Routledge.

Oja, S., & Smulyan, L. (1989). *Collaborative action research: A developmental approach.* London: The Falmer Press.

Olivero, J. (1982). Principals and their inservice needs. *Educational Leadership, 39*(5), 340–344.

Osterman, K. F., & Kottkamp, R. B. (1993). *Reflective practice for educators: Improving schooling through professional development.* Newbury Park, CA: Corwin Press.

Palanki, A., & Burch, P. (1995). *In our hands: A multi-site parent–teacher action research project.* (Report No. 30). Center on Families, Communities, Schools, and Children's Learning.

Peterson, K. D. (1995). *Teacher evaluation: A comprehensive guide to new directions and practices.* Thousand Oaks, CA: Corwin Press.

Sagor, R. (1997). Collaborative action research for educational change. In A. Hargreaves (Ed.), *Rethinking educational change with heart and mind* (pp. 169–191). Alexandria, VA: ASCD.

*Sagor, R. (1992). *How to conduct collaborative action research*. Alexandria, VA: Association for Supervision and Curriculum Development.

Schon, D. A. (1983). *The reflective practitioner: How professionals think in action*. New York: Basic.

Schon, D. A. (1984). Leadership as reflection-in-action. In T. J. Sergiovanni & J. E. Corbally (Eds.), *Leadership and organizational culture: New perspectives on administrative theory and practice* (pp. 36–63). Urbana: University of Illinois Press.

Schon, D. A. (1987). *Educating the reflective practitioner: Toward a new design for thinking and learning in the professional*. San Francisco: Jossey-Bass Publishers.

Starratt, R. J. (1995). *Leaders with vision: The quest for school renewal*. Thousand Oaks, CA: Corwin Press.

*Stringer, E. T. (1996). *Action research: A handbook for practitioners*. Thousand Oaks, CA: Sage Publications.

Stufflebeam, D. L. (1996, April). *Developing evaluation-oriented school principals*. Paper presented at the annual meeting of the American Educational Research Association, New York.

Taba, H., & Noel, E. (1957). *Action research: A case study*. Washington, DC: Association for Supervision and Curriculum Development.

Tuckman, B. (1988). *Conducting educational research*. New York: Harcourt.

Whitaker, K. S. (1995). Principal burnout: Implications for professional development. *Journal of Personnel Evaluation in Education, 9*, 287–296.

Wiersma, W. (1995). *Research methods in education: An introduction*. Boston: Allyn and Bacon.

**CHAPTER 2**

# Teaching and Doing Action Research Through General Semantics

*"All seeing is essentially perspective and so is all knowing."*

*(Nietzsche)*

*"To attack such problems, one must 'swarm all over them,' the way an infantry team might attack a machine gun nest."*

*(Arthur Foshay, 1994, p. 317)*

## Action Research and General Semantics

Before getting into some of the nitty-gritty of action research, you need to be aware of an important principle or mindset that should guide any action researcher. Action research, at its best, examines phenomena from a variety of perspectives. Much of what is characterized as action research today, unfortunately, suffers from a lack of in-depth analysis from a variety of perspectives. I believe that maintaining a multidimensional perspective when conducting any form of research, especially action research, is imperative. This perspective is so important I have devoted an entire chapter to explaining how I utilize the study of **general semantics** in both teaching and conducting action research.

# Introduction

I begin my course on educational research by relating a famous story told at Harvard Law School in which 175 eager, albeit anxious, first-year law students await their first professor in their first course.

A middle-aged, scholarly-looking gentleman dressed in a dapper suit enters the huge auditorium through one of the doors adjacent to the stage. As the professor approaches the podium he peers out at his students and selects his victim.

"You," pointing to a male student in the rear of the auditorium, "state the facts in the case before you." Nervously and hurriedly, the 175 students read the case. The student selected by the professor offers no response. Once again the professor repeats his request. The student again freezes. Again the request is made. "State the facts in the case before you." The student gives an inadequate answer.

The professor nonchalantly reaches into his pocket and takes out a dime and says "Take this dime, call your mother (it's an old story!), and tell her to pick you up because you'll never become a lawyer." Shocked, yet thankful they weren't called upon, the 174 other students anxiously await the student's reaction. No response.

"You heard what I said. Take this dime and tell your mother to pick you up." The student rises and walks slowly towards the stage. Hushed silence pervades the auditorium. Suddenly the student stops, looks up and shouts "Sir, you are a bastard." Without batting an eyelash, the professor looks up and says "Go back to your seat, you're beginning to think like a lawyer."

"This story," I inform my class, "epitomizes the purpose of law school, which is to instill habits of skepticism, verbal aggressiveness, and the readiness to challenge the authority of a lawyer." I continue by conveying my expectations and hopes for them this semester. "My purposes in teaching this course are very different from that professor at Harvard. I do, however, want to help you begin to *think and act* as action researchers." To accomplish this objective I not only provide hands-on activities that challenge my students to apply many principles of action research, but also incorporate the study of *general semantics* in order to help them avoid narrow frames of reference while conducting research.

Before discussing some implications of the study of general semantics for the teaching and practice of action research, I begin with an overview and short history of general semantics. Then I examine how I was introduced to the field of general semantics and explore some of its implications for action research.

## What Is General Semantics?

*"Action research is above all a matter of language."*
*(Gauthier, 1992, p. 192)*

Although defined variously, most agree that *general semantics* is concerned with ways of increasing the truth content of our language that inevitably influence our perceptions of the world. To achieve this, general semanticists examine the relationship between language, thought, and human behavior. More specifically, the field of general semantics is based on a fundamental principle that language is arbitrary. According to general semantics, there is no inherent relationship between a word and what it stands for. Because many of us only speak one language we unconsciously assume that there is some inherent relationship between words (verbal maps) and the things they represent. Calling an object a "chair" is arbitrary, for example. The word "chair" in English in no way more accurately describes what it is than calling it a "key say" in Hebrew. Anyone who speaks several languages knows there are as many words for things as there are languages; and there is no right one.

The arbitrariness of language, representing only one of many principles of general semantics, was first systematized by Alfred Korzybski (1879–1950) in a book that according to some is "one of the ten most influential books of the twentieth century" (as cited in Read, 1970). Korzybski's (1958) analysis in *Science and Sanity* laid the groundwork for what later became known as the field of study called "general semantics" (Bois, 1967). Korzybski, a Polish scientist and engineer, became convinced that discourse framed in right–wrong, yes–no, true–false, or what he called an "Aristotelian" way of thinking (a term he coined from the system of

deductive logical reasoning originating with Aristotle) was potentially limiting (de Bono, 1972). According to Korzybski, phenomena do not lend
themselves to such dichotomous thinking. For Korzybski, reality is too
complex and diverse to rely on one perspective in pursuing knowledge,
truth, and inquiry. Thus, Korzybski's non-Aristotelian formulations held
that we could never fully define reality, that all theories to some extent
were tentative, and that language is arbitrary. "Korzybski cryptically de-
nied the identity of theory and reality by saying, 'Whatever you *say* a
thing is, it is not'" (Pula, 1970, p. 153).

Emanating from this Non-Aristotelian premise is another one of
Korzybski's contributions known as "multiordinality." Given the
unreliability and inadequacy of language to precisely describe phenomena, Korzybski maintained that a word can often have very different meanings depending on, for instance, the context in which it is spoken and the
manner in which it is expressed. Multiple meanings (**multiordinality**) are
common and have significant implications for how we communicate.
According to the general semanticist, words are ambiguous and can be
used in many different ways. For example, I might ask you, the reader, the
following three questions: Who crosses the bridge on your nose?; How
can you sharpen your shoulder blades?; and Does the calf on your leg eat
the corn on your toe? (Berman, 1974). Although there is obviously a high
degree of social acceptance and agreement of meaning among people,
misunderstandings are too common because we unconsciously expect
people to have the same understanding as we do. Meanings are not in
words, they are inside people, according to general semanticists. Confusion of this basic premise often leads to errors in thinking, communication, and behavior.

The study of general semantics attempts to help people use language
more scientifically and accurately. General semantics is concerned with
increasing the correspondence between the words we use to describe reality and the structure of reality itself. Conceived as such, the study of the
field of general semantics has important implications for the teaching and
practice of action research.

I was initially introduced to the fascinating study of the relationship
between language, thought, and human behavior when a colleague, quoting Voltaire, said to me: "There are too many of us present." To which I
replied an incredulous, "what's that?!" He reiterated, "there are too many
of us here." "But there are only two of us in this room," I responded. "I'm
sure there are at least six of us," he said. "There is what you are, what you

think you are, and what I think you are. And there is what I am, what I think I am, and what you think I am." What did this mean? Momentarily stunned, I regained my composure and realized an inherent truth that I perhaps knew subconsciously but never articulated. I had taken for granted the multifaceted dimensions of reality. My assumptions erroneously shaped my perceptions and behavior. I also realized that the picture I have of myself is due to my unconscious assumptions. What I think I am is not me—it's an abstraction, a map of my real self. What did this mean for me as an action researcher?

Initial curiosity quickly turned into intrigue, fascination, and a compulsion. I read Korzybski's (1958) *Science and Sanity* (originally published in 1933), Chase's (1938) *The Tyranny of Words*, Hayakawa's (1939) *Language in Thought and Action*, and listened intently to Berman's (1974) audio cassette program "How to Think, Communicate, and Behave Intelligently: An Introduction to General Semantics." I learned the importance of increasing the correspondence between the structure of my verbal map of "what's out there" and the structure of reality itself. Aside from many personal lessons I learned, I became more interested in the implications general semantics had for my students engaged in action research. How might I help them become better researchers?

## Course Description

I begin my graduate-level research course by asking students to stand and walk over to the window. As they peer through the window I ask them to describe what they see. As they convey their perceptions, I record responses on the board. "Is there anything else you see?" "Is what you are seeing representative of what is out there?" "Is what you are describing an accurate assessment of what you have seen?" Students assume that their responses are accurate, if not definitive, descriptions of "what's out there." I ask them now to examine a chair at the front of the room. I inform them that on the underside of the chair the word "Taiwan" is imprinted. "Write down what you know about this object." Nearly every student writes that the object is a chair made in Taiwan. After a brief, albeit intense, discussion it is apparent that the students have not thoroughly examined their assumptions and perceptions. "Why did you assume that the object was made in Taiwan? Is this object a chair made in Taiwan or is it an object, we call a chair, that has the word 'Taiwan' printed on it?"

Our assumptions are lenses that affect what we see and how we interpret meaning. As researchers we should try to neutralize our assumptions, at least temporarily, in order to maintain objectivity. Doing research demands understanding that the chair may or may not have been made in Taiwan. Additional information is needed before a conclusive statement can be made about the origin of the object. Seeing things using multiple lenses or frames is a better way of ensuring a more accurate understanding of "what's out there."

Quoting Nietzsche, I explain that "all seeing is essentially perspective and so is all knowing." I read *It Looks Like This* (Webber, 1976) to them and have them peruse *The True Story of the 3 Little Pigs* (Wolf, 1989). We discuss the implications of these stories for their work as educational researchers. Researchers attempt to explain phenomena systematically through the application of the **scientific method**. To know something about anything necessitates a global or multidimensional perspective. One should acknowledge and consider a variety of perspectives or points of view before making a decision or reaching a conclusion.

Using the metaphor of detective can inform our work as action researchers. If a detective arrived on the scene of an automobile accident and proceeded to **interview** the drivers without attending to bystanders and even the elderly gentleman peering through the window of his apartment located above the scene of the accident, s/he would certainly not adequately ascertain the facts. Moreover, if one of the drivers was an elderly woman and the other a forty-year-old man dressed in a neat blue suit, possibly the detective would infer that a detailed investigation was unwarranted. In this case, the detective's assumptions and conclusions may have been misleading and inaccurate without the benefit of a thorough investigation.

Similarly, we as action researchers, I explain to my class, are detectives of sorts. We collect an array of data to inform the conclusions that we can justifiably make. To utilize a few **data collection** sources may lead to incomplete analyses, if not misevaluations. Although general semanticists originally questioned the truth claims of **quantitative research** (see, e.g., Payne, 1977), **qualitative research** too is particularly susceptible to misevaluations.

Questions about the "truth value" (Lincoln & Guba, 1985, p. 290) of qualitative research have emerged. Questions about the applicability, consistency, and neutrality of qualitative research persist. We need to ask questions such as "how truthful are the particular findings of qualitative investigations?"; "how applicable are these findings to other settings?"; "can other researchers replicate these findings?"; "how can we assure that the findings are not based on the researcher's unique biases and erroneous assumptions?"

The credibility of qualitative paradigms is enhanced by employing, for instance, a technique known as **triangulation**, first coined by Webb (1965). "Triangulation is the act of bringing more than one source of data to bear on a single point" (Marshall & Rossman, 1994, p. 146). As Marshall and Rossman continue to explain: "[D]esigning a study in which multiple cases are used, multiple informants or more than one data gathering technique can greatly strengthen the study's usefulness for other settings" (p. 146). I tell my students that incorporating multiple sources of data is critical to ensuring a more accurate view of reality. To reinforce this multidimensional framework that underlies triangulation, whether in regard to quantitative or qualitative analyses, I draw Figure 2.1 on the board and explain that multiple use of **data collection** methods will provide us with a more complete understanding of a given problem or **research question**.

To demonstrate the strength of **triangulation**, students, in groups of four, develop a problem and select a different **data collection** technique for each person in the group (e.g., **interview, questionnaire, historical analysis, unobtrusive measures**, etc.). They confer on defining the problem and later work independently for two weeks gathering data using only one technique. They reconvene to share observations, findings, and tentative conclusions. Students are then encouraged to address questions such as, "did my observations, findings, and conclusions coincide with those found by other members in my group?"; "in what way was my data collection limiting?"; "how can I more fully understand the problem?"; "how does the combination of techniques offer greater insights into the problem?" Students realize that triangulation rests on the assumption that the weakness in a single method will often be compensated by the strengths of another method. Triangulation therefore exploits the assets and neutralizes the liabilities of different data collection methods (Jick, 1979).

Not surprisingly, therefore, I encourage students in undertaking their individual projects to use a mixed-methodology **design** incorporating both qualitative and quantitative analyses (Creswell, 1994). Using one modality is limiting and will not reveal all that can be known about the impact of a particular **treatment**. Students begin to explore a specific issue or problem of concern to them in the classroom. They are encouraged to view the problem or topic from a multidimensional view. Students realize

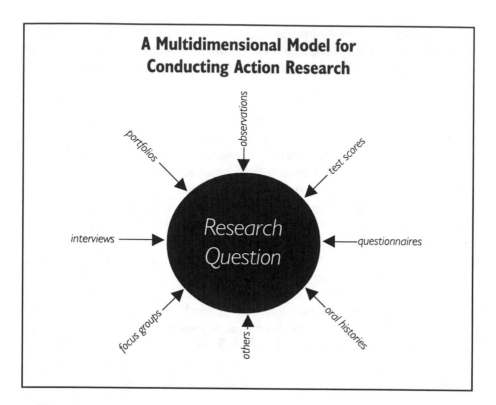

**Figure 2.1**

the complexity of the "world of reality" and that, although everything cannot be known about anything (a central premise of general semantics called the "allness principle"), assuming a multiple framed perspective gives a student a more realistic insight into a given educational problem.

Assignments, then, encourage students to use an array of data collection techniques that hopefully will preclude myopia and provincialism that often lead to uni-dimensional thinking about a given research topic. To this end, students complete two additional assignments prior to undertaking their own research project. First, I ask them to select a field site of some sort such as a health care facility, a restaurant, or a college cafeteria. They must describe the environment and interactions therein during a specified time frame using as many data collection techniques as is readily feasible. Students must report their findings and describe how each technique offers a unique dimension to the "reality" of their particular situation.

A second assignment is designed to help them view situations from different perspectives. Students are asked to describe how different people in given settings might view a particular situation. A student, for instance, would describe how a waitress, customer, and cash register attendant might view services offered in the restaurant.

Also, we watch Kurosawa's famous film "Rashomon," which recounts the same event through the eyes of several witnesses. Each witness tells a different story about how a murder took place. Students are asked to write four different versions of what happened and are encouraged, through class discussions, to realize and appreciate the social construction of reality and how "truth" depends on one's perspective.

Before proceeding with the remainder of the chapter, complete the following exercises that help reinforce some of the ideas expressed above.

---

## Exercises

1. How does the study of general semantics inform our work as action researchers?

   _____

   _____

   _____

   > Although answers will likely vary, a correct response should include the notion that action researchers should use a variety of data collection and research methods so that decisions will not be based on just one approach.

2. Here's a fun exercise: Korzybski discussed the term "multiordinality" and described that our use of language is often ambiguous and arbitrary. Here are some excerpts from an unknown author: "English is a crazy language, isn't it? There's no egg in eggplant nor ham in hamburger; neither apple nor pine in pineapple. English muffins weren't invented in England or French fries in France. Sweetmeats are candies while sweetbreads, which aren't sweet, are meat. We take English for granted. But if we explore its paradoxes, we find that quicksand can work slowly, boxing rings are square and a guinea pig is neither from Guinea nor is it a pig . . . How can a slim chance and a fat chance be the same, while a wise man and a wise guy are opposites? . . . your house can burn up as it burns down, . . . when stars are out, they are visible, but when the lights are out, they are invisible. And why when I wind up my watch, I start it, but when I wind up this essay, I end it."

Can you think of other examples of the "unique lunacy of a language"? And, what does all this have to do with action research anyway?

_____

_____

_____

Answers will vary

3. Define a problem you'd like to investigate and select four different data collection techniques you would use to better understand the problem you identified. Share your views with classmates.

_____

_____

_____

Answers will vary

4. Visit the video store and rent Kurosawa's famous film "Rashomon," which recounts the same event through the eyes of several witnesses. Each witness tells a different story about how a murder took place. Review the four different versions represented in the film and discuss the lessons relevant to action research.

_____

_____

_____

Answers will vary

# Another Lesson from General Semantics

A specific important lesson from general semantics that I review with my students as action researchers is to always test their hidden premises as they, for instance, observe principal–teacher interaction at a faculty conference. We all have beliefs and assumptions that shape our perspective. Often we react too impulsively. We make false assumptions and inferences based on inadequate data. "Avoid making snap judgments," I tell them.

As you observe a class ask yourself, "what am I assuming?" Typically an overly zealous student might arrive at some premature conclusions after perusing preliminary data. Withholding judgments until a thorough consideration of multiple data sources is suggested (Morain, 1969).

Misevaluations are not uncommon when analyzing data derived from **interviews**, for example. One student, seeking to ascertain a principal's attitude toward school reform, assumed that the principal suggested that bureaucracy as the organizational structure of schooling should be dismantled. The principal used the word "bureaucracy" when referring to his inability to obtain needed resources for a particular school program. "Bureaucracy" for the interviewer connoted red tape, waste, and inefficiency. He assumed that the principal concurred that the dysfunctional aspects of bureaucracy precluded successful school reform and that little, if any, substantive changes could occur until alternative forms of school organization were considered. At my suggestion, I urged this student to pursue this line of questioning with the principal and not to assume he disavowed bureaucracy totally. As the interview continued, the principal acknowledged the importance of bureaucracy in terms of providing stability and structure. He maintained that change within a bureaucracy was feasible. He was not, in fact, advocating a dissolution of the school bureaucracy.

The study of general semantics helps us use and understand language more scientifically. The unconscious assumptions we have about our language can result in many misevaluations, as in the case previously cited. Disagreements over meanings of words are not uncommon. Meaning is not in the words we use, but in the person's mind. Rather than asking the interviewee what he meant by "bureaucracy," my student assumed what he meant was based on his own assumptions of the meaning and implications of bureaucracy. General semantics offers much insight into interpreting meanings of words derived from interviews, case studies, surveys, and other qualitative sources. Action research is more meaningful and accurate when we become aware of some of the unconscious assumptions that we make in thinking, communicating, and behaving.

Similarly, misevaluations can also occur between the doctoral or master's degree advisor and student. Students are often anxious as they initiate their study. Numerous ideas flood their thoughts as they eventually narrow their focus to one fuzzy idea. Their thoughts may focus on the assumption that the professor will consider their idea foolish and unworthy of scholarly investigation. At the same time, the faculty advisor might have his/her own version of what topic deserves study and how the investigation should proceed. Unless meanings are articulated, confusion and misevaluations are inevitable. In my course, in which students must select an action research topic, I encourage them to share their ideas first with their peers and then with me. Shared meanings often lead to effective communication and successful research projects.

# Chapter Summary and Conclusion

One of the tasks of an action researcher is to understand that reality, language, and behavior are complex. Any attempt to understand and describe phenomena is necessarily incomplete given the multifaceted nature of reality. General semantics suggests that every point of view has built-in assumptions. While we attempt to gain wide perspective, we also understand the inherent bias of any investigation. Nevertheless, our goal as action researchers is to achieve perspective through the use of a multitude of data sources. As Kurman (1977) notes, "[A] shift of perspective is not a violation of the true order of things, but a viable alternative" (p. 267).

For instance, let's say you're interested in assessing the impact of the new stress reduction program implemented two years ago. You're interested in knowing the impact of these stress-reduction techniques on students' attitudes and achievement levels in mathematics. Before concluding that the program is a failure or success, you need to collect data or information to inform your decision. That's what research is all about, collecting data. However, if you were to only **interview** 30 students in one class or merely examine test scores on a given grade you would not get a true or valid picture of the program's impact. Examining scores of **teacher-made tests** and standardized tests, interviewing teachers, parents, and students, and reviewing anonymous surveys distributed to all participants would give you a much better picture of the current state of the program than merely looking at one narrow aspect. Once those data are collected and analyzed you're in a much better position to make a decision about the effectiveness of this program.

Examining a multitude of data before making a decision is what this chapter, in part, has tried to convey. This message may seem obvious and somewhat simplistic, but, in practice, action research has been plagued by a very limited use of alternate methods for collecting data. Employing qualitative and quantitative measures, and employing various data sources and **data collection** methods thereby achieving *triangulation*, the educational leader, as action researcher, is most certainly in a better position to arrive at an intelligent, thoughtful decision (O'Connor, 1990).

# References

Berger, P. L., & Luckmann, T. (1966). *The social construction of reality: A treatise on the sociology of knowledge.* New York: Doubleday.

Berman, S. I. (1982). *Words, meanings, and people.* San Francisco: International Society for General Semantics.

Berman, S. I. (1974). *How to think, communicate, and behave intelligently: An introduction to general semantics* (audiocassette program). San Francisco: International Society for General Semantics.

Bois, J. A. (1967). *Art of awareness.* Dubuque, IA: W. C. Brown & Co.

Bolman, L. G., & Deal, T. E. (1991). *Reframing organization.* San Francisco: Jossey-Bass.

Chase, S. (1938). *The tyranny of words.* New York: Harcourt, Brace, and Company.

Creswell, J. W. (1994). *Research design: Qualitative and quantitative approaches.* Thousand Oaks, CA: Sage Publications.

de Bono, E. (1972). *Po: Yes and no.* New York: Penguin Books.

Foshay, A. W. (1994). Action research: An early history in the United States. *Journal of Curriculum and Supervision, 9,* 317–325.

Gauthier, C. (1992). Between crystal and smoke: Or, how to miss the point in the debate about action research. In W. Pinar & W. Reynolds (Eds.), *Understanding curriculum as phenomenological and deconstructed test* (pp. 184–194). New York: Teachers College Press.

Hayakawa, S. I. (1939). *Language in thought and action.* New York: Harcourt, Brace, and Company.

Jick, T. D. (1979). Mixing qualitative and quantitative methods: Triangulation in action. *Administrative Science Quarterly, 24,* 602–611.

Korzybski, A. (1958). *Science and sanity* (4th ed.). Lakeville, Connecticut: The International Non-Aristotelian Library.

Kurman, P. (1977). Research: An aerial view. *Et Cetera, 34,* 265–276.

Lincoln, Y., & Guba, E. (1985). *Naturalistic inquiry.* Beverly Hills, CA: Sage Publications.

Marshall, C., & Rossman, G. B. (1994). *Designing qualitative research.* Newbury Park, CA: Sage Publications.

Morain, M. S. (1969). *Teaching general semantics: A collection of lesson plans for college and adult classes.* San Francisco: International Society for General Semantics.

O'Connor, B. N. (1990). About action research versus formal research. *Business Education Forum, 44*(4), 8–9.

Payne, D. (1977). The biases of inexact hypothesis testing. *Et Cetera, 34,* 330–338.

Pula, T. J. (1970). General semantics as an educative tool in the electrical curriculum. In L. Thayer (Ed.), *Communication: General semantics perspectives* (pp. 151–162). New York: Spartan Books.

Read, C. (1970). Alfred Korzybski: His contributions and their historical development. In L. Thayer (Ed.), *Communication: General semantics perspectives* (pp. 339–347). New York: Spartan Books.

Webb, E. J., Campbell, D. T., Schwartz, R. D., & Sechrest, L. (1965). *Unobtrusive measures.* Chicago, IL: Rand McNally.

Webber, I. E. (1976). *It looks like this: A point-of-view book.* San Francisco: International Society for General Semantics.

Wolf, A. (1989). *The true story of the 3 little pigs.* New York: Viking Press.

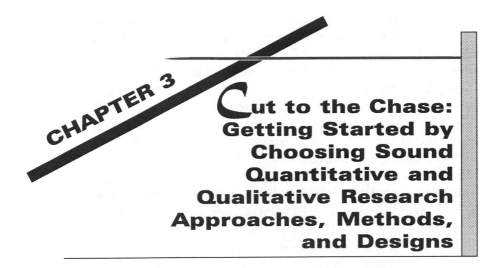

# CHAPTER 3

# Cut to the Chase: Getting Started by Choosing Sound Quantitative and Qualitative Research Approaches, Methods, and Designs

*"For those seeking whole-school improvement in terms of increasing student learning and creating a healthier professional workplace, action research captures the notion of disciplined inquiry (thus 'research') in the context of focused efforts to improve the quality of the organization and its performance (thus 'action')."*

*(Calhoun, Allen, & Halliburton, 1996, p. 1)*

Our discussion of **triangulation** in the previous chapter emphasized the importance of two approaches of research: quantitative and qualitative. Both approaches have different purposes, each having strengths and weaknesses. Current thinking in the field of educational research suggests that neither approach is superior to the other, although earlier views held that the quantitative approach, with its emphasis on traditions of positivism, was far more "scientific" than qualitative approaches. The predominance of this social science perspective has only recently undergone criticism in light of the emergence of qualitative, including ethnographic and biographical, analyses. Still, the quantitative research approach is appropriate in some situations, while qualitative research approaches are more suitable in other situations. Sometimes, both approaches can be applied in a given research project. Utilization of one particular approach depends on what is being researched, the aim of the project, and the researcher's preference, rather than the inherent superiority of one approach over another.

Quantitative and qualitative approaches have arisen from different research needs. The quantitative research approach seeks to establish facts through the utilization of the **scientific method**. In quantitative research, the researcher is considered to be "an outsider to the research" (Carr & Kemmis, 1986, p. 16) or an objective observer. Results from quantitative analyses are presented numerically, often using some statistical procedures. The research goal of this approach is discovery of some generalized truth (see **generalization** in the Glossary).

In contrast, qualitative research emphasizes the researcher's subjective viewpoint as integral to disciplined inquiry. Qualitative inquiry provides in-depth analysis into a given problem that might not otherwise be gleaned from statistical results derived from quantitative studies. Results, in qualitative studies, are verbally expressed in great detail. Qualitative approaches enable in-depth analyses into social, interpersonal, and cultural contexts of education more fully than do quantitative studies. For many educators, qualitative research provides richer and wider-ranging descriptions than quantitative methods (see Picasso story, related in the Epilogue).

Thus, rather than conceptualizing quantitative and qualitative approaches as diametrically opposed to research, both approaches should be seen as part of one naturalistic (qualitative)–positivistic (quantitative) continuum (see Figure 3.1).

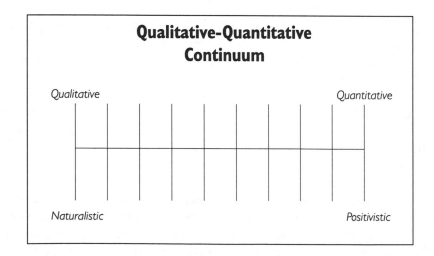

**Qualitative-Quantitative Continuum**

Qualitative                                                          Quantitative

Naturalistic                                                          Positivistic

Figure 3.1

An action researcher may, then, choose a variety of approaches from anywhere on the continuum. As you are introduced to various strategies below, keep in mind that both quantitative and qualitative approaches are equally viable and that use of both, if possible, is optimal. Your projects will be much richer and more meaningful.

# Getting Started:
# The Overall Research Plan

Thus far, we have learned that although action research is not complicated, educational leaders can apply rather sophisticated methods in order to solve practical problems they confront daily. Action research, as disciplined inquiry, can involve simple surveys to inform supervisory or teaching decisions or involve statistical analyses to determine the efficacy of given practices or programs. Educational leaders are professionals well-equipped to utilize research methodologies and strategies for school improvement.

Mindful of the importance of **triangulation**, as reinforced in the previous chapter, you're ready to get started. As a teacher prepares to teach a lesson, s/he must begin by planning. A teacher plans a sequence of learning experiences and activities centered around a goal and a number of objectives. In the same vein, an action researcher begins by developing a plan. This chapter will guide you through the steps in developing such a plan.

A **research design** is an overall plan for conducting action research. An action researcher begins by *clarifying the purposes* for undertaking a study and then *plans the logistics* or administrative items that are necessary to conduct a successful project. Selecting research *approaches* and *methods* are then considered. Planning and carefully considering an appropriate *design* are also essential elements in any action research project.

In order to get started by choosing a sound **research design**, several steps should be followed:

1. clarify the purposes of your research;
2. attend to administrative and logistical aspects of your study;
3. decide on a quantitative and/or qualitative *approach*;
4. select a *method* and *type* of research; and
5. choose a *design* that is appropriate for the area of investigation.

# Clarifying Purposes

The first step you need to consider is the purpose for undertaking action research. Four sets of questions should be initially addressed:

1. What is the purpose of my study or action research project?
2. What do I want to accomplish? or What are my objectives?
3. Why is such a study important? Why do I want to spend time doing this?
4. How will information gleaned from my study help improve the overall instructional program?

Here are some additional questions to ponder:

- Why do I want to conduct an action research study?
- What are the primary concerns about my current instructional program?
- What areas (instructional, curricular, administrative) need improvement?
- How do I know that our instructional programs are working at top efficiency and effectiveness?
- What is the impact of the new reading series on pupil achievement?
- Are the new computers and multi-media technologies being effectively used?
- Are parents adequately involved in instructional/curricular planning activities?
- What are student attitudes toward the new extracurricular after-school program?
- Are teachers adequately prepared to implement the new math series?
- Does the school climate foster a sense of collegiality?
- How might the recently mandated science program be effectively implemented?
- What other programs need implementation and how will I assess their effectiveness?
- Are instructional materials current and being optimally utilized?
- How do teachers feel about the new clinical supervisory methods incorporated by the principal?

- Are the needs of students, parents, and teachers met?
- Are school goals and objectives continually evaluated?
- How productive are the semi-annual parent/teacher conferences?
- Is portfolio assessment meeting its intended objectives in grades K–3?
- What alternatives are there to traditional grading practices in grades 7–9?
- Are discipline codes collaboratively developed and rigorously enforced?

These are only some of the questions you might consider *before* undertaking any study or research project. Before you begin, you must clarify your purposes for conducting the study by focusing on what needs are to be addressed in your school, what you hope to accomplish, and why this project is so important.

Before proceeding with the remainder of the chapter, complete the following exercise that helps reinforce some of the ideas expressed above.

---

### Exercise

1. What specific area(s) would you like to study as part of an action research project? Develop some ideas and share them with a colleague.

   Clarify your purposes for conducting action research by brainstorming and recording answers to the questions enumerated in the previous section.

   Articulate the overarching purpose of your study.

   Why and how will the action research project improve your school?

   What goals and objectives do you want to accomplish?

   Answers will vary

---

# Consider Logistics

You have now identified the overarching purpose of your study including why and how the study will further improve your school and what goals and objectives you want to accomplish. You also know that data should be gathered from a variety of sources. You will try to utilize both qualitative *and* quantitative measures, including experimental and non-experimental types of research, including a variety of data gathering **instruments** (see

Chapter 5). Before we consider the heart or essence of **research design** (deciding which specific form of research to use), we need to consider some logistical matters first:

- who will be involved in this study?;
- who will collect data?;
- how long will it take?; and
- what will it cost in terms of time and resources?

Additional concerns are knowing how data are to be collected, analyzed, and reported, by whom, and what will be done with the results.

In summary, then, the first step in choosing a sound **research design** is to develop an overall plan for your study so that you are clear about your purposes, you understand the value of this undertaking, and you have attended to some logistics. Therefore, the following questions will serve as a guide in developing any research plan:

- What research study will I undertake?
- Why am I conducting this study?
- How will this study help my school improve?
- What are my goals and objectives?
- Who will be involved in this study?
- What other logistical concerns should I prepare for?
- How will data be collected?
- How will data be analyzed?
- How will data be reported?
- What will I do with the results?

Answers to these questions will enable you to start framing and preparing a plan. You need *not* answer all of the questions above definitively. Just begin thinking about them as you continue to plan the project. You are now ready to select an appropriate **research design** matched to your particular needs and concerns.

# The Plan

Now that you have clarified the purposes for conducting an action research project and attended to various logistical concerns, a plan that specifies a **research design** must be articulated. Selection of a research design is really quite simple. The **design** used depends on the *question*(s) you ask and then selecting the appropriate research *methods* that can answer the questions you posed.

Preliminary steps in choosing a research design are:

1. specifying **research questions** and/or **hypotheses**;
2. selecting an appropriate **sample**; and
3. assigning individuals to **treatments**.

Specifying research questions and/or hypotheses will guide your study. Selecting an appropriate **sample** and assigning individuals or groups of individuals to various **treatments** are necessary.

- What questions will guide your research?
- Who will participate in your study?
- How will they be selected?
- Which group will be exposed to the treatment?

Answering these questions is a prerequisites for selecting a suitable **research design**. Refer to Glossary for explanations of **sample, sampling, treatment, research questions**, and **hypotheses**.

Before proceeding with the remainder of the chapter, complete the following exercise that helps reinforce some of the ideas expressed above.

---

### Exercise

2. Given the topic you chose in the previous exercise, what logistical areas will need immediate attention?

   Following the questions noted above in regards to *the plan*, describe your sample, how will participants of your study be utilized or assigned to a treatment, and what research questions will you attempt to answer as a result of undertaking your action research project?

   _____

   _____

   _____

   Answers will vary

The next sections of this chapter will delve more deeply into each methodological approach to research. Various *types* of quantitative and qualitative methods will be discussed as well as related strategies and techniques. Once an *approach* and *method* have been selected, an appropriate *design* can be applied.

# Quantitative Approaches to Action Research

I previously explained that three quantitative *methods* are commonly used in educational research: **descriptive**, **correlational**, and **group comparison research** (refer to Figure 1.6 in Chapter 1).

Descriptive research can be broken down further into two *types*: survey and observational research (refer to Figure 1.7 in Chapter 1).

Correlational research has no subdivisions, whereas group comparison research can be divided into three types: **experimental**, **quasi-experimental**, and **ex post facto research** (refer to Figure 1.7 in Chapter 1). Specific **research designs** that are employed to conduct experimental and quasi-experimental research will be explained later in this chapter.

## Descriptive Research

Descriptive research is one of three methods of research that assumes a quantitative approach in studying a given educational issue or problem. **Survey** and observational reports are *types* of descriptive research. Descriptive research may use statistics or numbers (usually percentages) to describe data.

Although descriptive research is treated as a quantitative method, survey and observational reports can, in fact, be reported qualitatively if nonnumerical findings are reported. Some authorities in the field of educational research consider descriptive research as nonexperimental and can be either quantitative or qualitative. Yet, in action research surveys and observations are usually reported quantitatively.

Let's say you distributed a questionnaire to teachers in your district and collected data about their attitudes toward bilingual education. To report your findings, you decide to note what percentages of teachers in various categories were favorably or unfavorably disposed to bilingual education. You report, in part for example, that 56% of elementary school teachers, as a group, are in favor of bilingual education as compared to 34% and 23% of middle school and high school teachers, respectively. This is an example of descriptive research because you describe findings of your study numerically.

Descriptive research may utilize simple mathematical notations such as percentages or more complicated statistical formulations (see Chapter 6).

Two types of descriptive research can be employed by action researchers: survey and observational.

## Surveys

**Survey** can be defined as a general term for any **instrument** used to assess attitudes or views of respondents. Discussion of surveys in this section will highlight the most common type of survey used in action research: **questionnaires**. Questionnaires are types of surveys that are distributed to a **sample** to ascertain attitudes about a particular issue or concern. Although questionnaires can, in fact, be assessed qualitatively, discussion of questionnaires has been included in this section because results are most often reported numerically.

Two other types of surveys, **interviews** and **focus groups**, whose results are reported verbally, will be discussed in the qualitative section.

Questionnaires are very useful tools to collect data about almost any given topic. Because they are relatively easy to construct and analyze, questionnaires are very popular in action research projects. Questionnaires, especially anonymously collected, provide keen insights that might otherwise be overlooked or unrealized.

Questionnaires can be used to describe how, for instance, teachers in your school feel about the new literature-based reading program recently adopted. Questionnaires are one of the most common types of **data collection instruments** (or data sources) used in action research projects.

Questionnaires, as a descriptive research methodology and as a data collection instrument, will be explained fully in Chapter 5.

Under what circumstances do you think you might utilize a questionnaire?

## Observations

Survey and observational research can really be considered *both* quantitative and qualitative in approach. The determining factor that categorizes one or the other is the way the data are reported. I have included survey and observational research as quantitative approaches because in action research projects they are often reported numerically. On the other hand, **ethnography**, as a qualitative form of observational research, uses verbal or non-numerical ways of reporting data.

Observational research, in this context, refers to studies that measure behavior of an individual or group of individuals by direct observation and report these observations in some numerical way.

Two common forms of observations are nonsystematic and systematic. When a supervisor, for instance, nonsystematically observes a classroom she may simply walk into a classroom unannounced and watch classroom interaction and may even begin taking notes on interactions observed. Nonsystematic observations are usually anecdotal and subjective. Systematic observation refers to a formal process of collecting data that is more scientific than nonsystematic observations in that data are collected with the aid of predetermined observation forms, audiovisual equipment, or some other observation instrument. Systematic observations are generally more accurate and desirable when conducting action research.

An example of observational research conducted systematically in action research projects is as follows:

An assistant principal and a principal observe three students in a classroom. These students have been identified as seriously disruptive. Both supervisors may simultaneously observe these students and record the number of instances of misbehavior within a predetermined period of time. Both observers must, of course, agree on what is considered "serious misbehavior." In advance of the observation they agree that serious misbehavior will be defined as any behavior that includes striking someone else in the class with one's body or any other object as well as verbal and non-verbal disruptions that include cursing, incessant calling out without permission, getting out of one's seat repeatedly, and so on.

During an observational research session both supervisors will record, for example, occurrences of misbehavior (i.e., target behavior) at various intervals or designated times using the Interval Recording Observation Form (see Figure 3.2).

---

# Interval Recording Observation Form

Student's Name: _____

Environment: _____

Target Behavior: _____

Start Time: _____

Observer: _____

Date: _____

*10-minute observation period: 30-second intervals*

| 9:00 | | 9:01 | | 9:02 | | 9:03 | | 9:04 | | 9:05 | | 9:06 | | 9:07 | | 9:08 | | 9:09 | |
|---|---|---|---|---|---|---|---|---|---|---|---|---|---|---|---|---|---|---|---|
| 1 | 2 | 3 | 4 | 5 | 6 | 7 | 8 | 9 | 10 | 11 | 12 | 13 | 14 | 15 | 16 | 17 | 18 | 19 | 20 |
| | | | | | | | | | | | | | | | | | | | |

*Key: + is marked for each occurrence of target behavior; − is marked if target behavior did not occur.*

---

**Figure 3.2**

Although **validity** is maintained by predefining "serious misbehavior," **reliability** is determined through interrater reliability measures (or percentages of agreements between observers) (see **reliability** in Glossary).

Any numerical recording of data collected through direct observation is considered observational research. Several noteworthy works describe in detail various ways or methods of collecting data through observational research. Consult, for example, Acheson and Gall, 1997; Glickman, Gordon, and Ross-Gordon, 1998; Moore, K. D., 1995; and Willerman, McNeely, and Koffman, 1991. This latter work provides detailed explanations of how to use seating charts, verbal flow charts, nonverbal communication patterns, and anecdotal recordings using audio- and videotapes. I usually require my students to read portions of their excellent book. See the next chapter for an example of a checklist observation technique.

## Correlation Research

Another possible *method* of research is known as correlational research (see **correlation** in the Glossary). Correlational research is used to explore the degree of relationship between two **variables** (an action researcher will rarely correlate more than two variables, even though it is possible to do so). For example, as an educational leader you might be interested in correlating students' scores on math and science tests. You might **hypothesize** that the higher a student scores on math tests, the higher she is likely to score on science tests. A correlational analysis will indicate the degree to which these two variables relate to one another. The strength of the correlation (or relationship) between two variables may warrant that a specific instructional measure be taken on a grade level or by an individual teacher.

Correlational research cannot indicate causality between variables. Therefore, any predictions made based on correlational research are tentative. Although not frequently employed by action researchers, correlational research might be useful, for example, to study the following questions:

1.   What is the relationship between leadership styles of principals and faculty morale?
2.   What is the relationship between levels of stress among high school freshman (or any group for that matter) and achievement levels (in a given subject)?
3.   What is the relationship between the availability of technologically oriented instructional materials in science and science achievement?

As will be indicated in Chapter 6, correlational analyses are relatively easy to compute with appropriate computer programs.

## Group Comparison Research

Group comparison research is one of three methods of research that assumes a quantitative approach in studying a given educational issue or problem. Group comparison research compares two or more groups according to some **variable**(s). Usually, action research involves comparing only two groups.

There are three types of group comparison studies: **experimental**, **quasi-experimental**, and **ex post facto**. Quasi-experimental research is most likely utilized in action research projects. The type of research chosen, however, depends, to a large extent, on the situation you are involved with and the degree of independence you, as researcher, have regarding your ability to assign individuals or groups to either **experimental** or **control groups**. Regardless of which type of group comparison research you employ, the same basic structure applies: i.e., two groups are formed, a **treatment** is administered, posttests are given after a reasonable period of time, statistical comparisons are made, and conclusions are drawn.

Let's say you randomly assigned students to two groups. One group (the **experimental group**) will receive computer instruction to reinforce writing skills, while the other group will learn the same writing curriculum without computers. After a 4-month period, you then compare the writing abilities of each group. Such comparisons enable you to assess the impact or effect of the **independent variable** (computer assisted writing instruction) on the **dependent variable** (writing achievement). In Chapter 6, I will discuss precisely how results from group comparison studies are analyzed.

As noted in Figure 1.7 in Chapter 1, **experimental research** is a *type* of group comparison research that may not be suitable for most educational researchers because of the requirement of **randomization**. Yet, some educational leaders might indeed want to undertake experimental research. Sometimes leaders do have an opportunity to randomize, as I did, when I was an assistant principal in New York City (see Glanz, 1994). I studied the effect of stress reduction strategies with fifth grade students by randomly assigning students to two groups: one group (experimental) received the **treatment**, i.e., stress reduction instruction, while the other group (control) did not receive the treatment. The **independent variable** was stress reduction training and the dependent variable was levels of stress exhibited by students during various times of the school year. The fact that randomization was incorporated indicates the experimental nature of the study.

How does **randomization** work? Although randomizing individuals or classes is not often very feasible in educational settings nor frequently employed in action research, opportunities may emerge in which randomization is possible and desirable. There are many ways of assigning subjects randomly to groups. While a detailed discussion of randomization and its variant forms (e.g., stratified random sampling, cluster **sampling**, etc.) is unnecessary (although explained to some degree in the Glossary), educators should know some rules when wishing to randomize:

1.  select the **population** you want to pull your **sample** from and make certain that all members of that population have an equal chance of being selected. For example, when I surveyed assistant principals in New York City (Glanz, 1994), I obtained a list of 3000 assistant principals. Then,

2.  I assigned each subject (assistant principal) a number from 0000 to 2999. Then,

3.  I consulted a table of random numbers (which can be found in almost any book on statistics) and arbitrarily selected a number. Then,

4.  I looked at the last four digits of the numbers.

5.  If that number was also assigned to a subject, that subject was selected for the sample; if not, I went to the next number.

    For example, notice this list of random numbers:

    | | |
    |---|---|
    | 21880 | 78677 |
    | 16899 | 90867 |
    | 22500 | 12490 |
    | 09823 | 73033 |
    | 23460 | 89780 |
    | 30494 | 23111 |
    | 92412 | 80003 |
    | 99780 | 00986 |

    If you start with the top number and look at the last four digits (1880), that represents the assistant principal who was assigned #1880; in other words, the 1,880th assistant principal on the list. S/he is then chosen for my study. I then look at the last four digits of the next number (6899) and realize that it is a larger number than the list of names of assistant principals (maximum of 3000), so I skip that number and continue with the next number. The last four digits of the next number is 2500, so I select the 2,500th assistant principal on my list and s/he becomes the second AP in my study.

6.  I continue this procedure until I have the desired **sample** (usually 10% of the **population** which, in this case, was 300 APs).

Other **sampling** techniques are alluded to in the Glossary.

Further discussion of group comparison studies can be found later in this chapter.

Before proceeding with the remainder of the chapter, complete the following exercises that help reinforce some of the ideas expressed above.

---

## Exercises

3. You are a superintendent who wants to sample teacher attitudes toward supervision and there are 5000 teachers in the population. Describe how you might select a random sample using the table of random numbers.

   _____

   _____

   _____

   Answer:

   POPULATION = 5000 teachers

   SIZE = 10% of 5000 = 500 teachers

   SELECT= assign each a number from 0001 to 5000;

   arbitrarily start in table of random numbers and look at first or last four digits and go down the list until you select 500 teachers. Note: Today, samples can be easily generated through computer printouts without the use of the Table of Random Numbers.

4. Can you think of a situation in which you might set up an:

   a. experimental study;

   b. correlational study; and a

   c. descriptive study?

   Describe each study in detail.

   _____

   _____

   _____

   _____

   Answers will vary

---

# Choosing a Research Design

Thus far, you have selected a topic or area of investigation, have clarified your purposes in undertaking this research venture, and begun to plan to conduct an action research study. At your disposal are quantitative and qualitative approaches to research. Within each approach, different methods (e.g., surveys, group comparison studies, or case study analyses) may be chosen. Selection of a particular method depends on a variety of factors such as the nature of the study, the kinds of questions asked, and the resources available. In this section of the chapter, in order to assist you in getting started, I will discuss another aspect of research design that is of utmost importance.

Why is a **design** necessary? As an educational leader, you'll likely have to implement various programs, establish certain procedures, and/or institute specific practices. Evaluating the efficacy of these instructional concerns will be a challenging, yet urgent task. Program evaluation, for example, is an essential responsibility of any professional supervisor. Evaluating a program with intelligence, thoroughness, and technical sophistication is essential. Any such **evaluation** requires attention to design as the foundation for setting up an action research project. Without attention to design, it would be like building a home without a blueprint.

Before you can choose a sound research design, you'll need to know what designs are readily available and when and how they should be used. Then, you can select the appropriate design to suit your objectives.

This section will discuss eight frequently used **research designs** that can be used, to varying degrees, in action research. These research designs are suitable for quantitative approaches, except for the single measurement design. In the next chapter, a design for evaluation research will be introduced.

# An Inadequate Research Design

There is really only one inadequate or unacceptable research design and that is called the unassessed treatment design (Popham, 1972). Unfortunately, this approach is often used by practitioners in school settings. A program may be implemented or practice established without thorough and thoughtful consideration of its efficacy. The program or practice is continued or discarded without undertaking any sort of evaluative measure. Sound familiar?!

An unassessed treatment design is characterized by an educator's inaction. The educational leader, for example, makes no effort whatsoever to assess whether the **treatment** is effective. Popham (1972) characterizes this design as T= nothing; i.e., no assessment is conducted to determine the impact of a given treatment. I knew a supervisor who once introduced a new procedure requiring teachers to more closely monitor student progress. At the end of the semester, he "felt" that the program was a good idea. He decided to expand the program to the entire grade. When I asked him why he decided to take this action, he replied "It sounds good, doesn't it?!"

Popham (1972) describes the unassessed treatment design as follows:

> In this approach, the instructional treatment developer simply implements a new instructional treatment or alters the existing instructional treatment without making any kind of systematic effort to measure whether the treatment is effective. Usually, of course, judgments have been made regarding whether the treatments are likely to prove worthwhile, but these evaluations are often made without any evidence whatsoever. A school administrator, for example, may introduce a new procedure requiring pupils to spend more time in the school library. At the end of the semester, he may "feel" it was a good idea and should be continued. Or a teacher may decide to alter the nature of his homework assignments so that students do half their assigned work during class sessions. Intuitively, he may decide that this new treatment worked out well, but he makes no attempt to measure the results produced by the innovation. (p. 140)

Popham concludes by cautioning against such an approach. "It is preferable for educators to remain open-minded, postponing all decisions about treatment until such time as appropriate measurements can be collected" (p. 142).

*Mini exercise:* Can you think of a situation in which such an approach was taken? Explain.

# Adequate Research Designs (or Simplified Designs for School Research)

A **treatment** (synonymous with **intervention**) is any specific instructional practice, program, or procedure that is implemented by a researcher in order to investigate its effect on the behavior or achievement of an individual or a group. A treatment might include, for example, a reading series recently adopted by P.S. X, use of computers to assist problem solving, or a behavioral contract system implemented to positively influence behavior of three seventh graders. As a researcher, you want to understand the impact these treatments have on various outcomes (e.g., achievement or attitudes). The following research designs adequately allow you to gather evidence to demonstrate the efficacy of the treatment. Below, eight research designs are discussed that might prove useful for action research projects.

## Single Measurement Design

Single measurement designs may be depicted as follows:

$$T \longrightarrow M$$

The "T" stands for treatment and the "M" indicates the measurement, i.e., the impact that the treatment has on the sample.

Although single measurement designs do not necessarily consider factors that may have influenced a particular outcome, these designs are frequently employed in action research projects because they are relatively easy to use.

When single measurement designs are employed, the educator introduces a treatment and, at least, attempts to measure its impact. Often the measurements take the form of some sort of traditional test.

Single measurement designs are also commonly employed in qualitative approaches. Let's say you were writing a case study to indicate the positive influence that behavior contracting had on the behavior of John, a fifth grader. A case study would involve detailed descriptions of John's behavior over time as a result of several observations. The researcher would provide anecdotal evidence demonstrating how, for instance, John's behavior has changed since the introduction of behavior contracting. Observations are recorded anecdotally in the sense that explicit descriptions of observable acts are recorded without interpretation. Note the following statements that are made anecdotally:

- Jerry got out of his seat at 9:15 A.M. and walked over to Susan and took her pen without permission.
- Juanita dropped her pen on the floor.
- There are 40 students in this class.

By the way, note the difference between anecdotal annotations and inferences:

- He is a trouble maker.
- The information on this test may be too difficult for Susan.
- She is hyperactive.
- Fred behaves very nicely.
- She appears neurotic at times.

Case study research will be discussed later in this chapter. As you learn about case study research you will note that the anecdotal records and interpretations of them are considered "measurements," albeit qualitative. Single measurement designs, whether quantitative or qualitative, are commonly applied to action research situations.

## One-Group Pretest/Posttest Design

A second design commonly used by practitioners is known as the one-group pretest/posttest design and is depicted as follows:

$$M \longrightarrow T \longrightarrow M$$

In this design, one group is selected and is pretested on some **variable**. A **treatment** is then introduced and its impact is assessed by a posttest of some sort.

This research design is not as powerful as the following designs, yet it is commonly used by action researchers because very often only one group is available for study. Growth from pretest to posttest can be assessed. The serious weakness, of course, of the one-group pretest/posttest design is that one can't be certain that an increase in achievement, for example, is a consequence of the treatment itself. No control is provided for intervening variables that might have influenced post-treatment findings. Suppose you find an increase from pretest to posttest, how confident can you be that the gain was attributable solely to your treatment and not due to some other factor? Learners could have gained due to maturation or experiences not associated with the intervention or treatment. Too many other plausible explanations exist.

Some people maintain that pretest–posttest comparisons may be effectively used to ascertain achievement gains. Yet, most researchers caution against such a procedure because it may be possible for one group with very low initial scores to make large gains as compared to another group that starts off with a high average and may make smaller gains. Groups who score higher on pretests will not always make as significant improvements as groups who start with lower averages. This fact is known as the "test ceiling factor."

Nevertheless, despite this serious flaw, use of this design is feasible if two conditions are met: (1) you don't rely only on this design but rather you *triangulate* (remember our discussion of general semantics in Chapter 2?; see **triangulation**) to every extent possible; and (2) you analyze data using the Sign Test, which will be explained in detail in Chapter 6.

## Static-Group Comparison Design

This is a **research design** used in **quasi-experimental research** involving two groups in which only one group, the **experimental group**, receives a treatment. Although a posttest is administered to each group (experimental and control), no pretest is usually administered. Individuals are not randomly assigned to groups. This design is schematically depicted as follows:

$$T\,1 \longrightarrow M$$

$$\longrightarrow M$$

Let's say you want to conduct a study with one class. This design is often used by action researchers who have only one class in which a study can be conducted. You divide the class into two groups. No pretest is used to accomplish this division. Rather, you, the lead-teacher, merely estimate two equivalent or comparable groups. Then, one treatment (e.g., use of stickers as positive reinforcement for math achievement) is administered to the group designated as experimental. The control group is intentionally not offered this form of positive reinforcement for their math work. At the end of a period of time (perhaps after a unit of instruction), you administer an **achievement test**. You would then use a statistical test (the **Mann-Whitney U-Test**; see Chapter 6) to determine whether or not there is a significant difference between the two groups.

## Non-equivalent Control Group Design

The next four designs are among the most powerful designs that can be used by action researchers (Popham, 1972). They include classic group comparison studies that, as you recall, involve two contrasting groups: the experimental group might receive one treatment, while the control group receives another.

The non-equivalent control group design is useful for educational leaders as action researchers. This design, frequently used in school research, involves administering one treatment (T1) to an experimental group and another treatment (T2) to a comparison (control) group. This design is schematically depicted as follows:

$$M \longrightarrow T\,1 \longrightarrow M$$
$$M \longrightarrow T\,2 \longrightarrow M$$

Non-equivalent control group designs usually involve intact experimental and control groups. For instance, if you taught high school English, you might select two classes (say, your fourth and sixth periods) to be involved in a study. You selected these two classes because both groups are somewhat equivalent in achievement levels or comparable in relation to the **variable** under study. (By the way, the word "non-equivalent" in the title of this design refers to the different or non-equivalent treatments both groups receive). Since non-equivalent control group designs involve intact classes, this design is associated with **ex post facto research** that involves group comparisons with intact classes (some consider this design quasi-experimental).

Non-equivalent control group designs can be used with two separate classes with or without the same teacher. You may even divide one class into two equivalent groups using the **matched pairs** technique.

Matched pairs is a technique used to divide a group of students into two comparable groups. Let's say you have a fifth grade class comprised of 28 students and you want to divide them into two equivalent or comparable groups to assess the impact of a particular instructional strategy. To divide the class using matched pairs, you would follow these steps:

1. Administer a test to the entire class. If the content area of your study involves mathematics, for example, you would administer a mathematics test.

2.  Rank the students who completed the test according to the grade achieved on the test. In other words, rank each member of the class from highest score to lowest score. For example, your results, in part, may appear as follows:

    | | |
    |---|---|
    | Mohammid B. | 97 |
    | Fred D. | 96 |
    | Juan S. | 96 |
    | Fran Y. | 93 |
    | Anita G. | 91 |
    | Kim W. | 88 |
    | Wendy L. | 83 |

    and so on

3.  You then take the first *pair* (Mohammid B. and Fred D.) and randomly assign them to the experimental and control groups as follows, for example:

    | Experimental Group | Control Group |
    |---|---|
    | Fred D. | Mohammid B. |

4.  Continue the same procedure for the next pair (Juan and Fran) and do so with all 28 students.

Using matched pairs ensures that you now have two comparable groups, at least in terms of mathematics achievement. You are then ready to conduct your study using, for instance, a non-equivalent control group design.

Non-equivalent control group designs can only work when you begin the study with comparable groups (although, as we'll discuss in Chapter 6, if comparability cannot be achieved for any reason, then a statistical procedure known as an **ANCOVA** can be used). Generally, the non-equivalent control group design is used when **randomization** is impossible, but groups are essentially comparable.

The next two designs are similar to the previous design except for the fact that randomization is possible. Randomization ensures equivalence between groups; i.e., whenever you randomize you can be certain that both groups are comparable. However, randomization is not easily used within classes because moving pupils from one classroom to another for research purposes may not be feasible or practical.

When could randomization be used? You may be able to randomly distribute students into classes before the start of the school year during reorganization, as I have done in some circumstances.

## Pretest/Posttest Control Group Design

The pretest/posttest control group design is a powerful design that incorporates randomization or **sampling**. This design may be depicted as follows:

$$\text{EXPTL} \qquad R\,M \longrightarrow T\,1 \longrightarrow M$$
$$\text{CONTRL} \qquad R\,M \longrightarrow T\,2 \longrightarrow M$$

The "R" indicates that the two groups have been formed by randomization procedures. As before, the "M" refers to the measurements taken prior to and after the introduction of the treatments (T1 and T2).

Since randomization ensures equivalence between groups, the pretest/posttest control group design allows you to draw conclusions about the effectiveness of the treatment. Statistically higher posttest scores of the experimental group as compared to the control group would indicate that, for example, the special use of a new mathematics series with the experimental group contributed to the higher achievement scores.

Why is a pretest necessary? It is not necessary to establish a baseline so that a comparison can be made when the posttest is given. As will be explained in Chapter 6, pretest to posttest gains are not made to ascertain the impact of a given treatment. Statistical work on posttest scores is all that has to be done once group equivalence is assured.

As stated earlier, randomization ensures comparability or equivalence between groups. Therefore, if randomization is employed, why give a pretest? One might respond that a pretest can confirm equivalence. But such an assertion is really unnecessary because it is readily acknowledged that randomization assures equivalence. Sometimes, however, a pretest may yield some important information about content validity. Sometimes a pretest might be a reactive measure that might produce a change in the subject's behavior. For instance, a pretest that is given orally may be reactive in the sense that respondents or subjects may obtain clues about possible answers from voice inflections of the tester. If pretests appear to be reactive, then an alternate design such as the posttest only control group design should be employed.

## Posttest Only Control Group Design

Posttest only control group design may be depicted as follows:

$$R\,T\,1 \longrightarrow M$$

$$R\,T\,2 \longrightarrow M$$

This design should be used when the pretest may be a reactive measure; i.e., participants completing a test or a survey may receive clues from the pretest that may influence a positive score on the posttest. If a pretest is potentially reactive, don't use it. Since randomization is employed, there is no need to worry about equivalence between groups. This design allows you "to make defensible judgments about the value of a given treatment" (Popham, 1972, p. 149).

## Interrupted Time Series Design

This next design is somewhat different from the previous designs. The **interrupted time series design** (also commonly known as the **single-subject design**) is schematically depicted as follows:

$$M\,1 \longrightarrow M\,2 \longrightarrow M\,3 \quad T \quad M\,4 \longrightarrow M\,5 \longrightarrow M\,6$$

In this design, one group is repeatedly pretested, exposed to a treatment, and then repeatedly posttested. In other words, in this design, a series of measurements is taken both before and after the introduction of the **treatment**. Measurements ("M") may be taken from existing archival data such as attendance records, standardized test scores, disciplinary records, and **school profiles**.

Interrupted time series designs usually involve *group* analyses with respect to a given **variable**, such as studying academic progress over time. When progress over time is assessed for *individuals*, another design is used. A **single-subject research design** allows a researcher to investigate one or just a few individuals with respect to a given variable (e.g., changes in behavior). Subjects are exposed to a treatment and then multiple measurements are taken over a period of time. The objective of this sort of research is to determine whether or not the treatment had any effect on the behavior of the subject(s). More detail about this design follows.

## Single-Subject Research Design

**Single-subject research design** is also a powerful method of studying the effectiveness of an intervention or treatment on a single subject or a small group. Measurements are repeatedly made until stability is established (a **baseline**), after which treatment is introduced and an appropriate number of measurements are made; the treatment phase is followed by a second baseline, which is followed by a second treatment phase.

Single-subject research design is popular for action researchers because it is very useful to monitor and assess a particular treatment on individual students. This design is advantageous because results are easy to interpret, usually by visual inspection of the charted data points. Statistical analysis is also unnecessary.

**A-B; A-B-A;** or **A-B-A-B research designs** are *types* of single-subject designs. Before we discuss A-B, A-B-A, and A-B-A-B designs, two basic terms must be explained.

1. **Baseline** condition (Condition A)—refers to information collected on a specific *target behavior* before an **intervention** strategy is employed (see Figure 3.3, which is discussed on page 76). The purpose of establishing baseline data is to provide a description of the target behavior as it naturally occurs without treatment. The baseline serves as the basis of comparison for assessing the impact of a treatment. Taking a number of baseline measurements to establish a pattern of behavior is known as baseline stability. For instance, observing Sarah for a period of three days in a row for 45 minutes each time and noting the number of times she gets out of her seat without permission would establish baseline stability.

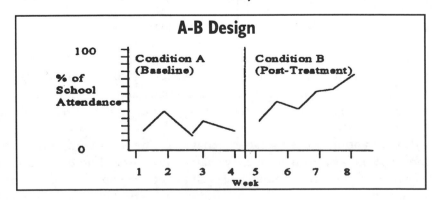

Figure 3.3

2.  **Treatment** (or **Intervention**) condition (Condition B)—during this phase, the treatment is introduced while **data collection** continues.

A word about *target behaviors:* Directly observing any subject in a school setting involves identifying a target behavior. The target behavior must be defined in such a way as to allow the observer to objectively and independently note and measure each behavior. Target behaviors must be observable and measurable. Independent observers must be able to see the behavior occurring and be able to quantify the behaviors by noting, for instance, the frequency and duration of each behavior. For example, observing Michael raising his hand in class, for any reason, is a target behavior because the observer can see the behavior occurring and is able to note the number of times Michael raises his hand in, say, a 45-minute period. An example of a nonobservable target behavior might be: Joshua will be cooperative during group work. The difficulty here, of course, is with the word "cooperative." What does "cooperative" mean? What does it mean to you? Can two independent observers agree that a particular student is being cooperative?

Here's a mini-exercise: Place a check next to the target behavior that can be observed and measured by two independent observers without defining the behavior prior to observation:

_____  1.  Johnny is acting out in class.

_____  2.  Natasha says "thank you" during the lesson.

_____  3.  Felicia is disruptive during art class.

_____  4.  Billy completes his class assignments.

_____  5.  Sally is behaving well.

_____  6.  Kisha raises her hand to ask or answer a question.

Numbers 2 and 6 are target behaviors that can easily be observed. The other choices require observers to define what they consider to be "acting out," "disruptive," "completes his assignments," and "is behaving well." Undertaking single-subject research design requires observers to clarify behaviors in advance.

A word about recording target behaviors: The most common way of recording data is by using frequency charts (checklists). These charts allow an observer to note the frequency of each target behavior. Interval recording is sometimes used to divide the observation period into equal intervals of smaller time periods (see Figure 3.4). Observers can then note whether the target behavior occurred (+) or had not occurred (–), during each interval. Note that the frequencies are not recorded, just the fact that the target behavior was noted during a specified period of time.

---

## Frequency Recording Observation Form

Student's Name: _____

Environment: _____

Target Behavior: _____

Start Time: _____

Observer: _____

Date: _____

*5-minute observation period: 30-second intervals*

| NAME | | 1 | | 2 | | 3 | | 4 | | 5 |
|---|---|---|---|---|---|---|---|---|---|---|
| Maria | | | | | | | | | | |
| Ronald | | | | | | | | | | |
| Steve | | | | | | | | | | |

Key: + is marked in the interval if the target behavior was observed; – is marked if target behavior did not occur.

---

**Figure 3.4**

A word about accuracy in recording behaviors: Here are some factors to consider that may potentially affect your **data collection** during **baseline** and **treatment** periods:

1. *reactivity*—The student observed realizes you are counting or noting the number of times, for example, she is talking to a neighbor. Reac-

tivity can be minimized by not staring at the student as observations are made.

2. *observer drift*—This occurs when an observer daydreams or when an observer is unclear as to when a target behavior is occurring. As alluded to earlier, operationally defining (see **operational definitions**) the target behavior is the best method to minimize observer drift. For instance, how might you operationalize "getting out of one's seat"? Answer: when his buttocks are approximately 12 inches from his chair.

3. *recording procedures*—Make certain that charts for recording data are available at the time of the observation.

4. *location of observer*—The best place to observe is usually from the back of the room, as long as you have an unobstructed view of the class.

5. *observer expectations*—Biased observations or conclusions are minimized when target behaviors are clearly defined in advance.

6. *lack of practice*—That the observer should practice recording behaviors prior to actual study is sound advice.

7. **reliability**—**Interrater reliability** is achieved when there is a high percent of agreement between two or more observers.

    Let's say two individuals are watching the number of times Jose leaves his seat without permission and the following data are collected by each observer:

Observer A—frequency = 5

Observer B—frequency = 10

Reliability could then be calculated by dividing $5 \backslash 10 = 0.5 \times 100 = 50\%$. You should strive for at least a 70% reliability factor.

Figure 3.3 (on page 73) depicts the first type of single-subject design known as **A-B**. Note Condition A (the **baseline** condition) and Condition B (the intervention condition). Don't forget, with single-subject research designs you are studying individuals, not groups of individuals.

The line in the center indicates that the treatment has been introduced. You'll notice that the **baseline** was kept over a 4-week period to establish stability before the introduction of the **treatment**. Measurements continue after the treatment is introduced to note any changes in attendance. From perusing the figure you may reasonably conclude that the treatment, indeed, had a positive effect on school attendance.

Can you draw a chart showing no change after the treatment is introduced? Can you think of a situation in which you as an educational leader might employ a single-subject research design? *Hint:* Think of a situation in which you want to monitor student behavior of some sort. Choose some target behavior; i.e., what exactly you are going to observe. Be very specific about target behaviors (e.g., number of times Howie gets out of his seat or the number of times Juan praises a fellow student in his cooperative group). Once a target behavior has been specified, start collecting **baseline** data during a specified period of time. Then introduce the **treatment** and keep collecting data. Record your data in chart or graph form.

One of the potential problems with an **A-B** design is how to determine that the change after the treatment was definitely due to the treatment and not due, perhaps, to some intervening **variable** or outside influence. That's why some researchers prefer a second type of single-subject design known as **A-B-A**.

This design is similar to the first design, except that you withdraw the **intervention** and then maintain **baseline** data. For example, as an educational leader you might want to introduce a program to increase attendance among students identified as at-risk of dropping out of high school. At a national convention you learn about a marvelous intervention strategy. You decide to implement this program (after, of course, becoming more familiarized with the program). How do you proceed? First, keep baseline data (Condition A) on each student's attendance records for a period of, say, 4 weeks to establish baseline stability. Then, introduce the treatment for a similar period of 4 weeks. You'll note, for example, that attendance rates dramatically increase. Before you conclude that the program is successful, what would you do? Right, withdraw the treatment and monitor student attendance rates by keeping additional baseline rates for 4 weeks. You might find a drop in attendance, but the attendance rates are better than they were prior to the introduction of the treatment.

An **A-B-A** design allows you to more confidently attribute the change in behavior to the treatment, as opposed to some extraneous factor or chance factor. Can you draw a chart or graph that illustrates the experiment described above?

The third type of single-subject research design is known as **A-B-A-B**. Again, this would be similar to the previous design, but would reintroduce the treatment. This design adds further credibility to your treatment. Can you explain why? Can you draw a graph illustrating this design? Can you think of a reason why an A-B-A-B design should not be used? *Hint:* Consider the ethics of removing a successful treatment.

A variation of the designs above is known as the Alternating Treatment Design (A-B-C-A-D-A) and is characterized by the introduction of three separate treatments (B, C, and D).

1.  Starts off the same way as **A-B**, with B representing the use of positive reinforcement through verbal praise.

2.  Then the first of two other treatments are introduced. The first treatment (B) is removed and a new treatment designated as C is introduced (e.g., positive reinforcement using only tokens, no praise) followed by A, which is a phase in which you record baseline data.

3.  Then treatment C is withdrawn, and a new treatment (D) is introduced (e.g. positive reinforcement offered by sending daily letters home), followed by a phase in which you continue to record baseline data, A.

This design can be used when you want to assess the impact of various treatments before you select one as your primary choice.

Can you graph an A-B-C-A-D-A design?

Graph and explain these other designs:

A-B-A-C-A-D and

A-B-C-B-C-B-C

How might these designs be used? Provide examples.

Another major category of single-subject designs is known as Multiple-Baseline Designs. These designs are modifications of single-subject designs. With the use of multiple-baseline designs you can:

1.  collect data on more than 1 subject, and/or

2.  collect data on more than 1 behavior, and/or

3.  collect data on more than 1 situation.

Multiple baselines are recorded because different subjects, behaviors, and situations are observed.

*Multiple-Baseline Across Subjects Design* involves utilizing one of the three single-subjects designs (A-B, A-B-A, or A-B-A-B) on two or more different subjects. For example, you may want to observe three of your students in terms of their frequency of violent behavior (i.e., your target behavior might be the number of times Steve, Maria, and Ronald hit some-one in the classroom). Baseline data for Steve might be graphed as shown in Figure 3.5. Completing similar graphs for Maria and Ronald will allow for comparisons to be made regarding the frequencies of hitting, pre-treatment and post-treatment, for all three students.

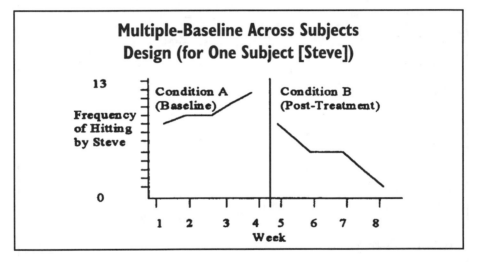

Figure 3.5

What conclusion might you draw from Figure 3.5?

*Multiple-Baseline Across Behaviors Design* involves utilizing one of the three single-subjects designs (A-B, A-B-A, or A-B-A-B) on one subject while observing two or more different behaviors. For example, you may chart the frequencies of hitting, yelling, and kicking for a given student or among three students. Comparisons, as before, can be easily made.

*Multiple-Baselines Across Situations Design* involves utilizing one of the three single-subjects designs (A-B, A-B-A, or A-B-A-B) in two or more different settings for one or more subjects. For example, you may chart the behavior of a given student or among three students in different settings (i.e., math class, cafeteria during lunch, and in the gymnasium). Comparisons, as before, can be easily made.

The reader is urged to consult Zirpoli and Melloy (1993) for an excellent overview of single-subject designs and other relevant information.

Table 3.1 contains a summary of research designs.

---

## Summary of Research Designs

### Design and Symbol

| Design | Symbol |
|---|---|
| Unassessed Treatment | $T \rightarrow$ |
| Single Measurement | $T \rightarrow M$ |
| One Group Pretest/Posttest | $M \rightarrow T \rightarrow M$ |
| Static Group Comparison | $T \rightarrow M$ |
| | $\rightarrow M$ |
| Non-Equivalent Control Group | $M \rightarrow T1 \rightarrow M$ |
| | $M \rightarrow T2 \rightarrow M$ |
| Pretest/Posttest Control Group | $R \ \ M \rightarrow T1 \rightarrow M$ |
| | $R \ \ M \rightarrow T2 \rightarrow M$ |
| Posttest Only Control Group | $R \ \ T1 \rightarrow M$ |
| | $R \ \ T2 \rightarrow M$ |
| Interrupted Time Series | $M1 \rightarrow M2 \rightarrow M3 \ T \ M4 \rightarrow M5 \rightarrow M6$ |
| Single-Subject | ___ A-B |
| | ___ A-B-A |
| | ___ A-B-A-B |
| | ___ Multiple Baselines |

---

Table 3.1

*Mini-exercise:* Pair and share with a colleague and describe each of these aforementioned designs, making certain to provide an example for each.

Before proceeding with the remainder of the chapter, complete the following exercises (culled, in part, from Popham, 1972) that help reinforce some of the ideas expressed above.

---

## Exercises

### 5. INTERRUPTED TIME SERIES DESIGN

Write in the space provided the letter or letters of the graph lines that support the conclusion that improvement was due to the treatment.

_____ In this hypothetical research situation, we have measured pupil performance on equivalent problem-solving tests every two months during the year, and we have introduced a three-week teaching unit (i.e., the treatment) on problem-solving procedures during the middle of the year.

Answer: C. Only to group C can we attribute the increase to the treatment. Groups A and B reveal fluctuating pre- and post-treatments performance records, thus indicating that the same stimuli causing the pre-treatment fluctuations could also have caused the post-treatment fluctuations.

6. IDENTIFYING TYPE OF DESIGN

Write the name of the design employed in this example, in the space provided.

A school superintendent introduces a new music appreciation program throughout her school district which depends heavily upon tape recordings of classical masterworks. Although rather costly, the new program is considered a success by the superintendent and her staff at the close of the year.

DESIGN EMPLOYED:

_____

_____

Answer: Unassessed treatment (because no attempt is made to investigate the program)

7. IDENTIFYING TYPE OF DESIGN

Write the name of the design employed in this example.

A tenth-grade biology teacher institutes a new approach to the teaching of one-celled animal life based on a series of seven-minute single-concept films. Prior to starting the new unit, she develops a test covering the material and administers it to her class before and after the unit, noting with satisfaction a dramatic improvement by her pupils on the test.

DESIGN EMPLOYED:

_____

_____

Answer: one group pretest/posttest

8. IDENTIFYING TYPE OF DESIGN

Write the name of the design employed in this example.

A researcher uses a table of random numbers to subdivide 15 junior high school classes into three groups of five classes each (30 pupils per class) as follows: "Treatment A," "Treatment B," and "Control." The treatments are administered during the first four months of the school year, and at mid-semester a posttest is given to all of the 450 pupils involved.

DESIGN EMPLOYED:

_____

_____

Answer: posttest only

## 9. IDENTIFYING TYPE OF DESIGN

Write the name of the design employed in this example.

A school principal has received a federal grant to institute a new mathematics enrichment program. Using school records, he computes the average mathematics achievement score on a nationally standardized examination for his fifth-, ninth-, and twelfth-grade pupils during each of the preceding three years. He plans to have the same tests administered for the two years following the institution of the new program. He wishes to compare the relative positions of the three classes during the five-year period.

DESIGN EMPLOYED:

_____

_____

Answer: interrupted time series

## 10. SELECTING THE APPROPRIATE DESIGN

Select the design best suited to the following research problem, and write its name in the space provided.

A school researcher hopes to test the merits of a new series of third-grade reading booklets. The booklets, commercially produced, are sold with a test which covers the skills ostensibly developed by learners during the four-week period when the booklets are to be used. The researcher suspects that the pretest may structure the thinking of the pupils if it is administered to them prior to their exposure to the booklets. Twenty third-grade teachers have indicated a willingness to have their classes involved in the research, as members of either the experimental or control groups.

BEST DESIGN:

_____

_____

Answer: posttest only (because of possibility for randomization and the potentially reactive nature of pretest)

11. SELECTING THE APPROPRIATE DESIGN

Select the design best suited to the following research problem, and write its name.

A high school government teacher wishes to conduct a study in his class of the difference that weekly issues of current events newspapers will make in his pupils' scores on a current events test. He realizes that pupils will learn about current events outside school, so he is particularly interested in their pretest to posttest growth. He has a series of literature selections which he can give to students in the class who are not assigned to read the current events newspapers.

BEST DESIGN:

_____

_____

Answer: pretest/posttest control group design or non-equivalent

12. SELECTING THE APPROPRIATE DESIGN

Select the design best suited to the following research problem, and write its name.

A school counselor wishes to test the influence on students' attitudes toward narcotics of a particular commercial film dealing obliquely with the use of narcotics. He devises a self-report questionnaire but is afraid that if pupils complete the questionnaire prior to viewing the film, they will become sensitized to the narcotics issue. Random assignment of pupils is possible.

BEST DESIGN:

_____

_____

Answer: posttest only (because of the reactive nature of questionnaire)

13. SELECTING THE APPROPRIATE DESIGN

Select the design best suited to the following research problem, and write its name.

Faced with the necessity for evaluating a new set of general science kits, members of a small high school science department decide that they cannot randomly assign pupils among their first semester general science classes because there would be conflicts. They have, however, administered science aptitude tests and have found that their four classes are remarkably similar. They hope to use the science kits with two complete classes, since two teachers have indicated unwillingness to use the kits with only a portion of their class.

BEST DESIGN:

_____

_____

> Answer: non-equivalent control group design (with previously administered aptitude test as pretest)

## 14. SELECTING THE APPROPRIATE DESIGN

Select the design best suited to the following research problem, and write its name.

> Ms. Barbara Lewis, a school principal, wishes to assess the interest-building contribution of a school club program instituted four years ago. She decides to use average daily attendance rates as an index of pupils' interest in school. She discovers that such data has been accumulated (in the school's archives) for every year since the club was inaugurated, as well as for the ten years before it was initiated.

BEST DESIGN:

_____

_____

> Answer: interrupted time series

15. Which statement is not true?

   a. Non-equivalent designs are used when randomization is not possible and groups are comparable.

   b. Posttest control group designs are used when randomization is possible.

   c. Interrupted time series designs are used when randomization is impossible or in a case in which two parallel treatments are not readily available.

   d. The purpose of matched pairs is to develop an accurate testing instrument.

> Answer: choice "d"

16. Divide into groups of three and consider that you are all principals who are evaluating some sort of program in your school. How could you use the following quantitative and qualitative approaches?
    a. observations
    b. surveys
    c. group comparison research
    d. ethnography

    Answers will vary

17. Identify the correct design:

    a. As a high school principal, I introduced a schoolwide restructuring program known as Housing. The high school was in desperate need to restructure because of high dropout rates and low SAT scores. The ninth grade has completed its first year in the Housing program. The program appears successful so I plan on including grade 10 next year.

    _____

    b. A supervisor of curriculum wanted to assess a new fourth-grade reading series used in two elementary schools in the district. Each school has three fourth-grade classes with comparable standardized reading test scores. She introduces the new reading series to one school in September, while the other school is monitored as they use the traditional reading series. Scores on the standardized reading test are compared at the end of May.

    _____

    c. An assistant principal wants to see the impact of a new in-school suspension program on the attendance record of selected students at-risk. She reviews attendance records for three years prior to the implementation of the in-school suspension program. She will compare these records to the attendance records for three years after the program starts.

    _____

    Answers: a) unassessed; b) non-equivalent control group design; c) time series

18. Write three realistic cases describing the use of any three adequate research designs. Cases should be drawn from either personal experience or an experience any supervisor or lead-teacher might encounter. Be specific, realistic, and practical.

    _____

    _____

    _____

    Answers will vary

19. MATCH

| X | Y |
|---|---|
| _____ A. unassessed treatment design | a. $T \rightarrow$ |
| | b. $T \rightarrow M$ |
| _____ B. single measurement design | c. $M \rightarrow T \rightarrow M$ |
| _____ C. one group pretest/ posttest design | d. $M \rightarrow T1 \rightarrow M$ $M \rightarrow T2 \rightarrow M$ |
| _____ D. non-equivalent control group design | e. $RM \rightarrow T1 \rightarrow M$ $RM \rightarrow T2 \rightarrow M$ |
| _____ E. pretest/posttest only control group design | f. $RT1 \rightarrow M$ $RT2 \rightarrow M$ |
| _____ F. posttest only control group design | g. $M1 \rightarrow M2 \rightarrow M3 \ T$ $M4 \rightarrow M5 \rightarrow M6$ |
| _____ G. interrupted time series design | |

Answers : A(a), B(b), C(c), D(d), E(e), F(f), G(g).

# Qualitative Approaches to Action Research

Qualitative research approaches "are used to examine questions that can best be answered by *verbally* describing how participants in a study perceive and interpret various aspects of their environment" (Crowl, Kaminsky, & Podell, 1997, p. 499). A study involving how a principal, for instance, fostered shared decision making in her school could be reported qualitatively. By interviewing key participants in the school, observing decision-making committees in action and describing in detail how participants interrelate with one another, and analyzing written documents and other sources about site-based management, the researcher may reach certain conclusions about the effectiveness of shared decision making in this particular school.

Qualitative approaches, as you recall, are just as viable as quantitative ones. While quantitative research attempts to describe outcomes, the "what" (product) of a study, qualitative studies examine the "how" (process) and the "why" questions. The power of qualitative research is in its ability to enrich our understanding of a given phenomenon.

Although results cannot usually be generalized to other schools, qualitative research offers a unique opportunity to conduct an in-depth analysis into the intricate processes at work when attempting to implement, for example, a collaborative model in a school, as described in the opening paragraph of this section. The value of qualitative approaches is that they provide rich detail and insight often missing from quantitative studies.

Other differences exist between qualitative and quantitative studies. Qualitative research captures behavior occurring in naturalistic settings and does not involve purposeful manipulation of subjects for experimental purposes as do many quantitative studies. Qualitative research is not just another methodology (a set of data collection and analysis tools), but can be conceived as a paradigm or a way of thinking about how knowledge is created and best understood. A fundamental belief that qualitative researchers espouse is that events cannot be understood unless one understands how they are perceived and interpreted by the people who participated in them. Moreover, quantitative approaches assume that social facts, in the first place, have an objective reality that can be studied scientifically. Qualitative modes, in contrast, assume that reality is socially constructed and is best represented, if you will, by the subjective perceptions or observations of individuals. Qualitative research can occur naturally by simply walking into a classroom, for instance, and recording behavior objectively or anecdotally without any prescribed or predetermined criteria. Qualitative research, in this vein, is more flexible and inductive than quantitative research that, by definition, requires a more structured, prescribed, and deductive format.

The quantitative researcher tries to maintain a degree of objectivity and detachment from whatever is examined. In contrast, a qualitative researcher may be more actively involved by participating at the same time observation, for example, is undertaken. While quantitative researchers attempt to identify a problem in advance of a study, qualitative researchers feel comfortable in waiting for problems or issues to emerge. In essence, quantitative research attempts to establish facts, while qualitative research tries to develop understanding of a problem.

*Situation:* Ms. Georgina Urbay, a lead-teacher in a suburban elementary school on the West Coast, just completed her master's degree at a local university. As a culminating project, she successfully completed her master's thesis on a topic relevant to her work situation.

For her project Ms. Urbay investigated gender influences on the quality of attention students receive in their class. Having reviewed the literature in this field, Ms. Urbay wondered whether gender biases existed in the classes she was responsible for supervising. When she observed some of the newer teachers, in the past, her observations focused on the quantity of thought-provoking questions asked during a lesson or identifying, numerically, which students were on- or off-task. In these previous visits, Ms. Urbay and the teachers predetermined the nature of each observation. This time she felt that she just wanted to get a general feeling about the classroom without previously established criteria for observation. She read about qualitative observation tools like the Wide Lens strategy (Acheson & Gall, 1997). With this procedure, the observer makes brief notes of events as they occur in the classroom. A favorite technique used by anthropologists, the wide lens strategy enables intensive, direct observations of behavior. No pre-arranged categories or questions are developed. The recorder may perceptively determine how wide a lens to make. The wider the lens, the more behaviors are observed. As narrow lenses are used, specific behaviors of individuals may be focused upon.

Anecdotal records usually consist of short descriptive sentences summarizing a particular event or situation. These recordings are usually made objectively and nonevaluatively. Rather than recording that "Susan was day-dreaming," Ms. Urbay might write "Susan was gazing out the rear window of the classroom." Ms. Urbay decides to reserve the right to make interpretive observations as well, but includes her interpretive comments in brackets. Although audio recordings would help capture the lesson, Ms. Urbay decides that such a recording would make the teacher feel uncomfortable and since she knows short-hand, recording data would not be a problem.

Ms. Urbay decides that rather than sitting in the back of the room as a detached observer, she would get a "better feel" for the classroom environment by participating to any extent possible in the lesson, at the same time she was recording observations. Ms. Urbay entered Mr. Jones' classroom. Eric Jones was a second-year teacher who was still receiving mentoring from Ms. Urbay. Ms. Urbay informed Mr. Jones that she would be observing and participating in his lesson. She informed Mr. Jones that this was not a formal observation, but merely an opportunity to just get a better sense of the classroom climate. She, in fact, spoke with Eric Jones about her research into gender-related issues in the classroom and suggested that she was curious about how gender might influence teacher behavior. It is important to note that Ms. Urbay is not responsible for personnel evaluation. She has established a good rapport with Eric Jones, as she has with the other teachers she mentors.

Ms. Urbay took the following notes during one segment of the lesson:

> 5th grade class; 13 boys and 12 girls; self-contained classroom; Eric Jones, teacher; 9:45 a.m.; I enter as Mr. Jones tells class to take out their readers; As Mr. Jones gives instructions for silent reading, three students (2 male and 1 female) are out of their seats hanging their clothing in the rear classroom closet; The girl is talking; Mr. Jones tells her to be quiet and sit down; During silent reading students are reading quietly; After about 3 minutes a monitor enters classroom and teacher is recording daily attendance; Noise level in class rises; Monitor leaves room; Teacher walks back and forth as students get quiet; At 9:49 a.m., Mr. Jones asks a boy to tell the class what the story was about; Student responds; Class attentive; Mr. Jones asks a girl, "Why do you think Billy in the story was so upset?"; Student responds; Teacher calls on a boy who also responds, albeit differently; Mr. Jones probes and asks boy to explain; Mr. Jones asks another thought-provoking question to a girl; Girl responds; Teacher asks another question to a boy and probes; . . . [10 minutes elapse and I note that it appears that Mr. Jones calls on boys and girls evenly, but that he consistently probes male responses, but rarely probes a female response, . . . curious, ask Mr. Jones about this!]; Time elapses; Teacher divides class into study groups; I join one of the groups with 2 boys and 1 girl; Teacher circulates; Students answer reading questions and discuss

story; I ask them if they liked the story and to explain why or why not; Teacher requests attention from class; Mr. Jones continues asking many thought-provoking questions and follows the same pattern of probing more for boys than for girls; Interestingly, when the boy sitting to my right in the group was asked a question, he was probed, but the girl to my left was not; I could not discern any concern among the students.

This situation is one in which the lead-teacher, Ms. Urbay, decided that a qualitative approach would be best suited for her observation of Mr. Jones' lesson. Her primary purpose was to obtain a better understanding of the lesson given by Mr. Jones. Although her observations focused on teacher questions and student responses, she had the flexibility to note any usual or unusual behavior in the classroom. Her format was flexible and unstructured. Her recordings occurred in the natural classroom environment without any manipulation of subjects or classes. What other features of the scenario above demonstrate its qualitative nature? Can you create a scenario, different from the example above, that illustrates a qualitative approach? Note that qualitative approaches are not always applied to observation of teachers' lessons. In the scenario you provide, describe qualitative research in a setting outside the classroom.

While qualitative and quantitative procedures differ in purpose, orientation, and, essentially, how research is conducted (see Figure 3.6), other differences center on how data are collected and analyzed, and how conclusions are reached. Unlike quantitative research, few authorities in the field agree on precise methods for data collection, analysis, interpretation, and, even, the reporting of findings derived from qualitative procedures (Creswell, 1994). Notwithstanding these differences, patterns or similarities emerge among those individuals who conduct qualitative inquiry. Although data collection and analysis are described in separate chapters later in this book, a brief overview of data collection and methods of analysis for qualitative studies is in order.

Data collection in qualitative approaches depends on the purpose for the study and the type of information sought. If the researcher is interested, for instance, in understanding meanings given to certain events such as reactions to faculty meetings, then a combination of direct observation,

---

## Characteristics of Quantitative and Qualitative Research

| *Quantitative* | *Qualitative* |
|---|---|
| numbers or statistics | verbal descriptions |
| generalization possible | specific to situation |
| describes the "what" | describes the "how" |
| positivistic | naturalistic |
| testable hypotheses | tentative hypotheses |
| structured | flexible |
| reality is objective | reality is constructed |
| detached | involved |
| deductive | inductive |
| predetermined | emergent |
| establishes facts | develops understanding |

---

**Figure 3.6**

participant observation, and interviewing may be used. On the other hand, if visual evidence of a particular situation is required (e.g., a student's behavior during a lesson), then a video recording may be more appropriate than distributing surveys. Although primary and secondary data collection techniques (such as observations, interviews, documents, and audiovisual materials) will be discussed in Chapter 5, some of the following data collection approaches in qualitative research (culled from Creswell, 1994) are commonly used:

- gathering observational notes as a participant-observer
- gathering observational notes by an observer
- conducting unstructured, open-ended interviews
- keeping a journal during a research project
- collecting personal documents (e.g., letters and official records)
- analyzing public documents (e.g., memoranda and minutes)
- videotaping a social situation of an individual or group
- examining photographs or videotapes
- watching and recording non-verbal behaviors

Can you think how you could use any of the data collection techniques above?

Data analysis in quantitative research, discussed in Chapter 6, is also varied. According to Patton (1980), "sitting down to make sense out of pages of interviews and whole files of field notes can be overwhelming" (p. 297). While data analysis can certainly be overwhelming, certain basic principles can be applied (these and other data analyses will be explained again in Chapter 6):

- *simultaneity*—Data analysis and even interpretation can be conducted at the same time as data are collected. Sorting similar pieces of information into categories and attaching meaning to them is commonly used in qualitative projects.

- *reduction*—Seemingly disparate pieces of data can be reduced into categories, patterns, or themes. Reduction is often accomplished by a procedure known as coding. Coding involves attaching meaning to a particular scene, document, or event. For example, in viewing different types of leaders in films, one may categorize the different leaders by their style by first coding each leader with a given leadership style. Reduction also involves **content analysis**, which will be discussed in Chapter 6.

The distinction between data analysis and data reduction should be made. Data analysis in qualitative research refers to the process of categorizing, describing, and synthesizing data. Data reduction is used to better describe and interpret data under analysis.

- *display*—Data can be displayed in numerous ways (visually and otherwise) to aid analysis and interpretation.

- *computer*—Data can be easily analyzed using qualitative text software packages.

Suppose you had carefully conducted some interviews with teachers and collected some open-ended anonymous questionnaires that dealt with teachers' perceptions of effective or "good" principals. After spending several weeks collecting data, you now wonder how you can make sense of it all. "Qualitative data analysis is primarily an inductive process of organizing the data into categories and identifying patterns (relationships) among the categories. Unlike quantitative procedures, most categories and patterns emerge from the data, rather than being imposed on the data prior to data collection" (McMillan & Schumacher, 1997, p. 501).

Calhoun (1994) describes qualitative data analysis as an inductive process this way:

> . . . Treat the responses and documents like a giant inductive set: At the simplest level you are searching for categories and their attributes—figuring out what things go together (convergence). For responses to open-ended survey or interview questions, read through the set quickly for a general impression. Then take each item, and list or group all responses together. Look at this list and decide if there are responses similar in content that appear frequently.
>
> For example, one team interviewed a sample of eighteen students . . . using four questions. . . . As the team looked at these eighteen responses on the first pass, they noticed immediately that projects of various sorts were mentioned frequently. On the next pass, they looked more closely at the comments students made during their discussion of projects. They noticed that students gave descriptions of projects across subject areas in science, social studies, math, and reading.
>
> As team members continued to distill these responses into information beyond the individual student, they discovered. . . . (p. 75)

Further discussion of this inductive process will be undertaken in Chapter 6.

Although we have been discussing the use of the qualitative research approach, **quantitative research** has for many years been the research of choice in the social sciences. The model of social research—the **scientific method**—and the logic that underpins it—positivism—have dominated educational and administrative theory. The predominance of this social science perspective has only recently undergone criticism in light of the emergence of qualitative, including ethnographic and biographical, analyses. The traditions of positivism and the scientific method in educational research, although still popular, have given way somewhat to alternative approaches for conducting research (Denzin & Lincoln, 1994).

Three *types* of qualitative methods that may be applied by the action researcher are: **historical, ethnography**, and **case study** inquiry. While other qualitative methods exist, I have personally used and found these forms useful. Qualitative methods do not, of course, utilize statistical or mathematical expressions. Qualitative approaches rely on detailed verbal descriptions of observed phenomena. Action researchers often find qualitative methods most suitable and more easily adopted in school settings.

No randomization is employed in nonexperimental qualitative studies. The researcher may select a particular individual to observe using "thick descriptions" (intensive, daily, observation over an extended period of time). For example, the day in a life of a city superintendent may be investigated by following the superintendent around for a day. Observations are recorded anecdotally (verbatim). Since this form of research is qualitative and nonexperimental, findings are primarily based on the investigator's perceptions and interpretations. (See discussion, in the Glossary, of ways of enhancing **validity** and **reliability** in qualitative approaches.)

## Historical Research

Historical inquiry is one of three methods of **qualitative research** (see Figure 1.5 in Chapter 1).

Briefly, historical research attempts to explain the past and its interconnectedness to present conditions. History can be understood as an attempt to study the events and ideas of the past that have shaped human experience over time in order to inform current practice as well as to make more intelligent decisions for the future.

Although historical inquiry would not usually be an action researcher's first line of research, historical study does have particular relevance, especially when undertaking a needs assessment prior to initiating a new program (see discussion of *needs assessment* in the next chapter). For example, a new principal would want to examine past records of levels of student achievement, records of dropout rates, or teacher attendance patterns. Data sources might include cumulative record cards, files, newspapers, original documents, and other archival information often found in **school profiles**.

Oral histories may be particularly useful for qualitative researchers. Oral histories involve open-ended **interviews** with a series of individuals involved in a particular issue. Can you think of an issue or situation in which an educational leader might want or need to undertake oral histories?

## Ethnographic Research

Ethnography is one of three methods of **qualitative research** discussed in this book (see Figure 1.5 in Chapter 1) and is perhaps the most common qualitative approach.

Ethnography, a branch of anthropology, is a method of research in which individuals are observed in natural settings and are described in detail. In ethnographic research there is no attempt to generalize findings. An example of an ethnographic study would be to ask: What is a typical week in the life of 5 city-school superintendents? One would follow or shadow these superintendents and take a lot of notes (called "thick descriptions" or "fieldnotes") describing anecdotally the activities of these individuals. After a week, you would have accumulated a plethora of notes. You would read and reread your notes and perform a **content analysis** to determine any themes that emerge from your data.

Note that it is possible to take detailed written descriptions of what was observed and, at the same time, make specific reflective or interpretative comments. As long as these subjective comments are kept separate from the descriptive data, use of the researcher's speculative comments is common in ethnographic research. In the brief excerpt that follows, note that the researcher's subjective comments are identified and kept separate from the descriptive, more objective portion:

Fieldnotes taken on October 27, 1998
at an after-school faculty conference at
Lakewood Middle School

"I walked into the Lakewood Middle School main auditorium at 3:10 p.m. as the principal, Mr. Ernest Malcomb, was calling the meeting to order. Twenty-six people were sitting in seats scattered about the large auditorium. The principal requested that those individuals in the rear of the auditorium sit near the front. Three individuals moved from the rear to the middle of the auditorium. Seven individuals remained in the rear. The principal began to read the faculty notes. After two minutes had elapsed, he requested that Ms. Chapman report on the curriculum committee's findings and recommendations."

Comments: The teachers in the rear of the auditorium seem defiant in their refusal to move their seats closer to the principal. As Mr. Malcomb read the faculty notes many teachers appeared bored.

Fieldnotes, then, are the researcher's written chronological account of what transpired during an observation session. Field notes consist of two parts:

1. an objective section that contains a detailed description of what has taken place and

2. a subjective part that contains the observer's reflections or speculations about what was observed.

Ethnographic research, then, clearly separates description from interpretation and judgment.

Some authorities in the field consider ethnography a form of descriptive research. Although ethnography does describe a particular situation, it does so usually without use of numbers, frequencies, or statistics. I have classified ethnography under qualitative research to indicate its non-mathematical orientation.

As an action researcher employing ethnographic research, you would identify a topic, pose a research question or two, and collect data by documenting and explaining in great depth what you are observing. Data sources for an ethnographic researcher might include:

1. study of the social behavior of individuals (examples might include: shadowing an associate superintendent during the course of her day; observing the occurrences of misbehavior among three special education students; or observing teachers during a grade conference);

2. communication patterns among individuals or groups (examples might include: observing interactions between faculty and a principal at an after-school conference or observing students as they play in the school yard);

3. environmental conditions (examples might include: studying the impact of block scheduling on student movement in the hallways or observing the impact of early dismissal procedures on the number of incidents of reported accidents).

Many detailed ethnographic studies have been published in education (see, e.g., Goodlad, 1984). Educational leaders, in their role as action researchers described in this volume, are unlikely to undertake an extensive ethnographic study. Readers who are interested in more in-depth analyses of ethnography, for purposes of doctoral work or otherwise, should consult other volumes such as Glesne and Peshkin (1992), Gay (1996), and Wiersma (1995).

Several principles related to ethnography as well as all qualitative research approaches can be reviewed. Ethnographic research:

- occurs in a natural setting
- attempts to explore the why, what, and, especially, how of an issue
- concentrates on fieldwork that may include observations, interviews, etc.
- focuses on a research problem and selection of a research site
- explores sites that are related to the problem, but not randomly selected
- stresses extensive use of field notes
- generates questions, collects data, and interprets data as a combined process
- generates theory from data (grounded theory)
- involves analyzing data as they are collected

Discussion of data collection methods useful in ethnographic research is presented in Chapter 5, whereas data analysis for qualitative approaches in general is discussed in Chapter 6.

## Case Study Research

This method of research is often used in qualitative approaches. Although case studies are actually ways of reporting ethnographic research, they are so common that I have included them as a separate category.

Case study research is one of three methods of **qualitative research** discussed in this book (see Figure 1.5 in Chapter 1). Case studies involve in-depth investigations of an individual, group of individuals, a site, or a scene. Findings are stated verbally, not numerically. Case studies are reported by describing in detail observations made of individuals, groups, or school settings. Special education teachers, for instance, who use IEP's (Individual Educational Programs) are actually involved in some aspects of case study research. Case studies are written so that a better understanding of a situation is likely and so that educators may discuss possible implications for an individual, group, or school.

Case study research can also be conducted by examining a specific phenomenon such as a program, an event, a process, an institution, or a social group (Merriam, 1997). An example of how a case study approach was used in an action research project can be found, for example, in Glanz (1995) in which a martial arts program for students at risk was implemented.

Case studies differ subtly from ethnographic research in that case studies are written descriptively and objectively, while ethnographic accounts may contain interpretive material. Case studies are also more narrowly focused on a particular person, place, or scene. Case studies may also tend to create an idealized situation by merely using descriptive accounts. Case studies are often guided by a series of questions that the researcher tries to answer. The case study, in the end, provides an in-depth, descriptive account.

Incorporating a qualitative research methodology through the use of portraits (Donmoyer, 1993; Lawrence-Lightfoot, 1983) has recently gained favor. Donmoyer and Kos (1993) have recently demonstrated the efficacy of this case study approach in examining the at-risk population. I would like to present, as an example, a brief, yet descriptive case study excerpt of one particular student who was in many ways representative of the students involved in the martial arts program mentioned above (Glanz, 1995). Data was gathered through the use of observations based on field notes, interviews, questionnaires, and video tape recordings. Information was gleaned from school personnel, especially the classroom teacher, the parent, the Sensei (martial arts teacher), and the student himself. Multiple observers, multiple data collection methods, and extensive "thick" descriptions were employed to attain as accurate a description as possible.

> Ernest is a ten-year-old African American fourth-grade student attending P.S. 563 in Elizabeth, New Jersey. Ernest was held-over once in grade 3 and is two years below grade level in reading and math. Ernest has had excellent attendance in school, but has been a severe discipline problem since the first grade. He has been suspended four (4) times within the last two years for the following incidents: striking another child across the face with his fist causing severe swelling and bleeding; throwing a chair at another student hitting the substitute teacher by accident; pulling the fire alarm during the school day; and threatening another child in his class with a knife.
>
> Ernest has had an unstable family life in that he has not seen his father for nearly five years. His father is incar-

cerated for robbery and attempted murder and is serving a fifteen year sentence. His mother, who has only reported to school once in the past three years, is a crack addict. Ernest lives with an "aunt" across the street from school. Ernest is an only child.

Ernest recently has been involved in a neighborhood gang of approximately fifteen other youth, mostly of junior high school age. Ernest is very intelligent and mature for his age. Although he is quite verbal, he does not participate in school. Teachers have reported the following comments appearing on report cards and cumulative record cards:

- Ernest is an active youngster who needs constant supervision. (grade 2)
- Ernest is intelligent and can do work if he wants to. (grade 1)
- Ernest is very aggressive and hostile to his classmates. (grade 2)
- Ernest needs help in reading and math. He does not participate and is very playful in class. (grade 3)
- Ernest threatens others and shows no interest in school. (grade 4)

Ernest has the potential, but clearly needs a more restrictive classroom environment.

Ernest has been referred to the guidance counselor, assistant principal, and principal without any significant, long-standing change in behavior and attitude. Psychological tests indicate that he is of above average intelligence. Standardized tests as well as teacher-made tests indicate that Ernest is low-achieving.

When the guidance counselor tried to explore Ernest's thoughts and feelings the conversation typically went like this:

GC:   How are you doing Ernest?

  E:   (no response)

GC:   Well?

  E:   Fine.

GC: Well, you know Ernest I have been receiving very disturbing reports about your behavior.

E: (silence)

GC: Do you like school?

E: Yeh.

GC: Well. if you like school, that's great, but

E: Do I have to be here? I wanna go.

GC: We know you are a very bright boy and want the best for you. Your teacher and Mr. XXXX really care about you.

E: (shrugs shoulders). I wanna go.

GC: Go where?

E: Out of here (storms out and runs through building for ten minutes before being apprehended by security and brought to the AP's office. At the AP's office, the same conversation repeats itself to no avail. Ernest is escorted back to class in time for lunch. He returns to class after lunch 30 minutes late. Excuse: playing basketball in the yard. . . .]

The case study continues to document attempts to assist Ernest. After participating in a martial arts class specifically designed to encourage greater self-discipline for students like Ernest, the following data were collected as part of the case study:

Ernest showed much enthusiasm about the Karate class in his discussions with the assistant principal (AP):

E: Yeah, I'm really interested. When can I begin?

AP: You know, martial arts are very demanding and require discipline and lots of hard work.

E: I can do it.

AP: Why are you so interested in the martial arts?

E: I don't know, just am.

AP: You like the violence and fighting?

E: Yeah, I guess . . . You know Karate?

AP: Yep.

E:   (nodding head in approval)

AP:  You know the Sensei, teacher, is very strict and will not tolerate fooling around.

E:   (no comment)

AP:  You also should know that you can continue in the class as long as you continue to receive good reports from your teachers and me. And that you'll have to do homework and all that . . . Sensei will explain all that. Okay?

E:   Okay.

[Two weeks into the program]

Mr. Shurack, a state-certified teacher and first degree black belt instructor, was interviewed about Ernest's progress in the Karate class. The Sensei reported that Ernest had much difficulty adjusting to the rigors and demands of the class. Ernest grew impatient and had difficulty maintaining concentration. There seemed to be a dramatic change in his atttitude and attention as a result of the number of visits to Ernest's classroom during the school day by the AP and Sensei where conversations were conducted about his progress. "It is due, I think," stated Sensei Shurack, "to the fact that Ernest received positive reinforcement and encouragement from his classroom teacher, the AP, the principal, and me that he was able to stick it out in class. The books and magazines (e.g. *Karate Illustrated* and *Kung-fu* which were ordered through our school library) seemed to sustain Ernest's interest in those early weeks."

As you can see from this excerpt, case studies provide descriptive and detailed information that is often missing from quantitative approaches.

Try writing a case study of your own school as an organization. The sample questions in Table 3.2 should serve as a guide. In the end, your case study will represent an attempt to describe your school as thoroughly as possible so that an outsider would be able to get a good sense of what your school is like.

# Some Guiding Questions in
# Writing a Case Study of Your School

1. Describe the area in which your school is located. How is it reached by transportation? What is the social class that predominates in the area? Is the school in a residential or business area? Do many students come from the local community? Where else do students come from? Are students bused to the school? What is the ethnic makeup of the student body?

2. Is the school plant in good condition? How old is the building? How is it decorated, outside and inside? How do students treat the physical plant? Are the corridors well-lighted? What are the colors of the walls? Are they clean? Are bulletin boards displayed in the hallways? What do they contain? How many floors are there in the building? What special facilities or equipment exist?

3. What is the makeup (number, ethnicity, gender, etc.) of the faculty, staff, and administration? What are the responsibilities of administrators? teachers? What hierarchical relationships exist, if any? What is the relationship between teachers and administrators?

4. What services exist in the school? Are there nurses, doctors, and custodians in the school? Where is the cafeteria? What is the quality of the food services? Who is in charge? Are teachers and administrators on duty? Is there a library? What library resources exist? Are multimedia technologies present? Does each class have computers? What are the different kinds of software and hardware?

5. Does the school have a written statement of philosophy? Is there a student and/or teacher handbook? Are parents welcome and involved in the school? How do faculty and administration involve parents?

6. How much emphasis is placed on constructivist instructional strategies? What motivational strategies are employed? Describe the state of student discipline. What classroom management techniques and strategies are employed?

7. How are decisions made in the school? Who is involved in instructional decision making? Who is involved in administrative decision making? Does a learning community exist in the school? What is the relationship of the district office to the school?

**Table 3.2**

These are only sample questions that might be framed. Many more questions about grouping practices, other instructional procedures, and logistical operations may be posed. Case studies provide an in-depth understanding of a particular situation. Remember, the action researcher is likely to use a case study to describe a particular situation that can be then discussed or analyzed by others. Once a school, for instance, is described in detail using a case study, discussion of educational and/or instructional implications may occur.

Can you think of a situation in which a case study might aid decision making? How might action researchers use the case study method?

Note that use of case studies by educational leaders, as action researchers, might be very specific and limited. For readers interested in a more detailed explanation of case studies, especially as they are used for doctoral theses, please consult Merriam, 1997.

# Chapter Summary

The following worksheet allows you to begin planning an overall research project by clarifying your purposes, specifying a research design, and choosing a sound qualitative and/or quantitative approach with appropriate methods. This worksheet is meant to allow you to brainstorm different ideas. Changes in your plan can always be made at a later date. This worksheet serves as a review of the ideas discussed in this chapter.

# Starting a Research Project

1. Why do I want to undertake this action research project? What do I want to investigate? What do I hope to learn? (Use additional paper to record your responses if necessary).

   _____

2. What preliminary information should I gather to help me get started? _____

   _____

3. What question or questions should I ponder? _____

   _____

4. What are my short-term and long-term goals? _____

   _____

5. Who will be involved in this research project? _____

   _____

6. What administrative or logistical concerns should I attend to? _____

   _____

7. How will data be collected, analyzed, and reported? _____

   _____

8. What will I do with the results? _____

   _____

9. Will I incorporate quantitative and/or qualitative approaches? _____

10. Check the methods and designs that may be used:

    ## QUANTITATIVE

    ___ Descriptive research    ___ surveys    ___ observational

    ___ Correlational research

    Group Comparison research

    ___ experimental    ___ quasi-experimental    ___ Ex Post Facto

    DESIGNS

    ___ Single Measurement              ___ One-Group Pretest/Posttest

    ___ Static-Group Comparison        ___ Non-equivalent Control Group

___ Pretest/Posttest Control Group     ___ Posttest Only Control Group
___ Interrupted Time Series     ___ Single-Subject

### QUALITATIVE

___ Historical (Needs Assessment)

___ Ethnography

___ Case Study

Purpose: _____

_____

Data Collection Methods: _____

_____

Data Analysis and Interpretation: _____

_____

Tentative Findings: _____

_____

# References

Acheson, K. A., & Gall, M. D. (1997). *Techniques in the clinical supervision of teachers.* New York: Longman.

Calhoun, E. F., Allen, L., & Halliburton, C. (1996). *A report on the implementation of and results from schoolwide action research.* Paper presented at the annual meeting of the American Educational Research Association, New York, April.

Carr, W., & Kemmis, S. (1986). *Becoming critical: Education, knowledge, and action research.* London: The Falmer Press.

Creswell, J. W. (1994). *Research design: Qualitative and quantitative approaches.* Thousand Oaks, CA: Sage Publications.

Crowl, T. K., Kaminsky, S., & Podell, D. M. (1997). *Educational psychology.* Madison, WI: Brown & Benchmark.

Denzin, N. K., & Lincoln, Y. S. (Eds.). (1994). *Handbook of qualitative research*. Thousand Oaks, CA: Corwin Press.

Donmoyer, R. (1993). The purpose of portraits: Rethinking the form and function of research on students at risk. In R. Donmoyer & R. Kos (Eds.), *Students at risk: Portraits, policies, programs, and practices* (pp. 37–48). New York: State University of New York Press.

Donmoyer, R., & Kos, R. (1993). *Students at risk: Portraits, policies, programs, and practices.* New York: State University of New York Press.

Gay, L. R. (1996). *Educational research: Competencies for analysis and application* (5th ed.). Englewood Cliffs, NJ: Prentice Hall.

Glanz, J. (1994). Redefining the roles and responsibilities of assistant principals. *The Clearing House, 67*(5), 283–288.

Glanz, J. (1995). A school/curricular intervention martial arts program for students at risk. *The Journal of At-Risk Issues, 2*(1), 18–25.

Glesne, C., & Peshkin, A. (1992). *Becoming qualitative researchers.* New York: Longman.

Glickman, C. D., Gordon, S. P., & Ross-Gordon, J. M. (1998). *Supervision of instruction: A developmental approach* (4th ed.). Boston: Allyn and Bacon.

Goodlad, J. I. (1984). *A place called school.* New York: McGraw-Hill.

Lawrence-Lightfoot, S. (1983). *The good high school.* New York: Basic Books.

McMillan, J. H., & Schumacher, S. (1997). *Research in education: A conceptual introduction.* New York: Longman.

Merriam, S. B. (1997). *Qualitative research and case study applications in education.* San Francisco: Jossey-Bass Publishers.

Moore, K. D. (1995). *Classroom teaching skills.* New York: McGraw-Hill.

Patton, M. Q. (1980). *Qualitative research methods.* Beverly Hills, CA: Sage Publications.

Popham, W. J. (1972). Simplified designs for school research. In R. L. Baker & R. E. Schutz (Eds.), *Instructional product research* (pp. 137–160). New York: American Book Company.

Wiersma, W. (1995). *Research methods in education: An introduction.* Boston: Allyn and Bacon.

Willerman, M., McNeely, S. L., & Koffman, E. C. (1991). *Teachers helping teachers: Peer observation and assistance.* New York: Praeger.

Zirpoli, T. J., & Melloy, K. J. (1993). *Behavior management: Application for teachers and parents.* New York: Macmillan.

# CHAPTER 4

# Easy Steps to Program Development and Evaluation Research

*"The challenge for today's educational leaders is to set an example that clearly demonstrates that schools can be the one institution where human relationships are enhanced . . . as it deals with internal and external evaluation processes and accountability requirements."*
*(DeRoche, 1987, p. ix)*

*"What should be clear is that . . . evaluation is a complicated endeavor, and that there is no single approach that will solve all problems."*
*(Herman, Lyons Morris, & Fitz-Gibbon, 1987, p. 24)*

*". . . evaluation conducted at the school level can improve the quality of information used to make management, program, and instructional decisions."*
*(Herman & Winters, 1992, p. 3)*

*"Successful program development cannot occur without evaluation. Program evaluation is the process of systematically determining the quality of a school program and how the program can be improved."*
*(Sanders, 1992, p. 3)*

*"Program evaluation projects provide educators with the information and insights they need to refine and improve the services and programs they provide to their students. And that is a worthy goal."*
*(Brainard, 1996, p. 57)*

As an educational leader, you'll most likely want to implement some sort of instructional program and then establish procedures for evaluation. Program development and evaluation are so common among those individuals in leadership positions that I have devoted this entire chapter to its discussion. I recall my first position as an assistant principal in an elementary school in New York City when I was confronted with some serious misbehavior in the upper grades by a few students at-risk. I decided to initiate a unique program to deal with this troublesome situation. I discussed this martial arts program briefly in the previous chapter in connection with case study research. In establishing this program, I also realized that its effectiveness had to be assessed. For a complete description of this program, how and why I implemented it, and how I undertook program evaluation, refer to Glanz (1995).

For an introduction into evaluation research, see the discussion in Chapter 1. The following eight steps will guide you in establishing almost any program in a school. My students, who have applied this design, have found these steps useful.

## Establishing a Program

What is the first step you would take to initiate a new program in your school/district? As a leader you realize that the success of any new program depends on understanding the unique culture and history of the school. Attempts at implementing reforms over the past twenty years have taught us that "reform through fiat" simply doesn't work. Meaningful and lasting change occurs best when implemented gradually at a grassroots level. Reform efforts that consider the unique culture and history of a particular school/district have a much better chance at succeeding (Cuban, 1984). Therefore, the first step in initiating any new program is not to "storm the fortress" and demand that teachers comply with newly mandated curricula or programs. The first step that any thoughtful, professional educational leader takes is to undertake a needs assessment.

In order to enliven this discussion about program implementation, I will relate these steps to a program that I tried to implement many years ago while undertaking a supervisory internship with the Curriculum Coordinator of a district that wanted to implement a gifted program in a particular school. This was my first experience at implementing a program that helped many youngsters achieve their potential.

## Needs Assessment

Leaders sometimes attempt to change or implement programs without considering many important factors. The first task of a competent educational leader who wants to start any sort of program is to analyze the situation by describing and identifying problems or areas of concern. In other words, a leader should undertake a needs assessment.

How should a needs assessment be undertaken?

1. Reflect by posing questions:
   - Does the school need a gifted program?
   - What evidence indicates that the school might need such a program?
   - Has a gifted program ever been implemented before?
   - If so, what happened to the program and why was it discontinued?
   - What will my new program contribute to addressing the needs of gifted students?
   - Who is considered a gifted student?
   - How do I (we) plan to implement such a program?

   Posing key questions is the first step in implementing any program. These questions should be addressed by the individual leader in collaboration with her/his supervisory staff and interested faculty.

2. Observe:

   Prior to making any decision about implementing the program, "walk around" the school getting to know the faculty, staff, students, and parents. Observe students and teachers at work. Get a sense of the culture of the school. We call this *MBWA*! You know what that is, right? *Management By Wandering Around*. This doesn't mean aimless wandering, but rather purposeful observation. Too many principals, from my experience, manage their schools from the main office, rarely observing and talking with their faculty and staff on a daily basis. Successful implementation of your program involves "getting out there" and finding answers to some key questions:

- What are faculty interested in?
- Who are the influential members of the faculty?
- What instructional strategies are commonly employed by teachers?
- Do students seem enthusiastic about learning?
- Are parents involved in the instructional/curricular program?
- Is there some grassroots support for the need of change?
- Who might you confide in and ask to participate in the initial stages of program implementation?
- What resistances to change exist?

Observing includes examining records, school files, and profiles. Examining records such as cumulative student folders, school profile sheets that provide summaries of standardized test scores, and teacher files may give you some valuable clues as to the direction you may take to implement this program. Such an analysis will help ascertain existing strengths and weaknesses that should be addressed during the initial stages of program implementation.

3.  Meet with key personnel:

Meeting with key school personnel, informally (through *MBWA*) and through formal invitation, will not only demonstrate your concern about faculty input into program development, but will provide valuable insights that observation alone cannot offer. Meet with the following personnel, among others: teachers, union representatives, parents (especially PTA president and board), superintendent, coordinators, guidance counselors, secretarial staff, lunchroom personnel, deans, and other supervisors. Speak with everyone! Why? For four reasons:

- to allow them to voice their concerns and opinions about the new program;
- to apprise them of possible future developments;
- to share information with them; and
- to invite their input in terms of suggestions, comments, and participation.

Although such attempts at shared leadership may be unusual and difficult to attain, my experiences have convinced me that

effective and lasting change occurs best through collaboration among faculty, staff, administrators, community, and students.

Public education has continued to receive voluminous criticism for being bureaucratic and unresponsive to the needs of teachers, parents, and children. One of the prominent proposals for disenfranchising bureaucracy is the dissolution of autocratic administrative practices in which overbearing supervisors rule by fiat. Favored is greater and more meaningful decision making at the grass-roots level. This translates into giving teachers more formal responsibility for setting school policies, thus enhancing democratic governance in schools. Susan Moore Johnson (1990) observed that "although schools have long been under the control of administrators, local districts are increasingly granting teachers more formal responsibility for setting school policies" (p. 337). The argument for greater involvement goes something like this: When teachers participate in decisions about their schools, there will be a significant improvement in their attitudes that will strengthen their commitment toward their work and that this will translate into better academic improvement. The new vision, then, calls for empowered teachers, democratic governance, and heightened professionalism (Glanz, 1992).

4.  Establish a needs assessment committee:

A final step in needs assessment might be to form a committee comprised of interested teachers, supervisors, parents, and students to assist in the implementation of the program. This committee can plan implementation of the project and engender support from other faculty and interested parties.

I was once asked to conduct a series of cooperative learning workshops for a school district in New Jersey. The principal, realizing the importance of faculty involvement in staff development, formed a needs assessment committee to ascertain interest in these workshops before I was hired. The committee designed a **questionnaire** to determine levels of experience with cooperative learning. The committee forwarded their findings to me prior to the start of the workshops so that I might have a sense as to the nature and level of sophistication needed in these workshops. My workshops were successful, in large measure, due to these preplanning strategies implemented by the needs assessment committee at this school.

Before proceeding with the remainder of the chapter, complete the following exercises that help reinforce some of the ideas expressed above.

---

### Exercises

1.  What steps would you take to assess the needs of your school/district? Whom would you contact and meet with? What sorts of data would you collect? Who might be involved in the process?

    _____

    _____

    _____

    Answers will vary

2.  Imagine that you are a principal who is interested in doing a needs assessment of your school. You want to survey how staff, parents, and students feel about the effectiveness of the school's goals in three areas: curriculum, organization, and school climate. Develop a questionnaire ascertaining how the staff, parents, and students feel about the school's curriculum, organization, and climate. Your questionnaire should include items about academic goals, monitoring of student progress, teacher effectiveness, administrative leadership, rewards and incentives for students, order and discipline, parent and community involvement, positive school climate, opportunity for student responsibility, among others. Describe how you would use these results to improve your school. Be specific, realistic, and practical.

    _____

    _____

    _____

    Answers will vary

---

## Goals

The second step you should take once you've decided that the program is needed is to develop short- and long-term goals. Framing a vision of what this new program has to offer is critical in program development. Goal development should be done collaboratively by involving as many stakeholders as possible. Setting up a committee for this purpose is recommended. This committee can be comprised of the same members as the

needs assessment committee, although involving others is advisable. This committee would be charged with:

- brainstorming goals or program objectives;
- prioritizing goals; and
- disseminating goals to faculty, staff, and community.

Whenever you form a committee to evaluate something, keep in mind these three questions:

- Why have we formed a committee? (purpose)
- What are our short-term plans? (objectives)
- What are our long-term plans? (goals)

Short-term goals should be accomplished within a 1- to 6-month framework. Examples of short-term goals are: establishing criteria for admission into the gifted program; forming a planning committee of two teachers, one staff developer, one parent, one assistant principal, and a student; and so on.

Examples of long-term goals are: increasing parental involvement by 10%; decreasing teacher-burnout; implementing a portfolio program next year for the upper elementary grades; raising standardized reading test scores by 15%; and so on.

## Administrative Aspects

Administrative or logistical concerns should be worked on throughout the implementation phase. As an educational leader, you should attend to the following concerns, among others:

- staffing considerations
- scheduling
- advertising
- room allocations
- ordering materials and supplies
- securing funding sources
- publicity
- delegating responsibilities

## Supervision

Supervision is a process that involves strategies to enhance instructional improvement. An educational leader is concerned with facilitating an environment conducive to learning.

A competent leader should attend to *PCOWBIRDS!*

*P* = Plans: Planning is integral to instructional success and an educational leader should help a teacher develop appropriate and meaningful instructional activities and learning experiences. Checking plans, offering suggestions, co-planning, reviewing procedures, and framing thought-provoking questions, among other important aspects, are essential. Supervision, then, involves assisting teachers to better plan their lessons and units of instruction.

*C* = Conferences: Conferencing with teachers, formally and informally, in order to share ideas and develop alternate instructional strategies is an essential supervisory responsibility.

*O* = Observations: An educational leader should offer her/his expertise by both formally and informally observing classroom interaction. A skilled leader who utilizes various observation systems (e.g., Acheson & Gall, 1997; Glickman, Gordon, & Ross-Gordon, 1998) can facilitate instructional improvement by documenting classroom interaction so that a teacher might reflect upon and react to what has been observed. Observations play a key role in supervision. As Yogi Berra once quipped, "You can observe a lot by watching."

*W* = Workshops: Educational leaders should conduct or organize various workshops for teachers on relevant instructional topics such as cooperative learning, alternative teaching strategies, and multiple intelligences.

*B* = Bulletins: Bulletins, journals, reports, and newsletters can be disseminated to interested faculty. One of my teachers became interested in cooperative learning after attending a reading conference. I sustained her interest by placing several articles about cooperative learning in her mailbox.

*I* = Intervisitations: Teachers rarely have the opportunity to visit and observe colleagues. A leader can facilitate intervisitations by rearranging the schedule so that teachers might observe one another and then share common instructional strategies or discuss common problems. Intervisitations, to be effective, must be voluntary and non-judgmental.

*R* = Resources: Leaders should make available for teachers a variety of instructional materials and technologies to enhance instructional improvement.

*D* = Demonstration Lessons: An educational leader presumably is a teacher-of-teachers. A leader is not necessarily the foremost teacher in a school, but s/he should feel comfortable in providing "demo" lessons for teachers, when appropriate. Providing such lessons enhances supervisory credibility among teachers and provides instructional support.

I once noticed, during a formal observation, that the teacher was not using wait time effectively. He posed good questions, but waited only about 2 seconds before calling on someone. As his supervisor, I suggested that he watch me teach a lesson and notice how long I wait after posing a question before calling on a pupil. These observations were the basis for a follow-up conference at which we discussed the research on "wait time" and the advantages of waiting before calling on a pupil. As the saying goes, "a picture is worth a thousand words." Having this particular teacher watch me demonstrate effective use of "wait time" was more valuable than had I merely told him what to do. Competent supervisors not only "suggest" how to do something, they also must "demonstrate" how it should be done.

*S* = Staff Development: Educational leaders can aid instructional improvement by providing staff development that is "purposeful and articulated," "participatory and collaborative," "knowledge-based," "ongoing," "developmental," and "analytic and reflective" (Griffin, 1997).

In establishing any new program, attending to supervisory issues is imperative.

## Curriculum

Curriculum includes all the planned experiences, programs, and subjects that are designed to enhance student learning. As an educational leader, you are always actively engaged in curricular and instructional matters. Too much time is often spent on what I call "administrivia." Administrative exigencies must, of course, be attended to, but instructional improvement will not be enhanced without direct and specific attention to curricular concerns. Suggestions include:

A.  reviewing current curriculum guidelines and other instructional materials;

B.  reviewing materials for instruction (e.g., texts, workbooks, comput-
    ers, etc.) making certain that curriculum materials are matched to
    appropriate instructional levels of students;

C.  arranging assembly programs, fairs, exhibits, contests, and other in-
    centives such as banners, t-shirts, buttons, etc.;

D.  facilitating interdisciplinary curriculum; and

E.  encouraging curriculum development and renewal (Glatthorn, 1994).

## Parents and Pupils

Implementing any program involves parental input in terms of advise-
ment and participation. While once being interviewed for an assistant
principalship, I was asked if I believed in parental involvement. Not want-
ing to offer the usual or typical canned response, I rose from my seat and
demonstrated for the committee my commitment to parental involvement in the following way:

"Let me show you what I mean when I say that parental involvement
is essential." *I held up a blank piece of paper (Illustration 4.1).* I continued,
"Within a school there are basically three groups of individuals. There are
faculty (including administration and teachers), there are students, and
there are parents." *As I mentioned each group, I drew a small oval until I
developed the configuration seen in Illustration 4.2.* "Quite often," I lamented,
"when faculty work on their side, and the parents work on their side, all
without partnership and commitment, the students are left in the middle."
*As I mentioned "the faculty," I placed a dot in the center of the left-hand oval;
as I mentioned "the parents," I placed a dot in the center of the right-hand
oval; and as I mentioned "the students," I merely pointed to the center oval. I
ended up with the configuration in Illustration 4.3.*

"When this happens," I continued, "when there is no communication
and teamwork between these two sides, the whole system can get looking
pretty unhappy." *As I said, ". . . when there is no communication . . ." I drew
the curved line above the three ovals. Then, as I said, "the whole system can get
. . ." I drew the curved line under the three ovals. The configuration now
resembled the sad face shown in Illustration 4.4.*

"But, let's add teamwork. Let's get everyone working together to help
our children. When parents and faculty work together constructively, the
whole school is unified." *As I mentioned "working together," I drew a large,
encompassing oval around the sad face so that it looked like Illustration 4.5.*

"Then," I concluded, "thanks to teamwork and spirit of cooperativeness, students will succeed and we will have a happy and functioning school; one we may all be justly proud of." *As I said the last words, I turned the drawing around 180 degrees. Before the eyes of the committee, it turned into the happy face as seen in Illustration 4.6.*

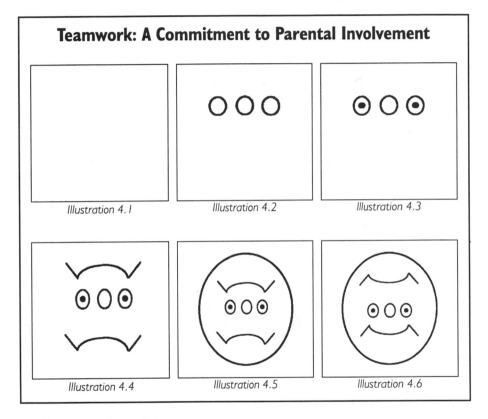

**Illustrations 4.1 to 4.6**
*From School Administrator's Public Speaking Portfolio by Susan Mamchak and Steven Mamchak. Copyright © 1983. Reprinted with permission of the Center for Applied Research in Education/ Prentice-Hall.*

Although this was a somewhat contrived and simple demonstration of my philosophical commitment to parental involvement, several committee members did smile and I'm certain I effectively communicated my point. Involve parents in any reasonable way possible. Here are some suggestions:

1. Invite their participation on needs assessment and goal committees through formal and informal invitations.
2. Sponsor an Open House at which you will provide refreshments and outline the nature of participation you desire.
3. Develop a "parent hotline" so that parents may keep abreast of "what's happenin'" in the school.
4. Invite parents to "parent-student" picture night.

Also, too often pupils are not considered in program development. Soliciting their participation on committees offers a unique opportunity to benefit from their keen insights and perspectives.

## Resource People

Program implementation involves the active participation of several other personnel, depending, of course, on the nature of the program. The following individuals may be valuable resources: guidance counselors, teachers with special expertise, social workers and psychologists, specialty coordinators from the district office or neighboring townships, lunchroom and office staff, health department officials, consultants, and so on.

## Evaluation

As defined earlier, evaluation is a decision-making process. In an era of accountability in which productivity is demanded, evaluation assumes greater priority and attention. How can we as educational leaders increase productivity?

1. Set goals;
2. Determine where we are; and
3. Identify strategies for getting where we want to be.

In a nutshell, when we evaluate we want to answer two fundamental questions:

1. How are we doing? and
2. How can we improve?

Evaluation is a comprehensive, ongoing process. Many consider evaluation synonymous with some sort of posttest and that's it. This volume has demonstrated the importance of taking a comprehensive approach to school improvement by incorporating quantitative and qualitative approaches.

Also, many individuals are not aware of the formative *and* summative nature of evaluation. Evaluation is ongoing to the extent to which you provide for formative evaluation. Assessing progress along the way makes sense. Why wait six months or a year before realizing that changes are warranted? Formative evaluation allows for program adjustments and modifications. Research has indicated that programs that incorporate formative evaluative measures are more likely to succeed.

Summative evaluation that is **triangular** in nature (see Chapter 2), leads to one of three conclusions:

1. modification of program or procedure;
2. elimination of program or procedure; or
3. continuation of program or procedure.

What should be assessed or evaluated? Any programs, practices, and procedures should be evaluated—such as, among others, school goals and objectives, parent-teacher conferences, assessment procedures (including report cards), faculty meetings, assembly programs, music programs, administrative procedures, dropout rates, attendance policies, schoolwide discipline plans, curriculum materials, pupil achievement, accounting procedures, school climate, and so on.

How to evaluate? Keep this mnemonic in mind: *ROTC.*

$R$ = records and rating scales—examine records, develop rating or attitudinal surveys, and checklists;

$O$ = observations, both formal and informal;

$T$ = tests, standardized and/or non-standardized; and

$C$ = conferences with everyone.

## A General Evaluation Plan

In developing a general evaluation plan, keep in mind these points:

1. What is the purpose of evaluation?
2. What needs to be evaluated?
3. What are your goals?

4. How will data be collected?

5. How will data be organized and analyzed?

6. How will the data be reported?

Problems are inevitable in program evaluation. Keep in mind these five steps for solving problems:

1. analyze the situation;

2. examine research (data collected or evidence);

3. examine results;

4. develop alternative solutions; and

5. act (modify, discard, or continue).

# Program Evaluation in Five Steps

The following steps of program evaluation were employed when I evaluated a program that I had established in a school while serving as assistant principal. The discussion that follows is based on information gleaned from Sanders, 1992.

The program I evaluated was first established at a public elementary school to address some of the needs of at-risk students. What made this program noteworthy was that martial arts training was incorporated as part of an overall curricular approach aimed at assisting selected 4th and 5th graders who were either currently involved in gangs or likely to join them. Program evaluation involved the following five steps:

## I.   *Focusing the evaluation* is composed of three steps:

1. clarify evaluation purposes;

2. clarify what is to be evaluated; and

3. identify questions to be answered.

In other words, in focusing our **evaluation** of the martial arts program, I attended to three aspects: clarifying the evaluation purposes, clarifying what was to be evaluated, and identifying the evaluation questions to be answered.

The purpose of our evaluation of the martial arts program was twofold:

1.  To monitor pupil progress academically and socially—The intent was to conduct formative (in-progress) evaluations of the students' academic and social progress.

2.  To monitor pupil motivation—The intent was to provide insights about the effort and persistence among student participants.

Our primary purpose for evaluating the program was to determine whether or not a program of this nature, which had never been attempted in our school before, should be continued and expanded to include other students at risk. Formative evaluative steps would enable us to monitor the program on an ongoing basis. Midcourse corrections could be made if necessary to improve the quality of the program. A summative evaluation was planned at the end of the school year by accumulating overall data relating to our two purposes outlined above as well as bringing in an outside consultant to provide his reactions to the program. The consultant was a principal of a school in another district who was also a black belt instructor in the martial arts.

After clarifying evaluation purposes, another set of decisions was needed to get a clear sense of what was to be specifically evaluated. Specific criteria were specified separately for each of the evaluation purposes noted above. Five specific aspects were identified for pupil academic and social progress:

1.  incidence of aggressive behavior (physical fights with other students and/or physical acts toward faculty and staff);

2.  degree to which basic school and class rules were adhered to;

3.  rates for tardiness and attendance;

4.  number of homework assignments completed; and

5.  number of in-class assignments completed.

Two specific aspects were identified for pupil motivation:

1.  degree to which students demonstrated effort and persistence in class; and

2.  degree to which students demonstrated effort and persistence in martial arts class.

Once we had a sense of what was to be evaluated, evaluation questions were posed:

A. What were the expected academic outcomes for students who participated in the martial arts program?

B. What were the expected social outcomes for students who participated in the martial arts program?

C. Were students motivated to participate in in-class and school-related functions as well as in the martial arts class itself?

D. How well were the students performing on the expected outcomes noted above?

E. To what extent was the program meeting expectations of principal, assistant principal, martial arts instructor, teachers, parents, and student participants?

## II.  *Collecting data*

In order to answer each of the evaluation questions, sources of information and evaluation methods for each evaluation question had to be identified. Scheduling the collection of data and assigning responsibility for collecting data was also attended to.

Sources of **data collection** were culled from existing resources such as school files and records, direct observation of the program, and people in any way connected to the program. Evaluation methods that were deemed appropriate and feasible were matched to each evaluation question as follows:

A. What were the expected academic outcomes for students who participated in the martial arts program?

> *Data collection methods:* teacher and pupil interviews, teacher-made tests, and checklists for completed assignments.

B. What were the expected social outcomes for students who participated in the martial arts program?

> *Data collection methods:* teacher, supervisor, and pupil interviews, number of reported suspensions, number of times students were reported to assistant principal's office for misbehavior, attendance reports, and observations.

C. Were students motivated to participate in in-class and school-related functions as well as in the martial arts class itself?

> *Data collection methods:* teacher, supervisor, and pupil interviews, attendance reports, observations, student journals and

portfolios, and visual anthropology or film ethnography (Marshall & Rossman, 1994).

D. How well were the students performing on the expected outcomes noted above?

   *Data collection methods:* methods noted above through formative and summative evaluations.

E. To what extent was the program meeting expectations of principal, assistant principal, martial arts instructor, teachers, parents, and student participants?

   *Data collection methods:* interviews and questionnaires.

## III.  *Organizing and analyzing the data*

Evaluation methods provided much qualitative information. Much data was especially gathered through the use of multiple observers, multiple data collection methods, and extensive descriptions. Field notes, thick descriptions, transcripts of interviews, written responses to questionnaires, student journal entries, and copies of written documents, files, and reports were organized and analyzed according to each evaluation question. My concern was to summarize the data collected as accurately and clearly as possible. At every opportunity, I attempted to verify and validate the findings by getting reactions from people involved in the project.

## IV.  *Reporting the data*

Results of this program evaluation revealed that the students at risk who participated in this integrated school/curricular martial arts program improved in the following ways:

A. Academically—Although teachers initially reported little, if any, change in the numbers of completed homework and in-class assignments, by the end of the sixth month of the program teachers did in fact state that these assignments were increasingly being completed. Teachers who were interviewed stated that they were pleased by this academic progress. Teachers attributed this success not necessarily to the martial arts program per se, but to the close contact with and supervision of these students by supervisors and the martial arts instructor. In fact, the martial arts program did provide an incentive for these students to improve academically.

B. Socially—Teachers and supervisors reported less incidences of aggressive behavior exhibited by these students. A reduction in the number of discipline referrals was clearly evident. Classroom teachers also reported greater adherence to rules and procedures, as did teachers on lunch duty. Improved attendance and tardiness rates were noted.

C. Motivation—Classroom teachers and the martial arts instructor related that these students demonstrated greater effort, interest, and enthusiasm.

D. Expectations—Results from interviews, questionnaires, and informal observations and talks with parents, teachers, supervisors, and students themselves revealed positive feelings about the curricular/martial arts program. Teachers and parents, in particular, asserted that they expected students to continue to improve.

Throughout the course of the evaluation, adult participants were informed about the evaluation process and the progress being made toward its completion. Time was spent obtaining comments from teachers, supervisors, and an outside consultant regarding any possible errors or omissions of evidence and other plausible interpretations that were missing. It was decided that the publication of an article describing our program could enhance efforts to expand the martial arts program to possibly include a larger sample and even expand the program to other schools. Reports of this evaluation, then, were to be disseminated throughout the district.

## V.  *Administering the evaluation*

Administering this evaluation plan was a complex and arduous undertaking. Many logistics had to be considered, including scheduling data collection, allocating time for data analysis, and budget. Although budget constraints were minimal, scheduling problems emerged fairly regularly. At times, certain teachers, due to their own pressures and concerns, did not readily provide needed data. Programs had to be occasionally adjusted and arrangements coordinated with participants. Establishing and maintaining open communications among all participants were a priority. Anonymity of participants was assured.

In sum, in order to assess the effectiveness of our martial arts program, I attended to five basic tasks in program evaluation (Sanders, 1992; also see Wholey, Hatry, & Newcomer, 1994): focusing the evaluation, collecting data, organizing and analyzing the data, reporting data, and administering the evaluation.

Before proceeding with the remainder of the chapter, complete the following exercises that help reinforce some of the ideas expressed above.

---

# Exercises

3. Using the steps described above implement and evaluate any program of your choice. Be as specific as possible in your descriptions.

   _____

   _____

   _____

   Answers will vary

4. A quasi-experimental design involving one group which is repeatedly pretested, exposed to an experimental treatment, and repeatedly posttested is known as a

   a. pretest/posttest design.

   b. posttest only design.

   c. time series design.

   d. revolving series design.

   e. none of these.

   Answer: choice "c". Explanations to this question and<br>the next five can be found in the preceding chapter.

5. A true experimental design which involves at least two randomly selected groups; both groups are pretested, one group receives a new treatment, and both groups are posttested is called a

   a. time series design.

   b. posttest only control group design.

   c. pretest-posttest control group design.

   d. non-equivalent control group design.

   e. none of these.

   Answer: choice "c"

---

6. Which is the weakest design?

    a. non-equivalent control group design

    b. posttest only control group design

    c. interrupted time series design

    d. single measurement design

    e. pretest-posttest control group design

    Answer: choice "d"

7. You take 50 4th grade students, assign 25 randomly to one class and 25 randomly to the other class. Both groups are measured beforehand. Two different treatments are presented, then a follow-up measurement is given. Which type of design is this?

    a. pretest-posttest control group design

    b. pretest-posttest only design

    c. one-shot case study

    d. non-equivalent control group design

    e. one-group pretest-posttest design

    Answer: choice "a"

8. Mrs. James teaches computers at P. S. 999. She has a new textbook which she wishes to use with her classes. She decides to test the effectiveness of the new textbook. She chooses two classes that rank similar in ability on a pretest in computer literacy. She gives her programmed text to group A, but with group B she continues her normal instruction. At the end of the semester, she gives a test on computer knowledge and discovers that the class using the new text outperformed the other group (B). She concludes that the new text should be incorporated in all the classes. What research design did Mrs. James use?

    a. non-equivalent control group design

    b. interrupted time series design

    c. pretest-posttest design

    d. pretest-posttest control group design

    e. control group only design

    Answer: choice "a"

9. Mr. Solomon is a supervisor in an elementary school. Mr. Jones, a 6th grade teacher, complains that one student, Billy, is disruptive and recalcitrant. Mr. Solomon tells the teacher to record Billy's behavior in anecdotal form for two weeks before a conference with the guidance counselor. During the first week, Mr. Jones discovers that Billy acts out 26 times. During the second week, he acts out 22 times. During the third week, Mr. Jones meets with the guidance counselor to work out Billy's problems. The counselor sets up a special reward system for Billy. During the fourth week, Billy acts out 18 times. During the fifth week, the disturbances decrease to only 5 times. Mr. Jones and the counselor conclude that the technique is successful. What research design was employed?

a. pretest-posttest control group design

b. control group only design

c. interrupted time series design

d. single measurement design

e. non-equivalent control group design

Answer: choice "c"

10. As an educational leader who wishes to establish a new science program in your school, what is the first step that should generally be taken?

a. consult with parents

b. hand out new textbooks and get feedback from teachers

c. establish summative evaluative criteria

d. disseminate goals and objectives to all staff

e. needs assessment

Answer: choice "e"

# Chapter Summary

The following worksheet allows you to plan a program and incorporate the steps in evaluation. This worksheet is meant to allow you to brainstorm different ideas. Changes in your plan can always be made at a later date. This worksheet serves as a review of the ideas discussed in this chapter.

# Starting a Program and Planning Its Evaluation

1. *What program do I wish to initiate? Why do I want to develop this program? What do I hope to accomplish? (Use additional paper to record your responses if necessary.)*

   _____

2. *What preliminary information should I gather to help me get started?* _____

   _____

3. *What question or questions should I ponder?* _____

   _____

4. *Who will be involved in this project?* _____

   _____

5. *How will data be collected, analyzed, and reported?* _____

   _____

6. *What will I do with the results?* _____

   _____

7. *What will I do when problems develop?* _____

   _____

8. *Complete the 8 steps in program development by being as specific as possible:*

   **Needs Assessment:** *What do I intend to do to adequately assess whether or not a need exists for my program?*

   **Goals:** *What are my short- and long-term goals? How do I plan on disseminating these goals?*

   **Administrative Aspects:** *What administrative or logistical concerns need to be addressed?*

   **Supervision:** *How will I facilitate instructional improvement?*

   **Curriculum:** *What curricular matters must be addressed? How will curricular changes be addressed?*

   **Parents and Pupils:** *How will I involve both of these groups?*

   **Resource People:** *How can specialists assist in program development?*

   **Evaluation:** *What is my evaluation plan?*

9.  Complete the 5 steps in program evaluation by being as specific as possible:

**Focusing the Evaluation:** *What are my purposes? What is to be evaluated? What questions will be developed?*

**Collecting Data:** *What data collection methods will be employed? (Match them to each evaluation question previously posed.)*

**Organizing and Analyzing the Data:** *How will I organize and analyze my data?*

**Reporting the Data:** *How will results of this program evaluation be reported?*

**Administering the Evaluation:** *What administrative and logistical items must be addressed?*

# References

[Note that references with an asterisk are annotated later in the book.]

Acheson, K. A., & Gall, M. D. (1997). *Techniques in the clinical supervision of teachers.* New York: Longman.

Brainard, E. A. (1996). *A hands-on guide to school program evaluation.* Bloomington, IN: Phi Delta Kappa Educational Foundation.

Cuban, L. (1984). *How teachers taught: Constancy and change in American classrooms, 1890–1980.* New York: Longman.

DeRoche, E. F. (1987). *An administrator's guide for evaluating programs and personnel* (2nd ed.). Boston: Allyn and Bacon.

Glanz, J. (1992). School-based management and the advent of teacher empowerment: One administrator's view of reform. *Record in Educational Administration and Supervision, 12,* 40–45.

Glanz, J. (1995). A school/curricular intervention martial arts program for students at risk. *The Journal of At-Risk Issues, 2*(1), 18–25.

Glatthorn, A. A. (1994). *Developing a quality curriculum.* Alexandria, VA: ASCD.

Glickman, C. D., Gordon, S. P., & Ross-Gordon, J. M. (1998). *Supervision of instruction: A developmental approach* (4th ed.). Boston: Allyn and Bacon.

Griffin, G. A. (1997). Is staff development supervision? No. In J. Glanz & R. F. Neville (Eds.), *Educational supervision: Perspectives, issues, and controversies* (pp. 162–169). Norwood, MA: Christopher-Gordon Publishers.

Herman, J. L., Lyons Morris, L., & Fitz-Gibbon, C. T. (1987). *Evaluator's handbook*. Newbury Park, CA: Sage Publications.

*Herman, J. L., & Winters, L. (1992). *Tracking your school's success: A guide to sensible evaluation*. Newbury Park, CA: Corwin Press.

Johnson, S. M. (1990). *Teachers at work: Achieving success in our schools*. New York: Basic Books.

Marshall, C., & Rossman, G. B. (1994). *Designing qualitative research*. Newbury Park, CA: Sage Publications.

*Sanders, J. R. (1992). *Evaluating school programs: An educator's guide*. Newbury Park, CA: Corwin Press.

Wholey, J. S., Hatry, H. P., & Newcomer, K. E. (1994). *Handbook of practical program evaluation*. San Francisco: Jossey-Bass.

# $\mathcal{D}$ata Collection
# Techniques That Work

*"As professionals, the process of reflecting, hypothesizing, and testing our theories about how students learn best is perhaps one of our most important undertakings."*

*(Linda Hanson, Superintendent,*
*quoted in* Journal of Action Research, *1995)*

## Popular Data Collection Techniques Used in Action Research

Having emphasized a triangular approach to action research that favors both quantitative and qualitative approaches, this chapter will continue along this same vein by discussing varied ways of collecting data. **Data collection** is the process of collecting information to answer one's **research questions** and/or confirm or reject an **hypothesis**. This chapter will highlight those data collection techniques (or **instruments**) that I feel you, as an action researcher, will find useful when conducting action research.

# Primary Data Collection Techniques

## Questionnaires

**Questionnaires** are one of the most common types of data collection **instruments** (or data sources) used in action research projects. Their ease of use and uncomplicated methods of data analysis make questionnaires an invaluable means of collecting data for an action researcher.

A questionnaire surveys respondents' attitudes toward a particular issue. Educational leaders may distribute questionnaires to assess attitudes of students, parents, teachers, or even other supervisors about a variety of issues, such as school climate and instructional supervision.

Sometimes, ready-made questionnaires that have been developed by companies are available for use. For example, the National Association of Secondary School Principals (NASSP, 1987) has developed several useful, ready-made questionnaires surveying school climate, teacher, student, and parent attitudes toward school. Also, you can call 1-800-228-0752 for the *School Effectiveness Questionnaire*, which can be hand-tabulated or computer-analyzed. In many cases, however, questionnaires may not be available to suit your unique needs. In such cases, you might have to construct your own questionnaire. See discussion below on questionnaire construction.

Two types of questionnaires are most common: closed ended and open ended. Open-ended questionnaires include questions that allow respondents to elaborate on a given question. A questionnaire, for instance, composed of questions to ascertain a teacher's attitude toward supervision may include the following open ended question: "Can you provide an example of a situation or experience in which you have benefited from supervision? Explain."

Note that while questionnaires are usually data collection instruments used in quantitative approaches, the responses to open-ended questions in questionnaires can be seen and interpreted as qualitative data. Very often comments generated from open-ended questions can prove very useful and even crucial in determining such things as the value of the program under study. (See Patton, 1990, p. 19, for a situation in which comments made in the open-ended portion of a questionnaire were the basis for a very important decision made by a school board, that would not have been made had only the closed-ended portion of the questionnaire been analyzed quantitatively.)

Closed-ended questionnaires, on the other hand, do not allow respondents to elaborate, but rather structure respondents' answers to predetermined choices. One of the most commonly used closed-ended questionnaires is known as the **Likert scale**. Many of us have taken a Likert scale questionnaire at one time or another. Right? You recall those choices it gives such as strongly agree, agree, disagree, and strongly disagree? A Likert scale is relatively easy to construct and easy to analyze.

### Likert Scale Construction: Some Guiding Principles

1. Limit the number of items to as few as possible (ideally between 15–20 items). Long surveys are unlikely to be completed by respondents.

2. Avoid ambiguously worded statements. Construct items so that they may be interpreted in the same way by every respondent. Why is the following statement worded ambiguously?

    "How often do you observe your fifth grade teachers?"

    *rarely        sometimes        often*

    Right. What is meant by "observe?" A casual look, an in-depth hour-long observation period, or some time in between? Moreover, what do the choices mean? How often is "sometimes"? Once a month, twice a month, or once a year?

    Sometimes statements are just phrased ambiguously due to sentence structure problems. Have a colleague or potential respondent proofread your items for ambiguity.

3. Avoid leading questions: i.e., don't suggest that one response will be more appropriate than another. For example, avoid using a question such as "Don't you agree that peer coaching is marvelous?"

4. Avoid sensitive questions to which respondents may not reply honestly. For example, don't ask: "Have you always acted so ethically?"

5. Statements should be concise, not overly lengthy.

6. Develop objectives before you write the items (see examples in sample questionnaire that follows).

7. Questionnaires should include statements that are conceptually related. If you are surveying attitudes of teachers toward bilingual education, then an example of a conceptually unrelated item would be:

"I get along with my supervisor." This statement has little, if anything, to do with the major purpose of your questionnaire. One way to ensure that items are conceptually related is to match each item with your objectives. Does each item address one of the stated objectives?

8. Avoid response sets. Sometimes respondents will not really read the survey, but merely go down a column circling all the "strongly disagree" choices. To avoid response sets you must word half the items positively and half negatively. Placement of positively and negatively worded statements should be random. Don't intentionally place an item in the order you think is best. As long as about half of the items are positive statements and the other half are negative statements, and the items are randomly distributed, you will have avoided the response set problem.

   Below is an example of two statements, one positively worded and the other in the negative:

   Directions: Circle the response that best indicates the extent to which you agree or disagree with each statement below, where

   SA = Strongly Agree
   A  = Agree
   D  = Disagree
   SD = Strongly Disagree

   1. Math is my favorite class.
   2. Learning math is a waste of time.

If someone really enjoys math, she will circle SA for the first item and SD for the second. If the respondent circles SA for both items, you might have a response set. Too many response sets affect the **validity** and **reliability** of your questionnaire.

9. Preparation of cover letter: A cover letter should be brief and neat. The letter should explain the purpose of your study, emphasize its importance, give the respondent a good reason for completing the survey, and ensure the respondent's anonymity.

10. Field test your survey to ensure consensual **validity**.

A sample Likert-scale questionnaire below illustrates the objectives that were written prior to developing the items. Note that your objectives would not be shared with respondents.

**SAMPLE QUESTIONNAIRE\***

Team Teaching Class

Objectives:

1.  Are students' physical needs met in the team teaching classroom?

    _____

    _____

    _____

2.  How is student achievement affected by team teaching?

    _____

    _____

    _____

3.  Does having two teachers increase your understanding of this topic?

    _____

    _____

    _____

4.  Are students finding their teachers more available for help?

    _____

    _____

    _____

5.  Are students comfortable participating in a team taught (larger) class?

    _____

    _____

    _____

6.  Does having two teachers help students to stay focused and attentive?

    _____

    _____

    _____

\*Developed by one of my graduate students, Ms. Jamie Horowitz.

Questionnaire:

# Millburn High School
# Mathematics Department

Place a check in the appropriate space below:

___ male  ___ female
___ freshman  ___ sophomore  ___ junior  ___ senior

This scale has been prepared so that you can indicate how you feel about the statements below. Please *circle* one of the letters on the left indicating how you feel about each statement. (SA strongly agree, A agree, D disagree, SD strongly disagree)

SA  A  D  SD    1. I understand explanations given by my teacher(s).

SA  A  D  SD    2. I can see the board and overhead screen clearly.

SA  A  D  SD    3. When something is unclear, I am not comfortable asking a question in class.

SA  A  D  SD    4. Being in a class taught by two teachers helps me to be more attentive.

SA  A  D  SD    5. I am not doing very well in this class.

SA  A  D  SD    6. My teacher(s) is available for extra help.

SA  A  D  SD    7. I am not comfortable participating in this class by responding to teacher questions.

SA  A  D  SD    8. I am confused by explanations given by my teacher(s).

SA  A  D  SD    9. It's hard for me to see the board and overhead screen from where I'm seated.

SA  A  D  SD    10. I am comfortable asking a question in class if I don't understand something.

SA  A  D  SD    11. I find it harder to pay attention in class with two teachers.

SA  A  D  SD    12. I am doing pretty well in this class.

SA  A  D  SD    13. My teacher is not available when I need extra help outside of the classroom.

SA  A  D  SD    14. I am comfortable participating in class by responding to teacher questions.

For more information about questionnaire construction, consult the following excellent references: Fink (1995), and Fink and Kosecoff (1985). On survey validity and reliability see Litwin (1995).

Before proceeding with the remainder of the chapter, complete the following exercises that help reinforce some of the ideas expressed above.

---

### Exercises

1. Explain why response sets might skew results from a questionnaire. How would you avoid a response set?

   _____

   _____

   _____

   See discussion above in point 8

2. You are a principal of Hartworth High School located in an affluent suburb with an enrollment of 2000 students and an active parent body.

   You are acutely aware that a successful school is one that has the following characteristics:

   A. a commonly held sense of mission/purpose

   B. a strong academic focus

   C. a strong administrative/instructional focus

   D. fosters collegial relationships and collaborative planning

   E. positive teaching/learning climate where success is recognized and rewarded

   F. a well-coordinated and articulated curriculum

   G. high expectations for all (equality of opportunity and excellence)

   H. high standards for all

   I. frequent monitoring

   J. parental and community involvement

   You sense that this school may be lacking in many of these areas. You see the need for improvement and would like to undertake a survey (needs assessment) of your school's "organizational health."

   Compose a questionnaire to assess the relative health of your school. Be certain to include all the essential ingredients of a good questionnaire (see

---

points explained above). Your questionnaire should include at least 15 items. For example:

Have participants respond to the following statements by noting "Strongly Agree," "Mildly Agree," "Mildly Disagree," or "Strongly Disagree."

1. teachers spend time working with students

2. teachers receive administrative help

3. problems are solved, not ignored

4. there is a pessimistic atmosphere in school

5. decision-making is undemocratic

6. teachers enjoy working in this school

Of course, items will depend on the nature of your objectives.

_____

_____

_____

Answers will vary

3. Principal's Rating Scale

You have been a principal of a school for nearly two years. You realize that an effective school is one that has a strong, competent leader. But how competent are you? Compose a rating scale to measure your effectiveness as principal. The rating scale will be distributed to all school personnel, parents, and students. For example:

Have respondents note "Always," "Sometimes," or "Never."

_____  a. your principal is accessible

_____  b. he/she encourages a positive relationship

_____  c. he/she encourages innovative programs

Discuss how you would utilize the findings of this rating scale to improve your performance. Discuss any shortcomings related to using a rating scale to measure the effectiveness of a principal.

_____

_____

Answers will vary

## Observation

A very common way to collect data in action research settings is to observe and record information. In Chapter 3 we discussed the difference between systematic and nonsystematic observation and explained that both forms of observation are valuable.

In qualitative research approaches, observation may take place in four ways:

1. *As a participant*—the researcher may conceal her or his role when gathering data. For example, a superintendent may want to study interactions among fellow superintendents at a conference. The researcher is able to observe firsthand social interactions among superintendents. Being actively engaged in the conference affords the researcher firsthand experience and data. Yet, the ethics of concealing one's purpose in interacting with others should be considered.

2. *As an observer-participant*—the researcher's purpose is known by all participants. The researcher may record data as they occur. Yet, participants may be reluctant to share information if they know that what they will say or do will be recorded.

3. *As a participant-observer*—the researcher's observation role is secondary to the participant role. The researcher records data; however, the researcher may not attend to all data.

4. *As an observer*—the researcher observes without participating. Recording data can be accomplished without distractions, yet those being observed may feel uncomfortable with the researcher's sole role as observer.

Regardless of the way you collect data through observation, several key questions should be kept in mind (thanks to my colleague Dr. Barry Friedman, a principal in the New York City Public Schools and an adjunct professor at the College of Staten Island, CUNY, for suggesting these questions):

1. What is the purpose of the observation?
2. Which individuals, events, settings, and circumstances are the focus of the investigation?
3. How are students, teachers, parents, and administrators behaving?
4. What activities are occurring?

5. How would you describe the social interaction?
6. How do people talk to each other?
7. What is the impact of my presence as an observer?
8. What instruments am I using to record data (e.g., pencil/paper, camera, video recorder, audio recorder, etc.)?

Two ways of collecting data through observation have been particularly useful for me. First, written descriptions are most often employed by educational leaders when collecting data. For instance, when a leader observes a teacher, she may record information by taking field notes or "thick descriptions." Taking field notes is a convenient and simple way of recording observations. Although field notes are subject to observer bias and subjectivity, recording data anecdotally (without drawing conclusions or making value judgments) is highly recommended. Still, this method of recording data is incomplete in the sense that it is impossible to record all events during a given lesson, for instance. Observations are therefore necessarily limited and should rarely be used as a sole means of collecting data. This is why qualitative researchers, as we discussed, emphasize the importance of triangulating on the basis of various data collection methods.

A second way of collecting data through observation is preparing a checklist of some sort to facilitate observations. A checklist allows you to record instances of a particular behavior or practice.

The checklist technique defines certain behaviors or events that can be checked off as they occur during a lesson, for example. Let's say that you are observing a teacher and want to keep a tally of the number of instances in which the teacher "gave directions," "praised," "criticized," "probed," and "asked questions" during a fifteen-minute segment of a lesson. Your checklist might look something like the one in Figure 5.1. Checklists such as this one can assist systematic collection of data through observation.

Glickman, Gordon, and Ross-Gordon (1998) review several useful techniques for collecting data through observation. I suggest that you review the quantitative and qualitative techniques described by these authors. Also, consult Willerman, McNeely, and Koffman (1991) for a thorough discussion of observation instruments.

## Interviewing

Seidman (1991) stated that interviewing is the most suitable **data collection** method if we are to understand the experiences of others and the

| Checklist Observation Technique | | | | | |
|---|---|---|---|---|---|
| Time | Giving Directions | Praising | Criticizing | Probing | Questions |
| Minute 1 | | | | | |
| Minute 2 | | | | | |
| Minute 3 | | | | | |
| Minute 4 | | | | | |
| Minute 5 | | | | | |
| Minute 6 | | | | | |
| Minute 7 | | | | | |
| Minute 8 | | | | | |
| Minute 9 | | | | | |
| Minute 10 | | | | | |
| Minute 11 | | | | | |
| Minute 12 | | | | | |
| Minute 13 | | | | | |
| Minute 14 | | | | | |

**Figure 5.1**

meanings they make of them. Interviews enable the researcher to learn the complexities of the participants' experiences from his or her point of view. Following the advice of Mishler (1986), the best interviews are flexible and open-ended, allowing for natural conversation. The goal is to understand each participants' experiences and perceptions related to a given situation in a non-threatening way such that "meanings emerge, develop, and are shaped by and in turn shape the discourse."

Interviews are often audio-recorded and subsequently transcribed. Transcription, however, can be laborious and time consuming. Action researchers are unlikely to have the time needed to analyze data in such ways. Still, interviewing is a common and invaluable source of data for action researchers.

Here are some guidelines to follow when using the interview technique for data collection:

1. Decide why you want to interview someone and what type of information you hope to glean from the interview.

2. Understand the difference between a structured interview and an informal one. A structured interview is one in which the interviewer has a high degree of control over the interview situation. A structured interview has an **interview protocol** which consists of a predetermined set of questions used by an interviewer. In contrast, an informal interview may occur without such a predetermined set of criteria or questions, but rather may be conducted informally, even casually, when speaking with someone. For those of you lacking interview experience, I recommend a structured format. As you develop confidence and skills, a more informal approach may be used.

3. Avoid the following: interrupting the participant; failing to pick up on a topic that the participant considered important; making inappropriate comments or jokes; asking irrelevant personal questions (e.g., "How many children do you have?" unless it comes up in the normal course of "small talk"); failing to check the tape recorder; asking leading questions such as "Don't you agree that principals should welcome teacher advice?"; asking multiple questions such as "Why was the supervisor union against shared decision making and what do you think about the superintendent who was against merit pay?"; and inferring something not said or meant by the participant.

4. Tips: Practice an actual interview with a friend, spouse, relative, or colleague; bring a tape recorder and extra blank tapes; organize your questions in advance; have fun; be a good listener; paraphrase the participant's main points; build rapport, especially at the beginning; probe when necessary; use a small inconspicuous tape recorder because a big one might make the participant self-conscious and consequently uncomfortable; ask questions when you do not understand what the participant meant; include open-ended questions such as "Take me through your day." or "Describe that meeting with the student . . ."; and send out thank you cards/letters as soon as you complete interviews. Also, read Chapter 6 in Seidman (1991) for more detailed suggestions and information. See also Chirban, 1996.

Note the difference between the way qualitative and quantitative researchers would use interviews. The typical qualitative interview would be unstructured and open-ended. Using a protocol with a predetermined set of questions would generally be avoided. Qualitative interviewers want to encourage a relaxed atmosphere wherein ideas can be exchanged freely and easily. Qualitative interviews are really chats, rather than formal procedures. Also, a qualitative interviewer would not necessarily feign objectivity, but may, at times, interact with the participant in an open, lively dialogue.

## Tests

Tests are perhaps the most common tools used to collect data by action researchers. Two typical tests are commonly used in data collection:

1. **criterion-referenced tests** are one of two major types of **testing** instruments that measure minimum levels of student performance. Teacher-made tests are one example of a criterion-referenced test. The teacher usually establishes an objective (or criterion) and then measures the extent to which students meet the objective. Criterion-referenced tests are one of many possible data collection sources. (In contrast, see norm-referenced tests).

2. **norm-referenced tests** (synonymous with **standardized tests**) are one of two major types of **testing** instruments that measure differences among individuals being tested. Each student's score is compared to the *norm* group, usually a nationally determined norm. A norm-referenced test, such as a standardized math test, can indicate how a given student, say 10-year-old Jerry, measures up against other ten-year-olds in the nation. For instance, if Jerry scores in the 65th **percentile**, this indicates that his score on the test was higher than 65% of ten-year-olds who took the test. Obviously, it also means that 35% scored higher than Jerry. Thus, norm-referenced tests compare students to other students on some pre-established norm or standard. Norm-referenced tests are usually used as important data collection sources.

Another data collection **instrument** (or data source) that is a kind of standardized or norm-referenced test is an **achievement test**. Achievement tests are commonly used measures or **assessment** tools in action research. An achievement test assesses an individual's knowledge or proficiency in a given content area. The Stanford Achievement Test and the Iowa Test of Basic Skills are examples of standardized achievement tests.

An achievement test is one form of **data collection** that may be used by an educational leader, for instance, to arrive at a decision about levels of student achievement in a particular content area. Analysis of results of these achievement tests may yield valuable information in terms of needed remediation in specific content areas.

Achievement or standardized tests are, unfortunately, overused sometimes by supervisors and teachers who consider them the most important pieces of data when trying to arrive at a decision about levels of pupil achievement. Although an invaluable source of information, achievement tests should be considered as part of a **portfolio** of other assessment tools. No single assessment device should be used in making a decision about a program or practice. This book advocates a multidimensional, **triangular** approach to data collection.

Another data collection instrument that is a kind of standardized or norm-referenced test is an **aptitude test**. This test is designed to predict someone's ability to perform. The use of IQ tests is an example of an aptitude test. The SAT (Scholastic Aptitude Test) taken by precollegiate students is another example of an aptitude test.

**School profile** sheets may contain many of these aforementioned test scores. School profile sheets frequently analyze test scores over an extended period of time for various groups of students in different grades. As such, they are an invaluable source of information for an action researcher.

Useful information may also be gleaned from tests that do not provide quantitative outcomes. Writing samples, for instance, are usually marked holistically and can be used as qualitative data. Although no longer as common as they used to be, oral examinations may be yet another kind of test used to collect data. Can you think of any others?

## Focus Groups

Focus groups (Krueger, 1994; Vaughn, Schumn, & Sinagub, 1996) are groups of individuals who are selected by a researcher and consent voluntarily to share their views and opinions on specific topics related to an action research project. As a type of **survey**, a focus group is not unlike a group interview.

For example, as an assistant principal in an elementary school, I asked my upper grade teachers to join me for a focused group session during lunchtime, during which I heard their opinions about the new textbook series adopted the previous year. Hearing their varied views provided an invaluable method of data collection that helped our textbook committee arrive at a decision about continuing or discontinuing the series.

Before proceeding with the remainder of the chapter, complete the following exercises that help reinforce some of the ideas expressed above.

---

## Exercises

4. Develop a set of criteria that can be used to observe your school organization. Use some of the sample questions posed in the "observation" section above. Describe your organization in detail.

_____

_____

_____

*Answers will vary*

5. Conduct an observation study for one of the following topics:

   A. observe a classroom teacher giving a lesson in a major subject area;

   B. observe a principal conducting a faculty meeting;

   C. observe an entire school and its basic set-up;

   D. observe a supervisor conducting a workshop or grade/department conference; or

   E. observe a district office and its basic set-up.

   Choose only 1 of the above and make an extensive observation of the situation. Feel free to incorporate any of the following data collection techniques described in the above sections: interviews, test data, and focus groups.

_____

_____

_____

_____

_____

*Answers will vary*

# Secondary Data Collection Techniques

## School Profile Data

School profile data sheets, generally available through the district office or state agencies, provide a wealth of important documentary information. These sheets provide reliable, clear data about a school's resources and students' needs in order to plan effectively for school improvement. These sheets provide achievement and background data over a period of years. Assessing student achievement over a four-year period, for example, is relatively easy. Data may include standardized reading and math scores by grade level over a four-year period; a statistical overview of a school's characteristics (percent utilization, capacity, staff-student ratio, repair orders, etc.); demographic backgrounds of faculty, staff, and students; teacher characteristics (e.g., certification or tenure status); student characteristics (including mobility, class size, attendance rates, etc.).

Data derived from such profile sheets are easily obtained and interpreted. Such information may prove invaluable for collecting data about a specific program, practice, or procedure.

Have you seen your school's profile sheet lately? Ask your principal to give you one to peruse and see how much information is readily available.

## Multimedia

Too often researchers neglect this valuable source for collecting data. Use of multimedia (including audiotape recordings, videotapes, films, photographs, electronic mail surveys, among others) has many advantages over more traditional methods for collecting data. Don't overlook using any of these mediums when collecting data.

For example, taking pictures of students showing how they feel about their projects is a wonderful qualitative way of communicating information. Pictures *are* worth a thousand words. Pictures that show a group of eager, enthusiastic, and smiling kindergarten students holding their "Big Books" indicate the pride they must have felt in creating them. Using videotapes to film students' reading skills in September and videotaping them again in June will provide striking qualitative evidence of reading growth.

Although many researchers may indicate that use of videotape and photography may reflect a subjective bias, these forms of media, if incorporated properly and judiciously, can provide unique evidence. As long as you **triangulate**, that is, incorporate other valid and reliable data collection methods, multimedia use makes sense.

How might you use multimedia to collect data?

By the way, do you recall why triangulation is important, based on our discussion in Chapter 2?

## Portfolios

**Portfolios** are **data collection instruments** (or data sources) that include a great deal of information about a particular individual or group of individuals. Portfolios may include a student's achievement test scores, book reports, homework assignments, art projects, in-class tests, oral presentations, self-assessments, art work, etc. (see Wolf, LeMahiew, & Eresh, 1992). Portfolios are excellent ways of collecting data from a variety of perspectives. Portfolios may later be analyzed qualitatively to arrive at a decision about the achievement levels, for example, of a particular student in language arts. Portfolio use is very much in consonance with the concept of **triangulation** introduced in Chapter 2. What's the connection?

How might you use portfolios to collect data?

## Records

School records, other than formal test data found in school profile sheets, are commonly referred to by educational leaders. Leaders, for example, may collect data by examining cumulative record cards (revealing information about students), teacher files (revealing professional data about teachers, such as record of service), anecdotal records, and diaries/journals/logs.

How might you use records to collect data?

While these data collection techniques are more than sufficient for the practicing educational leader, other researchers interested in more in-depth techniques will find these and other data collection methods more fully explained in Anderson, Herr, and Nihlen (1994) and Marshall and Rossman (1994).

---
# Chapter Summary
---

The following worksheet allows you to record the types of data collection instruments (or data sources) you intend to use. This worksheet is meant to allow you to brainstorm different ideas. Changes in your plan can always be made at a later date. This worksheet serves as a review of the ideas discussed in this chapter.

---

## Data Collection Instruments

1. Given the nature of my action research project, what kind of data do I want/need to collect? (Use additional paper to record your responses if necessary.) _____

   _____

2. Who will be responsible for collecting this data? _____

   _____

3. What administrative or logistical concerns should I attend to? _____

   _____

4. Will I incorporate primary and/or secondary data collection instruments? _____

   _____

5. Check the data collection instruments you are likely to need and record relevant information:

   ### Primary Data Collection Instruments

   #### QUESTIONNAIRES

   ___ open-ended    ___ closed-ended    ___ Likert Scale

   What are my objectives? _____

   What are some sample statements I may incorporate? _____

   _____

   #### OBSERVATION

   ___ participant    ___ observer-participant    ___ participant-observer    ___ observer

   Will I use systematic and/or non-systematic methods of observation? _____

   What type of observation checklist or form will I use? _____

## INTERVIEWING

___ structured (formal)      ___ informal

What questions will I include in my interview protocol? _____

_____

## TESTS

___ criterion-referenced   ___ norm-referenced

What specific types will I use? _____

_____

### Secondary Data Collection Instruments

### SCHOOL PROFILE DATA

Where are the profile sheets? _____

What information do I want to collect? _____

_____

## MULTIMEDIA

___ audiotape recordings    ___ videotapes   ___ films   ___ photographs
___ electronic mail surveys   ___ other

_____

## PORTFOLIOS

What items can I collect as part of the portfolio? _____

_____

## RECORDS

What kinds of records can I collect? _____

_____

## OTHER DATA COLLECTION INSTRUMENTS

_____

_____

# References

[Note that references with an asterisk are annotated later in the book.]

Anderson, G. L., Herr, K., & Nihlen, A. S. (1994). *Studying your own school: An educator's guide to qualitative practitioner research*. Thousand Oaks, CA: Corwin Press.

Chirban, J. T. (1996). *Interviewing in depth*. Thousand Oaks, CA: Sage Publications.

Fink, A. (1995). *The survey kit*. Thousand Oaks, CA: Sage Publications.

*Fink, A., & Kosecoff, J. (1985). *How to conduct surveys: A step-by-step guide*. Thousand Oaks, CA: Sage Publications.

Glickman, C. D., Gordon, S. P., & Ross-Gordon, J. M. (1998). *Supervision of instruction: A developmental approach* (4th ed.). Boston: Allyn and Bacon.

*Journal of Action Research*. (1995).

Krueger, R. A. (1994). *Focus groups: A practical guide for applied research*. Thousand Oaks, CA: Sage Publications.

Litwin, M. S. (1995). *How to measure survey reliability and validity*. Thousand Oaks, CA: Sage Publications.

Marshall, C., & Rossman, G. B. (1994). *Designing qualitative research*. Newbury Park, CA: Sage Publications.

Mishler, E. G. (1986). *Research interviewing: Context and process*. Cambridge, MA: Harvard University Press.

NASSP. (1987). *Comprehensive assessment of school environments*. Reston, VA: National Association of Secondary School Principals.

Patton, M. Q. (1990). *Qualitative evaluation and research methods* (2nd ed.). Thousand Oaks, CA: Sage Publications.

*Seidman, I. E. (1991). *Interviewing as qualitative research: A guide for researchers in education and the social sciences*. New York: Teachers College Press.

Vaughn, S., Schumm, J. S., & Sinagub, J. M. (1996). *Focus group interviews in education and psychology*. Thousand Oaks, CA: Sage Publications.

Willerman, M., McNeely, S. L., & Koffman, E. C. (1991). *Teachers helping teachers: Peer observation and assistance*. New York: Praeger.

Wolf, R. M., LeMahiew, P. G., & Eresh, J. (1992). Good measure: Assessment as a tool for educational reform. *Educational Leadership, 49*(8), 8–13.

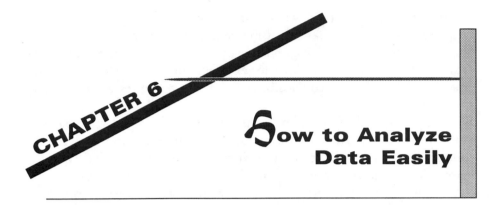

CHAPTER 6

# 5ow to Analyze Data Easily

*"Research brings light into darkness. Explications of meanings illuminate. Meanings of results truly matter."*

*(Davis, Jr., 1996, p. 296)*

Two people went out hiking on a foggy day when one of them fell over a cliff. The person at the top called down, "Are you all right?" "Yes, I'm all right," came back the answer. "Are you sure you have no broken bones?" his friend inquired. "No broken bones," came the answer through the fog. "Well, then, why don't you climb back up?" said the man at the top. "I can't," came the reply, "I'm still falling."

Moral of the story: don't make a decision until all results are in. Too often, many of us rush to conclusions because we "think" we know what the data are telling us. But without careful analysis, we may be shortsighted in our conclusions, arrive too quickly at judgments, and, even worse, make erroneous decisions that don't flow from the data. We should take an "I'm still falling" approach until we have adequately analyzed the data we so assiduously collected and, only then, can we begin to offer interpretations of the data and arrive at a conclusion or two.

Data analysis consists of looking for patterns, themes, associations, and interrelationships among the data collected. The process entails organizing and finding meaning in the mass of collected data. The process also involves presenting data in ways that will allow for easy interpretation. Displaying or summarizing data using tables, charts, and figures are useful ways of analyzing data. As we organize our data by displaying them using charts, for instance, we may look for emerging patterns. As these patterns emerge, explanations or conclusions can be drawn and research questions answered.

Data must be looked at holistically to determine a trend or pattern. Since we have relied on a multidimensional (**triangular**) approach to data collection, it is incumbent upon us to consider all data results. Some researchers sometimes rely on only one **instrument** before arriving at a conclusion. A significant **t-Test** finding, for example, doesn't necessarily mean that a particular program or practice should be implemented or adopted. Data analysis discussed in this chapter should involve consideration of all sources of data.

The purpose of data analysis is threefold:

1. to describe or summarize data clearly;
2. to search for consistent patterns or themes among the data; and
3. to enable us to answer our **research questions** and/or **hypotheses**.

As you know, this book has addressed two approaches to research: quantitative and qualitative. Since data derived from quantitative research are usually numerical and data derived from qualitative research are verbal, data analysis for each method will vary. Quantitative data are summarized statistically or mathematically, while qualitative data are analyzed through a logico-inductive process that includes grouping and comparing findings with research questions. Let's outline ways in which data might be analyzed quantitatively and, then, qualitatively.

# Quantitative Analyses

Data derived from descriptive, correlational, and/or group comparison research can be analyzed quantitatively. Some sort of statistical analyses are required to analyze quantitative studies.

## Statistical Analyses

Sadistic statistics?! Not really. With the advent of computer technology, use of statistical analysis has become relatively easy. No longer do you have to take out the abacus, calculator, or compute by longhand complicated formulae. Computers can conduct statistical analyses faster than you can say "hey, that's significant." Computers are readily available at campus computer lab centers and appropriate software packages are menu-driven for easy use.

The only slightly difficult thing to do is to be able to select the correct statistical calculation to match the type of research conducted. Programs exist today to help you do even that. So, as we discuss some statistics, don't fret since the computer can do it all.

Please note, therefore, that longhand calculations will not, for the most part, be described in this chapter. No educational leader would spend the time doing that kind of calculation. Learning how to analyze statistics on a computer is essential and will be part of your training in an action research course or workshop.

Two common types of statistics are:

1. **descriptive statistics** and
2. **inferential statistics**.

Descriptive statistics is one category or type of statistics that is used to describe and summarize data. Two of the most common ways to describe data statistically are by determining the **mean** and the **standard deviation**.

**Mean** is synonymous with average score. Mean indicates how a typical person scored on your test or survey. Mean is often represented either as simply $M$ or as $\overline{X}$ and is pronounced "X-bar." Mean is computed very simply by adding the numbers and dividing by the total number of numbers used. What would be the mean of these numbers: 23, 45, 12, 45, 23? Right, 21.4. Simply add the five numbers (23 + 45 + 12 + 45 + 23) and divide by five (since there are five total numbers).

See Figure 6.1 for the formula for mean.

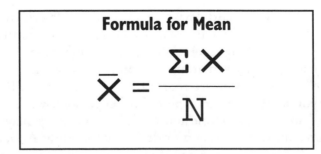

**Formula for Mean**

$$\overline{X} = \frac{\Sigma X}{N}$$

Figure 6.1

The Greek letter Σ (sigma) means the "sum of"; X equals the number of scores; and *N*, of course, signifies the number of subjects (*Ss*).

**Standard Deviation** (symbolized *S.D.*) indicates how much scores vary from each other.

For example, consider the means of these two sets of scores:

| | |
|---|---|
| Group X = 5 scores | Group Y = 5 scores |
| 50 50 50 50 50 | 100 50 45 35 20 |
| 250\5 = 50 | 250\5 = 50 |

Note that although both groups have the same mean, the scores in group X seem much more homogeneous than the scores in group Y. How do we describe the differences in the variation of the scores in both groups? Right, using standard deviation will indicate how much scores in this group vary. While standard deviation is more easily calculated quickly by computer, the formula in Figure 6.2 may be applied.

## Formula for Standard Deviation

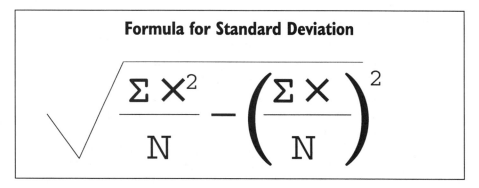

$$\sqrt{\frac{\Sigma X^2}{N} - \left(\frac{\Sigma X}{N}\right)^2}$$

Figure 6.2

Both mean and standard deviation are accurate **descriptive statistics** since they provide a good picture of a given distribution of scores. Means, of course, tell us the average score. Why do you think it may be important to know the mean of a given group of scores? . . . Knowing the standard deviation tells us how dispersed scores are in a given group. If you find a high *S.D.*, you might want to explore further reasons why scores in this group varied so much from one another. This knowledge may encourage us to examine our **treatment** and/or **design** of the study. Also, *S.D.* helps us draw conclusions about the **population** from what we know about the

**sample**. How mean and standard deviation can be used is described later in the chapter.

Percentages, as will be explained later, can also be considered descriptive statistics in action research projects.

Thus, descriptive statistics describe and summarize data numerically. For purposes of action research, the following are the most useful and common **descriptive statistics:**

(A) **Mean** (symbolized $\overline{X}$ or $M$)—a measure of central tendency indicating the arithmetic average;

(B) **Standard deviation** (symbolized *S.D.*)—a measure of dispersion indicating the amount scores vary from each other;

(C) Percentage (symbolized %)—a measure denoting "percentage" of individuals who gave a particular response or achieved a particular score;

(D) **Correlation coefficient** (symbolized $r$)—a measure of relationship indicating the degree to which two or more **variables** are related to each other.

In contrast to descriptive statistics, **inferential statistics** tell us how much confidence we can have in generalizing from a **sample** to a **population**. Although action research projects generally do not involve studies that seek generalization, certain useful and common inferential statistics are:

- Tests of significance (see **level of significance** in the Glossary) include:

    (A) **t-Tests**—determine significance of difference between means of two groups;

    (B) **sign tests**—determine significance of difference between means of one group;

    (C) **Mann-Whitney U-Tests**—determine whether two small groups differ significantly (works similar to a t-Test); and

    (D) **Chi square analyses**—(often symbolized by $X^2$) determine the relationship between two or more **nominal variables** (refer to **scales of measurement** in the Glossary).

The remainder of this chapter will be devoted to more fully explaining some of these descriptive and inferential statistics. An explanation of many other statistical analyses will not be undertaken because they are not usually utilized in action research projects. Note that many statistical operations can today be easily computed using a computer with a popular and easy-to-use statistical package.

For my action research projects, I find that computerized statistical packages are most desirable. For advanced students of research (usually those completing their doctoral dissertations), Statistical Packages for the Social Sciences (more commonly known as SPSS) is the most frequently used program. SPSS, in my opinion, is far too complicated and advanced for most statistical analyses that students enrolled in action research courses would need. A number of companies offer more user-friendly statistical packages. The professional educational leader, knowledgeable about applying action research, should become familiar with a statistical computer program.

I find that STATPAK, an acronym for "Statistical Package," is one such user-friendly package, but, in truth, any similar program will do. STATPAK is available for use with Macintosh and IBM-compatible computers. STATPAK can be obtained from Frisbie (1992) and Gay (1996). Installation procedures are supplied as well as directions on how to use STATPAK. STATPAK is completely menu-driven, is very, very easy to use, and best of all, it's free.

You can compute the following operations, among others, using STATPAK: **mean, standard deviation, correlation coefficients, t-Tests, ANOVAS,** and **Chi Squares.** I'm certain that as part of a course on action research you will have opportunities to use some of these computer software programs.

Other comparable statistical packages include, among others:

Stat-Star, (800) 541-0292.

GB-STAT automatic statistical graphs. Contact Dynamic Microsystems, (301) 384-2754.

PRO STAT. Poly Software International, (801) 485-0466.

MYSTAT for Windows (ISBN 1-56527-166-1).

## Application of Mean, Standard Deviation, and Percentage

In this section, results of a survey distributed to teachers about their attitudes toward supervision will be analyzed. Results that follow are fictionalized. The purpose of the analysis that follows will be to demonstrate how you, as an action researcher, can easily apply some basic descriptive statistics to analyze survey research. Other forms of descriptive statistics such as correlational analyses can be easily carried out by using one of the many computer programs.

Other than **standardized tests**, the most common **data collection** technique used by action researchers is the questionnaire. Let's illustrate how to apply three very common descriptive statistics: **mean, standard deviation**, and percentages. Let's apply them to a survey disseminated to teachers in Public School XY. The **Likert scale questionnaire** was designed to determine teachers' attitudes toward supervision.

The survey was disseminated to a group of 34 teachers. In order to analyze the data, you must develop an answer sheet of sorts that indicates favorable responses. Since the questionnaire is designed to assess attitudes toward supervision, which choices on the Likert scale questionnaire indicate favorable attitudes toward supervision?

Let's say you develop a 20-item questionnaire that includes, for example, the following two items, among others:

1. Your supervisor provides helpful feedback after a formal observation, and

2. Your supervisor offers little, if any, support in student disciplinary matters.

Since you've developed a Likert scale, the choices listed are Strongly Disagree (SD), Disagree (D), Agree (A), and Strongly Agree (SA). Choices are stated as follows:

SD  D   A   SA    1. Your supervisor provides helpful feedback after a formal observation.

SD  D   A   SA    2. Your supervisor offers little, if any, support in student disciplinary matters.

What response for each question indicates a favorable attitude toward supervision? Well, for the first question the most favorable response would be *SA* and least favorable response would be *SD*. Since four choices are provided (*SD, D, A, SA*), you would award 4 points to the most favorable response (*SA*), 3 points to the next favorable response (*A*), 2 points to *D*, and 1 point to *SD*, the least favorable response.

How might you code the second question? . . . Right, the most favorable response this time is *SD* which receives a 4, *D* receives a 3, and so on. Notice that the value awarded for each response varies depending on the question. You determine favorable responses based on what would be considered to be generally accepted among educators.

If your questionnaire has 10 items, what would be the highest possible favorable score? . . . Right, 40 (10 items, each receiving a 4 for the most favorable response equals 40). And what would be the lowest possible score, indicating the least favorable attitudes toward supervision? . . . Right, 10 (10 items, each receiving a 1 for the least favorable response equals 10).

*Mini-exercise:* What would be the highest and lowest scores for a questionnaire that has 20 items?

Here's an example of how a researcher coded the following questions indicating favorable attitudes toward supervision (note that the higher the score, the more favorable respondents' attitudes are toward supervision):

1.  Supervision facilitates instructional improvement.

    SA      A       D       SD
    4       3       2       1

2.  Supervision is a waste of time.

    SA      A       D       SD
    1       2       3       4

Now, if 32 individuals completed the questionnaire, you would have a total score for each of them as follows, for example:

       S1 = 40
       S2 = 34
       S3 = 10
       S4 = 18
       S5 = 26
       S6 = 30
       S7 = 14
       S8 = 20
       S9 = 10
       S10 = 30
       and so on

Obviously, subject 4 (S4) has a more unfavorable attitude toward supervision than subject 1 (S1). Who has the least favorable attitude toward supervision?

Now, how would we apply the three basic descriptive statistics to analyze these data? The results below, for two questions, is one common and easy way to indicate results.

## TEACHERS' ATTITUDES TOWARD SUPERVISION: SURVEY RESULTS

1. *Your supervisor provides helpful feedback after a formal observation.*

N = 32
21.9% Strongly Disagree (Raw score = 7)
75.0% Disagree (Raw score = 24)
3.0% Agree (Raw score = 1)
0.00% Strongly Agree (Raw score = 0)
Mean = 1.81
Standard Deviation = .47

*Conclusion:* An overwhelming percentage of respondents maintain that the supervisor doesn't provide helpful feedback after an observation.

2. *Your supervisor offers little, if any, support in student disciplinary matters.*

N = 32
0.00% Strongly Disagree (Raw score = 0)
15.6% Disagree (Raw score = 5)
62.5% Agree (Raw score = 20)
21.9% Strongly Agree (Raw score = 7)
Mean = 1.94
Standard Deviation = .62

*Conclusion:* An overwhelming percentage of respondents maintain that the supervisor offers little, if any, support in student disciplinary matters.

Notice in the example above that we first note the percentages. N = 32 for the first question indicates that 32 individuals responded to the first question. Therefore, *N* signifies the *number* of respondents. Raw scores indicate the number of respondents who filled in a given choice (e.g., 7 individuals responded "Strongly Disagree" to the first question).

Percentages are calculated by dividing the raw score (e.g., 7 in the first question above) into *N* (therefore, 7/32 = 21.9%). Calculate the other percentages on your own now. . . .

Many action researchers only rely on percentages for analyzing data. However, use of means and standard deviations are also commonly employed. Means and standard deviations are calculated easily using a calculator or by using a computer program such as STATPAK, as follows:

You would enter the STATPAK's main menu and select calculations for Mean and Standard Deviation. You will then be asked to enter a number for the first entry. Note that you will have 32 entries because 32 individuals responded to the first question. To calculate the mean and standard deviation, you need to look back at your key to determine how many points are awarded for a given choice. In the first question above, we awarded 4 points for a "Strongly Disagree" response because that would be considered the most favorable response to the first question. We also need to note the raw score for each response.

Since a "Strongly Disagree" response gets 4 points and 7 individuals respond "Strongly Disagree," we would enter the number "4" seven times into the STATPAK program. Why? Because seven individuals are awarded 4 points each for the "Strongly Disagree" choice.

The next choice, "Disagree," is awarded 3 points. How many individuals responded "Disagree"? . . . Right, 24. Enter 3, twenty-four times. The next category is "Agree." How many respondents chose "Agree"? . . . Right, only 1. Therefore, enter the number 2 (indicating 2 points) only once. Since no one responded "Strongly Disagree," no entry is made for the next choice.

Follow directions on the STATPAK menu and in a few seconds you will see the following page:

| Standard Deviation for Samples and Populations | |
| --- | --- |
| STATISTIC | VALUE |
| No. of Scores (N) | 32 |
| Mean | 3.19 |
| Standard Deviation | 0.47 |

Compute the mean and standard deviation for the second question above using a calculator or the STATPAK program (or any similar program, for that matter).

Sometimes, a Likert Scale may incorporate other choices such as *Very much, Somewhat,* or *not at all.* Also, results are often stated simply using percentages rather than means and standard deviations. Examine the analysis of results derived from a questionnaire (below) which indicates results based on student attitudes toward school:

1. *Indicate the degree to which your classes were informative and educational.*

N = 27
61.0% Very Much
28.0% Somewhat
11.0% Not at all

2. *Indicate the degree to which you enjoy your academic studies.*

N = 34
70.0% Very Much
20.0% Somewhat
10.0% Not at all

3. *Counseling has met my expectations.*

N = 35
11.0% Very Well
61.0% Well
28.0% Not at all

Can you, for extra credit (just a joke), figure out how many people responded for each choice above?! It's really quite simple. Multiply each percentage by N (the total number of respondents). For example, for question number one: multiply .61 by 27 = 16.47, rounded off to 16 people. That means that 16 people responded "very much" to the first question. Then, multiply .28 by 27 = 7.56 = 8; and .11 by 27 = 2.97 = 3. Thus, 16 + 8 + 3 = a total of 27 people who responded to the first question.

Whenever you want to determine a raw score, you multiply the percentage by the number (in this case, the number of total respondents). Therefore, for example, if I told you that Jeremy received an 70% on his math test and that there were 20 questions, what would be his raw score (i.e., number of correct responses)? That's right, multiply .70 by 20 = 14 correct responses. Now, figure out the number of people who responded for each choice in questions two and three above (answers can be found after exercise 2 below).

The examples illustrated above analyze results for one group. Sometimes, however, you might want to compare attitudes of two different groups, such African American parents' attitudes toward the school versus attitudes of Hispanic American parents. To analyze results from two groups, you would follow the same procedures for each group as you did before. You would now have, however, two sets of scores, one for each parent group. Although you could analyze each group using percentages, means, and/or standard deviations as explained above, you might consider another approach, such as the use of **correlational analysis** or **t-Test** analysis on both groups.

A correlational analysis would indicate the degree of relationship between both sets of group scores. You might conclude, for example, that there is a significant relationship between the way African American parents feel about the school and the way Hispanic American parents feel. To ascertain whether there is a significant statistical difference, however, between the two groups, a t-Test analysis should be undertaken, as will be explained in the next section.

Before proceeding with the remainder of the chapter, complete the following exercises that help reinforce some of the ideas expressed above.

---

### Exercises

1. You've analyzed the results of an AIDS questionnaire distributed to 70 high school freshman as follows:

   A. AIDS can reduce the body's ability to fight disease.

   | SA | A | D | SD |
   |----|----|----|----|
   | 53 | 14 | 3 | 0 |
   | 75.7% | 20% | 4.3% | 0% |

   $\overline{X} = 3.71$
   $S.D. = .54$

B. AIDS attacks the immune system in the body.

| SA | A | D | SD |
|---|---|---|---|
| 50 | 18 | 2 | 0 |
| 71.4% | 25.7% | 2.9% | 0% |

$\overline{X}$ = 3.69
S.D. = .53

C. A person can be infected with the AIDS virus (HIV) but not have the disease AIDS.

| SA | A | D | SD |
|---|---|---|---|
| 41 | 20 | 7 | 2 |
| 58.6% | 28.6% | 10.0% | 2.9% |

$\overline{X}$ = 3.43
S.D. = .79

Describe how you would compute the percentages, means, and standard deviations. Based on this excerpted data, describe what the survey indicates. What do the means and standard deviations tell us?

_____

_____

_____

Check answers in sections above

2. Develop a 5-item questionnaire, a coded answer sheet, and provide some dummy data. Compute means, standard deviations, and percentages for each item.

_____

_____

_____

Answers will vary; Answers for questions two and three in the previous section are, respectively: 24, 7, and 3 people; and 4, 21, and 10 people.

3. Examine the table below and draw four comparisons between the Cooperative Learning experimental group and the Whole Class control group. This table is culled from a study of a group of secondary school teachers in Israel conducted by Sharan and Shachar, 1988 (Reprinted with permission, Springer-Verlag, Inc.).

## Effects of Complex Cooperative Learning in a History Course by SES

| | Groups | | | |
| | Experimental Cooperative Learning | | Control Whole Class | |
| Test | High SES | Low SES | High SES | Low SES |
|---|---|---|---|---|
| (Pretest) | | | | |
| M | 20.99 | 14.81 | 21.73 | 12.31 |
| S.D. | 9.20 | 7.20 | 10.53 | 7.05 |
| (Posttest) | | | | |
| M | 62.60 | 50.17 | 42.78 | 27.03 |
| S.D. | 10.85 | 14.44 | 14.40 | 13.73 |
| Mean Gain: | 41.61 | 35.36 | 21.05 | 14.92 |

_____

_____

_____

Answer: Any of the following comparisons can be made: (1) In the pretests the lower-SES students scored significantly lower than the higher-SES students; (2) The lower-SES students taught by cooperative learning achieved over two times higher than those of the lower-SES students taught by whole class instruction; (3) Lower-SES students taught with cooperative learning scored higher than High-SES students taught with whole class instruction; (4) High-SES students scored higher than High-SES students with whole class instruction.

## The t-Test

A t-Test is a popular and common statistical technique that determines the degree of significance between the **means** of two groups. In other words, the purpose of a t-Test is to determine whether the difference between two means is statistically significant (see **statistical significance**).

Let's say you've divided your class into two equivalent groups using the **matched pairs** technique previously described in Chapter 3. Or, let's say you are a middle or high school teacher who wants to compare two equivalent classes (say, periods 4 and 6) in terms of science achievement. Both groups or classes would be exposed to a **treatment** and then a posttest would be administered. The results of the posttest are indicated in Figure 6.3 for two classes of five students each. Parenthetically, a t-Test would not ordinarily be used for groups less than 15 participants. I've used five students in each class to merely simplify the explanation of the t-Test. For groups less than 15, a **Mann-Whitney U-Test** should be conducted (see discussion in the next section).

| Posttest Results for t-Test Computation ||
|:---:|:---:|
| **CLASS I** | **CLASS II** |
| S1 = 85 | S1 = 73 |
| S2 = 82 | S2 = 76 |
| S3 = 78 | S3 = 80 |
| S4 = 75 | S4 = 70 |
| S5 = 72 | S5 = 65 |

Figure 6.3

The numbers in Figure 6.3 represent raw scores or interval data (see **scales of measurement**) based on posttest results. A score of 85, for instance, in Class I indicates a student's raw score on a science achievement test.

A cursory perusal of the data in Figure 6.3 may lead one to conclude that the students in the first class scored higher posttest scores than students in the second class. In other words, students in the first class have higher achievement in science than the other students. However, can we conclude that this difference is statistically significant? No, we can't.

To determine statistical significance requires that some sort of statistical operation be conducted. In this case, a t-Test would be the appropriate choice.

Computation of a t-Test can be performed using a calculator with a square root function or, more simply, using STATPAK, a computer-based statistical program that was introduced earlier in this chapter. It seems to me that no supervisor, teacher, or other practitioner would choose to expend the effort to compute any statistical calculations other than by using a computer-based program. Therefore, an explanation of any "long-hand" statistical computations will not be undertaken in this text.

To determine whether or not the posttest scores of these classes are significantly different from one another, one would simply input the raw scores in a computer-based program, such as STATPAK, by pressing a couple of keys. STATPAK is very user-friendly and all you need to do is follow the menu-driven instructions on the screen. (Your professor will certainly demonstrate the ease of computer-based programs and you will have the opportunity to practice t-Test calculations on your own.)

While some programs actually indicate whether or not the t-Test result is significant, STATPAK does not. To determine significance, you must consult a t-Test Table that is, by the way, very easy to interpret.

After inputting the information in Figure 6.3 (using a t-Test for non-independent means), you will find that the t value equals 2.49 (ignore the minus sign). The **degrees of freedom** *(df)* equal 4. Now, all you have to do is consult a t-Test Table that can be readily found in almost any statistics book. I have, however, included an abbreviated t-Test set of values in Table 6.1 for your use in this chapter. You would go down the left column *(df)* to the number 4 and look across at the values noted. Since your t-Value was 2.49, you would look for the value that is less than 3.00. In other words, to be significant, your t-Value must be higher than the values noted on the table. In this case, a t-Value of 2.49 is higher than the value under the .05 column (2.48), but lower than the value under the .01 column (5.02). Therefore, there is a **statistically significant** difference between the posttest results of these two classes at the .05 level. One may, therefore, conclude that the differences between the two classes may be attributed to the **treatment** and not to a chance error factor (see **level of significance**).

In other words, there is a significant difference in achievement between the two groups. If these were posttest scores on attitudes toward
science, and not achievement scores, then you could conclude that one
group had more favorable attitudes toward science than the other group.
The level of significance is indicated in the following statement:

$$t = 2.49, p < .05$$

This statement indicates the obtained t-Value (3.00) and the probability
(p) that differences between the two groups were due to chance error factors is less than 5%. In other words, you can conclude with 95% certainty
that the differences between the two groups were true differences that
resulted from the treatment.

| **Abbreviated Table of t-Values** | | |
|---|---|---|
| **Number of Subjects (df)** | **.05** | **.01** |
| 4 | 2.48 | 5.02 |
| 5 | 2.35 | 4.54 |
| 6 | 2.13 | 3.75 |
| 7 | 2.02 | 3.37 |
| 8 | 1.94 | 3.14 |
| 9 | 1.90 | 3.00 |
| 10 | 1.86 | 2.90 |
| 11 | 1.83 | 2.82 |
| 12 | 1.81 | 2.76 |
| 13 | 1.80 | 2.72 |
| 14 | 1.78 | 2.68 |
| 15 | 1.77 | 2.65 |
| 16 | 1.76 | 2.62 |
| 17 | 1.75 | 2.60 |
| 18 | 1.75 | 2.58 |
| 19 | 1.74 | 2.57 |
| 20 | 1.73 | 2.55 |
| 22 | 1.73 | 2.53 |
| 24 | 1.72 | 2.51 |
| 26 | 1.71 | 2.49 |
| 28 | 1.71 | 2.48 |
| 30 | 1.70 | 2.47 |
| 40 | 1.68 | 2.42 |
| 100 | 1.65 | 2.35 |
| *Note: t-values for directional hypotheses are presented.* | | |

Table 6.1

Before proceeding with the remainder of the chapter, complete the following exercise that helps reinforce some of the ideas expressed above.

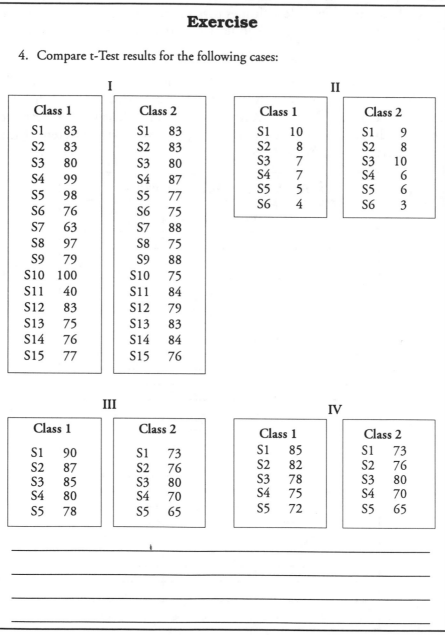

## Exercise

4.  Compare t-Test results for the following cases:

### I

| Class 1 | | Class 2 | |
|---|---|---|---|
| S1 | 83 | S1 | 83 |
| S2 | 83 | S2 | 83 |
| S3 | 80 | S3 | 80 |
| S4 | 99 | S4 | 87 |
| S5 | 98 | S5 | 77 |
| S6 | 76 | S6 | 75 |
| S7 | 63 | S7 | 88 |
| S8 | 97 | S8 | 75 |
| S9 | 79 | S9 | 88 |
| S10 | 100 | S10 | 75 |
| S11 | 40 | S11 | 84 |
| S12 | 83 | S12 | 79 |
| S13 | 75 | S13 | 83 |
| S14 | 76 | S14 | 84 |
| S15 | 77 | S15 | 76 |

### II

| Class 1 | | Class 2 | |
|---|---|---|---|
| S1 | 10 | S1 | 9 |
| S2 | 8 | S2 | 8 |
| S3 | 7 | S3 | 10 |
| S4 | 7 | S4 | 6 |
| S5 | 5 | S5 | 6 |
| S6 | 4 | S6 | 3 |

### III

| Class 1 | | Class 2 | |
|---|---|---|---|
| S1 | 90 | S1 | 73 |
| S2 | 87 | S2 | 76 |
| S3 | 85 | S3 | 80 |
| S4 | 80 | S4 | 70 |
| S5 | 78 | S5 | 65 |

### IV

| Class 1 | | Class 2 | |
|---|---|---|---|
| S1 | 85 | S1 | 73 |
| S2 | 82 | S2 | 76 |
| S3 | 78 | S3 | 80 |
| S4 | 75 | S4 | 70 |
| S5 | 72 | S5 | 65 |

Answers: I, t = 0.12; II, t = 0.25; III, t = 5.72; IV, t = -2.49. Consult a t-Test Table to determine whether or not differences are significant. By the way, do you know what **degrees of freedom** are? Refer to the Glossary.

## The Sign Test

One of the common statistical techniques or procedures used in action research to determine whether the posttest scores are different from the pretest scores in **one-group pretest-posttest designs** is known as the Sign Test. Although we cautioned against using one-group pretest/posttest designs because of the inability to control for extraneous factors or **variables** that might have influenced results on the posttest, this **design** is still popular in action research and can be utilized if analyzed properly.

Let's say you are working with a teacher who wants to encourage her pupils to read more books and write more book reports (this example is culled from Willerman, McNeely, & Koffman, 1991). The method the teacher has traditionally used is the "Stars on the Chart" method. You remember that chart, don't you? A chart is displayed on a wall in the classroom with an alphabetical listing of all the names of the students. Stars are placed next to names to indicate the number of books read. As an educational leader, you notice Ms. Smith's use of these charts and you surmise that many students are simply turned off to reading because the competition inherent in this "Stars on the Wall" approach is too much to bear for some students. You recommend another approach that you recently read about in *Instructor* magazine. You clip out the article for Ms. Smith and encourage her to try the new method.

Ms. Smith is intrigued by this new method of writing and publishing class newspapers that includes book reports written by the students. Newspapers are to be published weekly and disseminated throughout the school and community. Ms. Smith decides to try this approach. She wonders if this new method for encouraging book reports will significantly increase the number of books read by her students.

She states her **hypothesis** in null form: "There will be no difference in the number of books read by students whose book reports are rewarded by charting them with stars on the classroom bulletin board and students whose book reports are printed in a classroom newspaper."

Note that there are not two separate groups in this case. One group at a time will be treated with a method for encouraging students to read more books. She now collects her data in the following way:

1.  For one month she counts the number of books read by students in her class. This is considered the pretest.

2.  During the second month she begins to publish book reports in the classroom newspaper and disseminates them throughout the school. She records the number of books read by students. This is considered the posttest.

## Sign-Test Computations

| Student | Pretest Score | Posttest Score | Sign |
|---------|---------------|----------------|------|
| Mary | 6 | 4 | − |
| Zakia | 4 | 5 | + |
| Juan | 6 | 7 | + |
| Michael | 5 | 6 | + |
| Rochelle | 6 | 4 | − |
| Natasha | 3 | 4 | + |
| Jacob | 3 | 4 | + |
| Jessie | 4 | 6 | + |
| Kevin | 6 | 5 | − |
| Carlos | 5 | 5 | 0 |
| Marisa | 6 | 7 | + |
| Cynthia | 5 | 6 | + |
| Huan | 7 | 8 | + |
| Linda | 5 | 6 | + |
| Tim | 4 | 7 | + |
| Karim | 5 | 5 | 0 |
| Rolanda | 4 | 5 | + |
| Joseph | 6 | 7 | + |

Figure 6.4

3. She charts results by comparing pretest scores (number of books read using the star method) with posttest scores (number of books read using the newspaper technique). A plus sign (+) (see Figure 6.4) indicates an increase from pretest to posttest; a minus sign (–) indicates a decrease from pretest to posttest; and a zero (0) indicates no change in scores.

Then, she follows these next steps to carry out the **sign test** to determine if there is a significant difference between pretest and posttest scores:

1. As you note in the chart, Ms. Smith has 18 students who are identified as N =18 (number of students equals 18). She counts the number of scores that were *not* the same, which happens to be 16 (18 – 2). Therefore, N now becomes 16 (N = 16).
2. She counts the number of pluses and minuses and assigns the smaller number the X value. Therefore, there are 13 pluses and 3 minuses; X = 3.
3. Now that you have N = 16 and X = 3, you refer to the "Sign Table" that can be found in a statistics book. I have, however, included an abbreviated Sign Test set of values in Table 6.2 for your use in this chapter. Find where on the table the X value and the N value intersect. You'll note that the table shows a probability value of .011.

How do we interpret this value? We learned earlier that in education the generally accepted level of significance is .05; i.e., only a 5 percent chance error factor. For the **sign test**, the minimum **level of significance** is .10, which means a less stringent level of significance is used. To find a significant difference between the two sets of scores, the number found on the table must be lower than .10. Since .011 *is* lower than .10, we can therefore reject the null hypothesis that no difference would be found between the pretest and posttest scores. We may conclude, then, that the use of classroom newspapers to encourage students to read more books was a more effective approach than using the star method.

As a general rule, one-group pretest/posttest designs use the **sign test**. The weakness of this design, of course, is that there is no **control group**. However, the sign test does provide the educational leader with empirical data to help make a good educational decision.

## Abbreviated Table for the Sign Test

| N | \multicolumn{7}{c}{X values} | | | | | | |
|---|---|---|---|---|---|---|---|
|   | 0 | 1 | 2 | 3 | 4 | 5 | 6 |
| 5 | .031 | .188 | .500 | .812 | .969 | | |
| 6 | .016 | .109 | .344 | .656 | .891 | .984 | |
| 7 | .008 | .062 | .227 | .500 | .773 | .938 | .992 |
| 8 | .004 | .035 | .145 | .363 | .637 | .855 | .965 |
| 9 | .002 | .020 | .090 | .254 | .500 | .746 | .910 |
| 10 | .001 | .011 | .055 | .172 | .377 | .623 | .828 |
| 11 | | .006 | .033 | .113 | .274 | .500 | .726 |
| 12 | | .003 | .019 | .073 | .194 | .387 | .613 |
| 13 | | .002 | .011 | .046 | .133 | .291 | .500 |
| 14 | | .001 | .006 | .029 | .090 | .212 | .395 |
| 15 | | | .004 | .018 | .059 | .151 | .304 |
| 16 | | | .002 | .011 | .038 | .105 | .227 |
| 17 | | | .001 | .006 | .025 | .072 | .166 |
| 18 | | | | .004 | .015 | .048 | .119 |
| 19 | | | | .002 | .010 | .032 | .084 |
| 20 | | | | .001 | .006 | .021 | .058 |

Table 6.2

Before proceeding with the remainder of the chapter, complete the following exercise that helps reinforce some of the ideas expressed above.

---

### Exercise

5. Describe a situation in which you, as an educational leader, would use the sign test. Create a scenario and provide dummy data. Apply the test and determine whether significant differences are found.

_____

_____

Answers will vary

## The Mann-Whitney U-Test

A second type of statistical test commonly used in action research is known as the Mann-Whitney U-Test. The Mann-Whitney U-Test can be used to analyze results for small groups of students (under 15 per group) when two groups are formed by:

1. dividing one class into two groups using the **matched pairs** technique described earlier; or

2. comparing two separate classes that are comparable (e.g., two sections of a math class in high school).

The **Mann-Whitney U-Test** is used for small groups and operates not unlike a **t-Test**. The t-Test is preferable for groups larger than 15 students per group.

Let's examine how a Mann-Whitney U-Test might work (this example is also culled from Willerman, McNeely, & Koffman, 1991):

Let's say you'd like to assist a teacher to assess the effect of computer-assisted instruction on mathematical computation skills among third graders. You'd suggest that the teacher follow these steps:

1. Administer a pretest and with the results divide the class into two groups using **matched pairs**.

2. One group would be allowed to use computers to assist them in computational work (the **experimental group**), while the other group would learn computation the traditional way without use of computer-assisted instruction (the **control group**). (A null **hypothesis** could be framed that there will be no difference between the two groups). Of course, to avoid the Hawthorne Effect (see **confounding factors**) you might want the latter group to have equal access to computers, but not to assist them in mathematical computations. You might allow them to use computer-assisted instruction to enhance vocabulary development.

3. At the end of a given period of time (for instance, two months), a posttest is administered to both groups and scores are ranked. See Figure 6.5.

## Control and Experimental Group Test Scores and Rank Order for a Mann-Whitney U-Test

| Control | | | | Experimental | | |
|---|---|---|---|---|---|---|
| Student | Score | Rank | | Student | Score | Rank |
| Fran | 87 | 11.5 | | Al | 98 | 20 |
| Bob | 72 | 4 | | Paul | 93 | 15 |
| Tania | 65 | 2 | | Margie | 76 | 6.5 |
| Jerry | 54 | 1 | | Stacey | 88 | 13 |
| Ralph | 67 | 3 | | Allison | 96 | 18 |
| Renaldo | 73 | 5 | | Melissa | 90 | 14 |
| Ro | 78 | 8.5 | | Candida | 87 | 11.5 |
| Vivian | 82 | 10 | | Mark | 76 | 6.5 |
| Sharon | 95 | 17 | | Cary | 94 | 16 |
| | | | | Helen | 99 | 21 |
| | | | | James | 97 | 19 |
| | | | | Noreen | 78 | 8.5 |

**Figure 6.5**

The table in Figure 6.5 indicates that the first group consists of 9 students (N = 9) and the second group consists of 12 students (N = 12).

Scores are on the posttests are ranked as follows:

Considering both groups together, the *lowest* score achieved regardless of group would receive a 1. The second lowest score receives a 2, and so on. Jerry, with a score of 54, has the lowest score of either group and therefore is awarded a rank of 1. Tania has the second lowest score and thus is awarded the rank of 2.

In the event of a tie, as occurs with Margie and Mark, you would compute their ranks as follows:

Since one subject would have received a rank of 6 and the other a 7 if their scores had not been the same, you add 6 plus 7 and divide by 2 (the number of subjects involved). Therefore, 6 + 7= 13; 13 ÷ 2 = 6.5. Both Margie and Mark are awarded a rank of 6.5. If three scores were to be tied, then you would add them together and divide by three to attain the rank score for each subject.

Try to complete the table by ranking the other scores and check your answers with Figure 6.5.

Now the Mann-Whitney U-Test can be calculated as follows:

**Step 1.** Once scores have been ranked, multiply the number of subjects in the control group by the number of subjects in the experimental group. Thus, $9 \times 12 = 108$.

**Step 2.** Calculate the U1 and U2 with the following formula:

$$U1 = N1\,N2 + \frac{N1\,(N1 + 1)}{2} - R1$$

$$U2 = N1\,N2 + \frac{N2\,(N2 + 1)}{2} - R1$$

KEY:

N1 = number of subjects in Control Group
N2 = number of subjects in Experimental Group
R1 = sum of ranks for Control Group
R2 = sum of ranks for Experimental Group

Try the calculations on your own using a calculator. Now that you have attained U1 and U2 values, you are ready to check the "Table of U-Values."

U1 should equal 91 and U2 should equal 17.

You should consult a U-Value Table, which can be found in many statistics books. I have, however, included an abbreviated U-Value Table in Table 6.3 for your use in this chapter. Select the smaller U-value to estimate the level of significance. If the value of the table is *larger* than the lower U-value, then the groups are statistically significant.

Look where 9 and 12 intersect on the table. You'll notice two points identified on the chart. The 26 is the lower limit and the 82 is the upper limit. Now, you notice that our U1, which was 91, falls above the upper limit on the table, whereas the U2, which was 17, falls below the lower limit. Since we are looking at the lower U-value (U2 in this case) and since the values on the table (26 and 82) are larger than U2, we conclude that there is a significant difference between the posttest scores of both groups. We, therefore, reject the null hypothesis and conclude that computer-assisted instruction had a significant effect on pupil achievement in mathematical computational skills.

## Abbreviated U-Value Table for the Mann-Whitney U-Test

|     | 1 | 2 | 3 | 4 | 5 | 6 | 7 | 8 | 9 | 10 | 11 | 12 | 13 |
|-----|---|---|---|---|---|---|---|---|---|----|----|----|----|
| 1   |   |   |   |   |   |   |   |   |   |    |    |    |    |
| 2   |   |   |   |   |   |   |   | 0/16 | 0/18 | 0/20 | 0/22 | 1/23 | 1/25 |
| 3   |   |   |   |   | 0/15 | 1/17 | 1/20 | 2/22 | 2/25 | 3/27 | 3/30 | 4/32 | 4/35 |
| 4   |   |   |   | 0/16 | 1/19 | 2/22 | 3/25 | 4/28 | 4/32 | 5/35 | 6/38 | 7/41 | 8/44 |
| 5   |   |   | 0/15 | 1/19 | 2/23 | 3/27 | 5/30 | 6/34 | 7/38 | 8/42 | 9/46 | 11/49 | 12/53 |
| 6   |   |   | 1/17 | 2/22 | 3/27 | 5/31 | 6/36 | 8/40 | 10/64 | 11/49 | 13/53 | 14/58 | 16/62 |
| 7   |   |   | 1/20 | 3/25 | 5/30 | 6/36 | 8/41 | 10/46 | 12/50 | 14/56 | 16/61 | 18/66 | 20/71 |
| 8   |   | 0/16 | 2/22 | 4/28 | 6/34 | 8/40 | 10/46 | 12/51 | 15/57 | 17/62 | 19/69 | 22/74 | 24/80 |
| 9   |   | 0/18 | 2/25 | 4/32 | 7/38 | 10/44 | 12/51 | 15/57 | 17/64 | 20/70 | 23/76 | 26/82 | 28/89 |
| 10  |   | 0/20 | 3/27 | 5/35 | 8/42 | 11/49 | 14/56 | 17/63 | 20/70 | 23/77 | 26/84 | 29/91 | 32/97 |

Table 6.3

Before proceeding with the remainder of the chapter, complete the following exercise that helps reinforce some of the ideas expressed above.

---

### Exercise

6. When would you employ a Mann-Whitney U-Test?

   a. in collaborative planning
   b. assessing posttest results in a quasi-experimental study
   c. assessing posttest results in a single measurement design
   d. when randomization is impossible

   Answer: choice "b"

---

## The Chi Square and Other User-Friendly Statistics

A third common statistic, the **chi square** (pronounced kiy-square and represented by $X^2$) is used for **nominal** data (see **scales of measurement**). Nominal data refer to categories such as gender (male, female), ethnicity, socioeconomic status, etc. Any study that uses nominal data is analyzed using the chi square statistic.

Let's say you are a principal of a high school and want to know if there's a relationship between gender and teacher morale in the school. You would use the $X^2$ to determine, for instance, whether low morale is more closely associated with femaleness or maleness.

We will *not* outline the steps for calculating a chi square but will only mention that such calculations can easily be conducted using statistical programs such as STATPAK. More important is to know when to use each statistic. A summary of relevant and friendly statistics will conclude this section.

Aside from the use of means, standard deviations, sign tests, t-Tests, and Mann-Whitney U-Tests, which have previously been explained, only four other statistics may likely be used by action researchers: the Spearman Rho, Pearson r Correlation Coefficient, **ANOVA**, and **ANCOVA**.

The Spearman Rho (also known as Rank Correlation) shows the degree of relationship between two sets of scores collected from the same group. According to Willerman, McNeely, and Koffman (1991), "the Spearman Rho correlation is useful to teachers who do action research because it can be used with groups that have small numbers of subjects and with data that are in either interval or ordinal form" (p. 139).

The Pearson Product Moment Correlation Coefficient (better known as simply the Pearson r) is a common statistic used to correlate two variables. In other words, the Pearson r would be used to determine the degree of relationship between two variables, such as science test scores with math test scores.

Suppose you wanted to correlate (i.e., examine the relationship) between two **variables** such as teachers' attitudes toward supervision and years of teaching experience. You might have **hypothesized** that teachers with more years of experience have less favorable views toward supervision. Yet, a correlational study or analysis of these two variables might indicate no significant relationship or correlation. If that were so, you might find a .15 **correlation coefficient**.

**Correlation coefficients** are expressed from +1.00, which indicates a perfect correlation between two **variables**, to −1.00, which indicates a perfect negative correlation between two variables. A 1.00 coefficient indicates that as one variable increases, the other increases proportionally. The most common statistic used to calculate correlation is the Pearson Product Moment Correlation Coefficient (usually abbreviated as $r$; i.e., coefficients of correlation are expressed by the mathematical symbol $r$). Another statistic, used with ranked data, is the rank order **correlation coefficient** (called *rho*), but can be computed through computer analysis.

Correlation is NOT causation. A relationship between two variables does not necessarily mean that a cause and effect relationship exists. Research may indicate a strong correlation (i.e., relationship) between teacher use of positive reinforcement and positive pupil behavior in the classroom. Praise, for instance, may be a potent force to mitigate misbehavior, however, one cannot conclude that praising a student will *cause* a positive change in behavior. Any experienced teacher will testify to the fact that effective use of praise doesn't always yield positive student behavior. For some students, praise is ineffective. Yet, correlational studies do indicate a strong relationship that may warrant teachers to learn how to effectively and judiciously use praise and other forms of positive reinforcement.

Correlational analyses usually involve one group and two variables (e.g., fourth grade students' math scores correlated with science achievement scores).

The **Analysis of variance** (ANOVA, sometimes called the F test) is a statistical technique for determining whether or not significant differences can be found among the **means** of *three* or more groups.

Suppose you want to determine possible differences in social studies achievement among three separate groups of eighth graders taught by three different teachers using different methods of instruction. An analysis of variance (ANOVA) statistical test would be applied to determine whether or not a statistically significant difference in social studies achievement exists among the three different groups of students. This statistic operates not unlike the **t-Test**. The ANOVA computes statistical differences for three or more groups, while the t-Test, as you recall, only works with two groups. Although not frequently used in action research, the ANOVA can be effectively used under certain circumstances.

Another statistic, although not commonly employed by action researchers, yet nevertheless valuable, is an **Analysis of covariance** (**ANCOVA**). The ANCOVA is a statistical technique used in **group comparison** research when equivalence between the groups (usually only two in action research) cannot be ascertained.

Let's say you are comparing the achievement levels of two groups of seventh graders, one of which is treated with computer-assisted instruction. In **group comparison** research, posttest scores of both groups are compared to determine which group had higher achievement scores. (We don't measure growth between pretests and posttests, as was explained in Chapter 3). Yet, without assuring that both groups were initially comparable or equivalent (i.e., had somewhat equivalent achievement levels to begin with), you cannot draw any conclusions from posttest scores.

Why can't comparisons be made? Comparisons cannot be made because one group may have started with higher achievement levels than the other group. How, then, can anyone conclude that the **treatment** (i.e., computer-assisted instruction) had any effect on achievement? How do you know that, for instance, high achievement levels can be attributed to the treatment as opposed to the fact that the **experimental group** had higher achievement scores initially? Thus, such comparisons cannot be made.

The analysis of covariance statistic can be used when you cannot ascertain group equivalence at the outset of a study. ANCOVA would be conducted with posttest results of both groups. This statistical procedure takes the pretest scores and adjusts them statistically so that they can be treated identically.

You don't have to understand how this works mathematically or statistically. All you need to understand is that the analysis of covariance statistic can be used when noncomparable (non-equivalent) groups are being studied.

The statistics mentioned above can be easily computed using STATPAK or any other computer program. Inputting data and following menu-driven instructions is all you have to do. Your professor or workshop leader will likely demonstrate the ease of using such computations.

The following references are very useful in more fully explaining these statistics as well as providing easy-to-follow instructions for computations: Crowl, 1996, 1986; Fitz-Gibbon and Morris, 1987; Willerman, McNeely, and Koffman, 1991. Note that the Crowl, 1986 work is especially useful, in that easy-to-follow step-by-step calculations are provided in his appendixes.

Before proceeding with the remainder of the chapter, complete the following exercise that helps reinforce some of the ideas expressed above.

---

### Exercise

7. Describe a study that you, as an educational leader, might undertake in which the chi square would be used to analyze data. Set up a scenario and provide dummy data. Apply the test and determine whether significant differences are found.

   _____

   _____

   _____

   Answers will vary

---

# Qualitative Analyses

Analyses of qualitative data differ from analyses of quantitative data. Data analysis, as was explained, is the process of bringing structure and meaning to the mass of data collected. Remember, qualitative research, relying on extensive fieldnotes, yields a bulk of data that is not easily analyzed. Analyzing such data, especially for practicing educators, can be time consuming and arduous, albeit, at times, fascinating and creative. Whereas data analysis of quantitative data is straightforward, logical, and statistical, data analysis for qualitative studies is often complex and not readily convertible into standard measurable units.

In addition, while quantitative analyses are conducted at the end of a study, qualitative analyses are ongoing; that is, they may occur as data are being collected. Moreover, qualitative analyses tend to be somewhat eclectic in that there is no one "right way" or pre-established criteria to follow. Data analysis "requires that the researcher be comfortable with developing categories and making comparisons and contrasts" (Creswell, 1994, p. 153). Creswell delineates several guiding principles, however, when undertaking qualitative data analysis:

1. Simultaneity—In contrast with quantitative data analyses, qualitative data may be analyzed simultaneously with data collection. As you interview various people, for instance, certain phrases or themes may be readily apparent. Making note of these phrases or themes, as you continue data collection, will aid thematic development in subsequent interviews. A summary chart at the end of this chapter can be used to record such data.

2. Decontextualization or reduction—These terms refer to the qualitative researcher taking the voluminous data collected and reducing them to patterns, categories, or themes. Reduction is often accomplished by a procedure known as coding. Coding involves attaching meaning to a particular scene, document, or event. For example, in viewing different types of leaders in films, one may categorize the different leaders by their style by first coding each leader with a given leadership style. **Content analysis** is a process that makes decontextualization or reduction possible.

   Content analysis is a method of data analysis in which you analyze the content in a given document according to prescribed categories or criteria while following explicit rules of coding. When conducting content analysis of any document, categories should emerge naturally based on your analysis rather than using the analysis to verify preexisting categories. As you peruse the data in a document, you would identify key words to create research categories. Krippendorf (1980) reports that content analysis allows for making inferences from the data context using the procedure above.

   Let's say you wanted to investigate whether principals were favorably depicted in popular culture (e.g., television and film). You would first obtain several television shows and movies for viewing. You would then identify several categories that would guide your viewing. These categories would depend on the purposes of your research. Let's say you were interested in understanding the different ways principals were depicted in these forms of popular culture. You could identify the following three categories: (a) favorable scenes about principals; (b) unfavorable or unflattering scenes; and (c) neutral scenes. As you watch these shows and movies, you would describe each scene thoroughly and might even transcribe dialogues. You would then classify each scene into one of the aforementioned categories. Frequencies of scenes in each of the three categories are tabulated, and on the basis of content analysis, you would arrive at a conclusion about the way principals are depicted in the television shows and films you watched.

Content analysis, then, is a method of analyzing data through a process of categorization.

How might you use content analysis to analyze data?

3. Grounded theory—This refers to the comparison of collected data to extant theory or literature in search of a pattern or theme. Themes emerge as a consequence of collecting data. One should not develop a theme and then look for data to confirm one's expectations (Strauss & Corbin, 1990).

## Analytic Procedures

Let's apply the principles explained above by reviewing the main analytic procedures used in qualitative studies. Drawing from the work of Marshall and Rossman (1994), analytic procedures essentially fall into the following three categories:

1. *Organizing the Data*—Accumulate your data collection types (e.g., observations, interviews, documents, and audiovisual materials) and read and reread all the data. Make notes of anything that strikes you as significant or unusual. You should also make a list of all the main topics you have covered and may begin to cluster together similar topics. Major topics and sub-topics may emerge. This stage familiarizes you with all the data you have collected. Computer analysis, as will be described below, may be helpful at this initial stage.

2. *Generating Categories, Themes, and Patterns*—This phase of data analysis can be most cumbersome, yet interesting. Often simple scanning the data several times will result in some emerging pattern or theme. Feel free to make educated guesses or hunches at this stage.

Developing coding categories occurs at this stage. Our discussion of decontextualization or reduction above comes into play at this phase. Coding systems enable you to see themes emerge from the data. You can choose from a "family of codes" (Anderson, Herr, & Nihlen, 1994; Bogdan & Biklen, 1992). I will introduce some of these codes. Further discussion of these codes can be found in the previous citation.

a. Perspectives held by participants—includes codes of ideas or perspectives held by individuals (e.g., liberal or conservative views).

b. Activity codes—includes codes that demonstrate a regularly occurring behavior (e.g., smoking, cutting class, or attending faculty meetings).

c. Event codes—includes codes that occur infrequently or only once (e.g., a teacher's strike or a teacher's dismissal).

d. Strategy codes—includes codes that refer to methods and techniques that people use to accomplish various things (e.g., behavior management strategies or various instructional strategies).

Working data into codes is an especially laborious process that, to be honest, educational leaders as action researchers are not likely to attempt with as much rigor as someone undertaking a doctoral research project. For more detailed information, consult Wiersma (1995).

3. *Testing Emergent Hypotheses*—As categories or themes begin to emerge you will want to initiate the process of framing some sort of hypothesis in order to determine whether or not the theme or category is consistent with the data. What kinds of questions can you pose to verify that the theme you selected is indeed inclusive of most, if not all, of your data?

As themes emerge and are verified, separating each one onto index cards, in folders, or into a data base is a matter left to the discretion of the researcher. Themes, at this point, can be compared to extant theory. Let's say bureaucratic themes have emerged in your study of the way district office supervisors relate to school personnel. That is, a consistent pattern emerges in a particular district in which district office supervisors, by and large, do not relate to teachers in professional, collaborative ways, but are rather officious, aloof, and bureaucratic. You might review literature to determine whether this observation or theme that has emerged from your data is representative of the way, for instance, most district office personnel relate to school faculty. In other words, does the literature support your findings? This inductive process of collecting data, developing a theme, and comparing the theme to extant literature is known as grounded theory. That is, your findings are "grounded" in real and verifiable data you have collected. You did not develop some theme and then look for data to support it. I should add that, at times, referring to literature as you collect data in an attempt to discover a theme is also an accepted practice in qualitative research.

An application: Imagine that you have collected data on the attitudes of parents and teachers toward inclusion. The qualitative data collection types include observations, interviews, documents (minutes of teacher/parent council meetings), and audiovisual materials (photographs and videotapes of students in inclusive settings). How might you incorporate the data analytic procedures described above?

Note that many different and personalized ways exist to analyze qualitative data. The first step you might take is to separate the written data into three groups: observation data, interview data, and document data. A fourth group would include the visual data from the photographs and videotapes. You would then read and view all the data. As you do so for each group, you would make both mental and written notes highlighting interesting and possibly significant pieces of information or even obvious emerging patterns. This might include underlining key words, phrases, or sentences in text or even color coding different pieces of data. Any logical and workable method can be applied. Whether you use index cards, folders, or a laptop is a matter of personal preference.

Note that analytic procedures can also be applied during, and not only after, data collection. The purpose of this initial stage in data analysis is to take all the data that have been collected and to organize and separate them into workable units.

> *Remember: The goal of analysis is to discover patterns, ideas, explanations, and understandings.*

Familiar with the data and having taken preliminary notes that have identified key words, phrases, or events that seem relevant, you would now be ready to generate categories or themes that might emerge from the data. For each group, you would select appropriate codes that highlight appropriate information and better organize the data. Use of codes and subcodes would be in order. For example, from the interview data a major code might be "Friendships" and sub-codes might include "with other included students" or "with paraprofessionals." The idea is that a particular interview reveals that included students have developed friendships with other students and paraprofessionals in the inclusive classroom. Each interview might have many different codes and sub-codes. If a qualitative researcher has interviewed five individuals, then several pages of coded data might be taken. This procedure would be followed for each data group. How do you think coding might work for videotaped data?

Once categories or themes emerge such as "teachers' resistance to, inclusion" (note that several different, even competing themes may emerge, such as teachers against inclusion, but parents for inclusion), the researcher might review the themes and compare them to extant literature or theory in order to uncover a general theoretical framework that would explain the data. This process is known as grounded theory.

A brief word about the credibility of qualitative data analysis is in order. **Triangulation** enhances the credibility of qualitative data analysis. The use of varied data collection instruments and the comparison of emerging themes in one data collection instrument to other instruments contribute to the credibility of the analysis. If the pattern, for example, emerges consistently in the videotaped data as well as in interviews, observations, and documents, then the trustworthiness of the analytic procedures is apparent. As alluded to earlier and explained in the Glossary, **reliability** and **validity** of qualitative data also contribute to its credibility. How do you think reliability and validity of qualitative data is achieved? Here's a bonus question: How does the concept of grounded theory contribute to **internal validity**?

## Computer Applications

Qualitative analyses are enhanced by state-of-the-art computer applications. Software programs are available to sift through qualitative data (e.g., "thick descriptions" from field notes) to locate specified words and phrases, creating indexes, attaching codes to various parts of the text, developing categories, etc. The possibilities of computerized data analysis for qualitative research are currently being considered (see, e.g., Fielding & Lee, 1991; Weitzman & Miles, 1995).

General and useful programs include word processors, data base managers, spreadsheets, and text retrievers. Word processors are designed for production and revision of text and thus useful for taking, writing, and editing field notes. Most of you are likely quite familiar with the advantages of a word processor. How might a word processor help in data analysis of qualitative material? At what phase or phases of data analysis would a word processor come in handy?

A data base program can input text data according to a structured format. Let's say you wanted to use a data base program to keep track of interview data. You could set up a data base that records and keeps records of each interview subdivided into important pieces of information including name of interviewee, date of transcription, time of interview, and other information. Retrieval of various files aids in data analysis.

A spreadsheet program, although established for accounting purposes, can be used to create tables. A spreadsheet allows you to record information in each vertical column and in each horizontal row. Keeping track of your research project will be easier using a spreadsheet. Think of two specific ways a spreadsheet may help analyze data.

A text retriever is a sophisticated text search program that allows you to locate all instances of words, phrases, and combinations of phrases in one or more files. How might a text retriever assist in data analysis?

## Tables, Graphs, and Charts

Whether you employ quantitative and/or qualitative analyses, using tables and graphs, whenever possible, to summarize your findings will not only better facilitate data interpretation (see next chapter), but will serve as a way to display data after analysis, and serve as an easy, convenient, and visual way for reporting your data to others. "A picture (i.e., table or graph) is worth a thousand words." Use your imagination to devise tables and/or figures to summarize your findings. A sample of a table, a graph, and a chart are included to demonstrate how data can be displayed visually.

Table 6.4 illustrates how data can be presented in a table. This table indicates that two groups were comparable at the start of the project. How do we know this? The means and a t-Test (t = .19) did not indicate a significant difference. Yet, after the administration of the posttest, presumably months later, a significant difference between both groups was apparent (t = 8.69). Therefore, the original hypothesis ("failing sixth grade math students who participate in the after-school tutorial programs will have higher math scores than failing math students who do not participate in the after-school m-ath tutorial programs") was supported.

See Figure 6.6 for a sample graph. Graph your data whenever possible.

## Means, Standard Deviations, and t-Tests for the Experimental and Control Groups for Reading Comprehension Scores

| Test | Group | | |
|---|---|---|---|
| | Experimental | Control | *t* |
| (Pretest) | | | |
| *M* | 24.10 | 23.90 | .19* |
| S.D. | 2.93 | 3.59 | |
| (Posttest) | | | |
| *M* | 40.90 | 31.60 | 8.69** |
| S.D. | 2.80 | 3.88 | |

\* *p* > .05
\*\* *p* < .05

Table 6.4

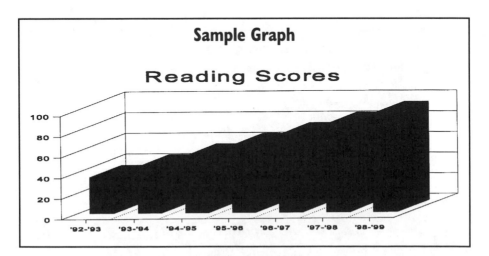

**Figure 6.6**    Bradley School Reading Scores. Percent of Students Reading on Grade Level in the Fourth Grade from 1993 to 1999.

When analyzing qualitative data, I recommend charting data collection techniques with key findings as follows:

| Data collection technique | Key findings |
|---|---|
| Questionnaire | 58% of parents dislike idea of inclusion |
| Interview | Teacher X: "I don't think inclusion will work." |
| School Profile | Test scores indicate . . . |
| Multimedia | Videotapes demonstrate . . . |

How do you think this chart might help data analysis and interpretation?

# Chapter Summary

The following worksheet allows you to easily analyze your data. This worksheet is meant to allow you to brainstorm different ideas. Changes in your plan can always be made at a later date. This worksheet serves as a review of the ideas discussed in this chapter.

---

### Data Analysis Worksheet

1. *What is the purpose of analyzing the data I collected? (Use additional paper to record your responses if necessary.)* _____

    _____

2. *Will I use both quantitative and qualitative analyses?* _____

    _____

3. *Which computer program will I use to analyze my data?* _____

4. *Who will be responsible for analyzing and presenting the data?* _____

5. *What tables and/or figures might I develop to summarize my data?* _____

    _____

6.  *Statistical and Non-statistical Analyses:*

**QUANTITATIVE**

___ *Descriptive statistics*
___ *mean*    ___ *standard deviation*    ___ *percentage*    ___ *correlation coefficient*


___ *Inferential statistics*
___ *t-Tests*    ___ *sign tests*    ___ *Mann-Whitney U-tests*    ___ *chi square*
___ *Spearman Rho*    ___ *Pearson r*    ___ *ANOVA*    ___ *ANCOVA*    ___ *Other*

**QUALITATIVE**

*Organizing the data:* _____

_____

_____


*Codes for data:* _____

_____

_____


*Themes that emerge from my data (make certain to note which instrument you are using, e.g.,*
*interview, observation, focus group, questionnaire, etc.):* _____

_____

_____


*How do these themes that emerged relate to the extant literature or theory?* _____

_____


*Computer analyses:* _____

_____

_____


*Other ideas?* _____

_____

Before proceeding with the next chapter, complete the following exercises that help reinforce some of the ideas expressed above.

---

## Exercises

8. A researcher wished to test the effectiveness of a new reading program as compared to an older one. If the difference between the two programs was statistically significant at the $p < .05$ level, this means that

   a. the new program made less than meaningful changes in the student's reading skills.

   b. the results are probably due to the researcher's program and not a chance occurrence.

   c. the probability of being incorrect is 95 chances out of 100.

   d. the new program should be introduced to all grades.

   e. the statistical analysis used was the correct one and the program has educational significance.

   Answer: choice "b"


9. When you find that there is a statistically significant relationship between two or more variables, you are indicating that

   a. your statements of conclusion are not warranted.

   b. your statements of conclusion should be taken with a grain of salt.

   c. your statements of conclusion can be considered valid considering the degree of significance.

   d. this is a correlational study.

   Answer: choice "c"


10. A test of significance used to determine whether there is a significant difference between two means is known as a(n)

   a. t-Test.

   b. self-report research project.

   c. ethnographic study.

   d. quantitative study.

   Answer: choice "a"

11. Triangulation is helpful in judging which aspect of qualitative studies?

    a. researcher bias
    b. credibility
    c. grounded research

    Answer: choice "b"

12: Describe qualitative analytic procedures to someone who has never conducted qualitative research before.

    _____

    _____

    _____

    Answer: Refer to sections above

13. An educational leader is interested in conducting research on the nature of instruction in two different schools. One is a blue-ribbon school and the other is not particularly noteworthy. Set up an ethnographic study that examines the organization, culture, and instructional program in each school. What phenomena would be observed in each school? What data collection instruments (or data sources) would be used? How would data be analyzed?

    _____

    _____

    _____

    Answers might vary

# References

Anderson, G. L., Herr, K., & Nihlen, A. S. (1994). *Studying your own school: An educator's guide to qualitative practitioner research.* Thousand Oaks, CA: Corwin Press.

Bogdan, R. C., & Biklen, S. K. (1992). *Qualitative research for education: An introduction to theory and methods.* Boston: Allyn and Bacon.

Creswell, J. W. (1994). *Research design: Qualitative and quantitative approaches.* Thousand Oaks, CA: Sage Publications.

Crowl, T. K. (1996). *Fundamentals of educational research* (2nd ed.). Madison, WI: WCB Brown & Benchmark Publishers.

Crowl, T. K. (1986). *Fundamentals of research: A practical guide for educators and special educators.* Columbus, OH: Publishing Horizons, Inc.

Davis, Jr., O. L. (1996). Some brambles and briars and snares in the paths of research and its reports. *Journal of Curriculum and Supervision, 11,* 295–298.

Fielding, N. G., & Lee, R. M. (1991). *Using computers in qualitative research.* Newbury Park, CA: Sage Publications.

Fink, A. (1995). *How to analyze data.* Thousand Oaks, CA: Sage Publications.

Fitz-Gibbon, C. T., & Morris, L. L. (1987). *How to analyze data.* Newbury Park, CA: Sage Publications.

Frisbie, L. H. (1992). *STATPAK: Some common educational statistics* [Computer software]. Columbus, OH: Merrill.

Gay, L. R. (1996). *Educational research: Competencies for analysis and application* (5th ed.). Englewood Cliffs, NJ: Prentice Hall.

Knapp, T. P. (1996). *Learning statistics through playing cards.* Thousand Oaks, CA: Sage Publications.

Krippendorf, K. (1980). *Content analysis: An introduction to its methodology.* Beverly Hills, CA: Sage Publications.

Marshall, C., & Rossman, G. B. (1994). *Designing qualitative research.* Newbury Park, CA: Sage Publications.

Sharan, S., & Shachar, H. (1988). *Language in the cooperative classroom.* New York: Springer-Verlag.

Strauss, A., & Corbin, J. (1990). *Grounded theory: Basics of qualitative research.* Newbury Park, CA: Sage Publications.

Weitzman, E. A., & Miles, M. B. (1995). *Computer programs for qualitative data analysis.* Thousand Oaks, CA: Sage Publications.

Wiersma, W. (1995). *Research methods in education: An introduction.* Boston: Allyn and Bacon.

Willerman, M., McNeely, S. L., & Koffman, E. C. (1991). *Teachers helping teachers: Peer observation and assistance.* New York: Praeger.

# CHAPTER 7

# *P*utting It All Together: What Does It All Mean?

*". . . be modest in reporting action research. We live in a time when exaggerated claims for educational accomplishment are almost the norm . . . Education is not yet a science and may never be, given the differences in individual human behavior. There is very little about education that we can claim with certainty. Action research continues to be promising, but we must be aware of its limitations as well as its possibilities."*

*(Foshay, 1994, p. 325)*

## Interpreting Data

Having collected and analyzed your data, you are ready to reach certain conclusions so that you can take some action. The graphs and figures you've accumulated merely present the data in visual form, but do not indicate how this data is to be used or interpreted. The fact that you have found, for example, statistically significant findings regarding a particular **treatment** does *not* necessarily mean that a change in educational programming is inevitable. There is a distinction between **statistical significance** and educational significance. A .05 statistical difference may not necessarily warrant implementation of a new textbook series, because other factors may need to be considered before investing money and expending additional efforts. What other factors may possibly influence your decision to adopt or discard the new textbook series?

Maybe data collected qualitatively indicate that teachers find the teacher's editions complicated and not very useful. Perhaps parents complain that the textbook doesn't represent the cultural diversity of the community. Perhaps the cost of the textbook series is prohibitive. Despite statistically significant findings that the **experimental group** who used the new textbook series increased reading comprehension levels, adoption of the series may be precluded by other factors. Obviously, then, the decision to adopt or not adopt the textbook series depends on a variety of factors. Interpretation of data must be viewed as a decision-making process that includes these many possible factors.

How, then, does one decide whether to adopt or discard the new textbook series? In other words, how can we best interpret our data to make informed decisions about the instructional program in our school?

Ultimately, interpreting data must be based on those decisions that are likely to help achieve your goals and objectives. What do you eventually hope to accomplish? Will this program, product, or procedure move you closer to your goals? What evidence exists that this program, product, or procedure is effective? Is this evidence overwhelming or are there conflicting findings? (One of my mentors once quipped: "If in doubt, do without!"). Reflecting on these and similar questions will assist in appropriately interpreting data from your study.

I have found that establishing a steering committee that is in charge of interpreting data is quite helpful. The steering committee is provided with relevant data summaries that they can peruse and discuss. After a period of time, the committee makes recommendations for your consideration. Parenthetically, in **collaborative** or **schoolwide action research** projects, the steering committees would actually decide on the efficacy of a given program or practice.

Another strategy for interpreting data is using prespecified standards. You would chart expected results for each **data collection** instrument employed and note the extent to which the standard was met. Conclusions are then drawn. Final decisions are then made based on the conclusions drawn. For an excellent guide to interpreting data, see Chapter 5 in Herman and Winters, 1992. Table 7.1 has been adapted from the aforementioned work.

## Using Prespecified Standards to Interpret Data

| Instrument | Standard | Percentage Meeting | Conclusion |
|---|---|---|---|
| Science Aptitude Test | 50% above 50th % | 61% above 50th % | Above goal; success |
| Problem-solving science question | At least 50% scoring "acceptable" or above | 37% last year; 52% scored acceptable, but only 20% for girls | Met goal overall, but examine achievement for girls |
| Portfolios | Average rating: 4 out of 6 | 20% were rated 4 out of 6 or higher | Problem here; let's examine |
| Parent survey | At least 80% registered satisfaction with new program | 90% approval rate | Met goal; success |

Table 7.1

You'll notice that Table 7.1 displays data and compares results with prespecified standards for an elementary school science program. The table demonstrates various instruments, standards established, percentages met, and appropriate conclusions that can be drawn. Your perusal of the table will allow you to interpret results fairly easily. Multiple indicators should always guide your decision making.

A cautionary, albeit parenthetical, note should be made about the interpretation of test scores. Test scores are still the most frequently used data source in many schools. Misinterpretations of test scores are too common. Although test score interpretation goes beyond the purview of this text, pointing out a few general cautions that apply to the interpretation of any test score is in order (for more detailed information consult, e.g., Gronlund & Linn, 1990):

- A test score should be interpreted in terms of the specific test from which it was derived. In other words, look beyond the test title to evaluate a pupil's performance in terms of what the test actually measures. For example, one type of **achievement test** may measure a pupil's ability to compute mathematical problems, yet another achievement test may measure problem-solving ability. To use, for instance, the former test and thus conclude that the pupil needs remedial assistance in mathematics may be an inaccurate generalization. The evidence more accurately indicates that the pupil may need help in computational skills, but that her/his ability to problem-solve may be, in fact, satisfactory.

- A test score should be interpreted in light of all the pupil's relevant characteristics. In other words, consider such factors as motivational levels, physical health, and any disabilities that may impair performance. Test performance may be affected by these and other factors.

- A test score should be interpreted according to the type of decision to be made. Attempting to predict, for example, a pupil's success in college from a **criterion-referenced test** is not justified when **norm-referenced tests** more accurately provide such information. Remember to match the test score to the type of decision that needs to be made.

- A test score should not be interpreted as a specific value. A grade equivalent score of, say, 5.3, doesn't indicate that a pupil is exactly one month ahead in reading of a pupil who scores 5.2. These scores, as well as other types of scores, should be considered as merely small differences and not significant in and of themselves. To make a decision about a pupil's performance based on a specific value will lead to erroneous conclusions.

- A test score should be considered along with other supplementary evidence. Making a decision about a pupil's academic performance should involve a variety of data sources. Relying solely on test score information is shortsighted and will lead to erroneous conclusions. **Triangulation** of data sources is essential for judicious data interpretation.

Using prespecified standards to interpret data may fit nicely with quantitative data, but how do we interpret qualitative data? As with data analysis, interpretation of qualitative research is different than for the quantitative approach. While generalizations can usually be drawn from quantitative research (although as you recall not all quantitative approaches in action research lend themselves to generalization, see Chapter 3), no generalizations may be made for qualitative findings due, in large measure, to the small samples that are used. Conclusions that are drawn from qualitative studies are tentative and speculative and must be viewed within a unique context. In other words, findings from an ethnographic study might be applicable to the particular school under study, but may not be applied to all similar schools.

Since a triangulated approach to research has been advocated in this book, findings from both quantitative and qualitative studies should be carefully examined. Overall results from quantitative studies might yield numerical or statistical evidence to support the use, for example, of a particular textbook series, but qualitative findings that present detailed insights into "how" these books are being used on a daily basis might add some important information as well. It is not a matter of deciding that one approach yields more reliable findings than another. Rather, the cumulative effect of both approaches or methodologies provide the best insight into whether or not a district or a school should expend thousands of dollars to adopt the textbook series. Sometimes quantitative and qualitative findings support similar conclusions and sometimes different ones. Ultimately, you, as action researcher, will have to decide (perhaps along with your steering committee) what the weight of evidence suggests. The important point is that employing a mixed methodology (both quantitative and qualitative approaches), when feasible, is the best way to conduct research.

# Reporting Data

Too often little attention is paid to reporting data in a clear, cogent manner. This lack of attention to reporting your findings doesn't make sense considering all the time and energies you expend. I'm not suggesting that formal written reports are always necessary. In fact, most action research studies will not necessarily need a formal follow-up report. Still, reporting and documenting findings in some way is highly recommended.

Informal reports may take the form of reviews of findings to parents at local PTA meetings or to faculty at faculty conferences. Informal reports may be distributed to faculty, staff, and parents through a one- or two-page summary of the study, along with findings and recommendations.

At times, however, a formal report may be required. If the superintendent has charged you with the responsibility of evaluating the district's gifted program, you will likely have to submit a formal written report. In my courses, I always require my students to submit a formal summative evaluation report of their action research projects. Such report writing is good practice and also serves to summarize one's project in a disciplined way.

For some useful advice about creating effective reports, see Table 7.2, which has been excerpted from Herman and Winters (1992).

For those of you undertaking a master's degree action research project (thesis), the method of reporting your findings will be prescribed by your professor and/or department. (See the next several sub-sections for steps I advise my students to follow).

## Writing the Research Report

The rest of this chapter is devoted to outlining the formal steps for writing a **research report**. No single standard for report writing exists; still the following outline has proven helpful for beginning students to organize their thoughts and data.

Too often students take courses on research, evaluation, and **assessment** without actually engaging in a project of some sort. Students who take courses that don't encourage application of research techniques may learn elements of **research design** and data analysis, but are unlikely to internalize the lessons learned. According to constructivist theory, people learn best when they are given opportunities to construct meanings on their own. I'm reminded of the story of the fellow who, when taking an undergraduate course in ornithology (the study of birds), was quite surprised by the way in which the professor conducted the course.

> Students entered the large lecture hall expecting to learn about birds by visiting nearby forests and outdoor reserves. To their astonishment and dismay, the professor would only lecture about the multitude of species of birds by reading from his notes, rarely looking up at the large, disinter-

# Hints for Creating Useful Reports

*Both school principals and school board members say that a useful report*

- *is brief,*
- *contains narrative or explanatory information,*
- *presents trends over time in graphic form to support conclusions, and*
- *has a technical appendix for those interested in more detail.*

*There are some differences in report content found useful by the two groups.*

- *School-level administrators are most interested in the why and how of student outcomes. They seek information clarifying relationships between school policies, curriculum and instruction, and school outcomes.*
- *At the board level, not unexpectedly, the central concern is with the status of school performance and a description of progress rather than the nuts and bolts of planned improvements or reasons for performance.*
- *When sharing information with school boards, there is a danger in presenting information at a level of detail and complexity that is not needed.*

*Both audiences use and value qualitative information in decision making.*

- *Written reports that include summaries of carefully conducted observations, interviews, or attitude surveys will provide powerful information for program improvement.*
- *Teachers, principals, and others form conclusions about school effectiveness and hypotheses about how programs succeed or fail based on impressions and experiences.*
- *A few well-selected anecdotes also can be a powerful device for communicating the meaning of your findings.*
- *Explanations of school results generated during the data interpretation process form yet another source of useful information for school-level decisions.*
- *Qualitative data form an important part of the decision making process; summaries of these data belong in written reports.*

*Reprinted with permission, Sage Publications.*

**Table 7.2**

ested audience. Jerry, an otherwise studious undergraduate, soon became irritated by the way the professor conducted the class. After about three weeks of lecture, the professor began showing slides of birds. Although he was still lecturing, at least the students had some visual stimulation provided by these black and white photographs. Jerry remained silent and dutifully took copious notes.

About three weeks before the midterm exam, the professor announced that for the examination he would show them a particular bird and the students would have to identify the species. Well, this infuriated Jerry as it did many of the other students. Still, they passively took notes. However, a week before the scheduled exam the professor declared: "I changed my mind. Instead of showing you the whole bird, I'm going to just show you its beak and leg." Then the professor continued his lecture.

Jerry could no longer contain himself. He rose from his seat in the rear of the auditorium and voiced his dissatisfaction: "I can't believe the way you've conducted this class. We entered the course expecting to learn about birds by actually going out into the field and observing. But no, all you do is lecture and show us outdated black and white photographs of birds. Then you decide to give us a ridiculous exam. To make matters worse," continued Jerry as his fellow students sat in a mild state of shock, displaying glimpses of delight, "you have the gall to change your mind and show us portions of the bird's anatomy!"

The professor, at this point, was red-faced and boldly retorted, "Young man, stand up and tell me your name because you just failed this course!"

Jerry rose from his seat, turned sideways, pointed to his nose and lifted his pants, pointing to his leg, and said "You figure it out!"

I tell my students that unlike the way this professor conducted his course, I would indeed give them ample opportunity to apply concepts and theories learned in the course. To this end, I require my students to plan and conduct an action research project. I believe Eleanor Duckworth (1986) said it best: "All people ever have is their own understanding; you can tell them all sorts of things, but you can't make them believe it unless they also construct it for themselves" (p. 495).

As part of their project requirement, the students must write a summative evaluation report. Although action research projects can be conducted without a formal report, sometimes you may have to report your findings to a larger audience (e.g., faculty, superintendent, and school board). Formal reports are often written for program evaluations.

Although many acceptable formats exist, the format below is the one I recommend that my students follow for completing my course requirements. Students have commented that having these steps to follow makes their report writing much easier.

# Overview of Steps for Quantitative and/or Qualitative Studies

TITLE PAGE

CONTENTS

CHAPTER 1: INTRODUCTION
  Background
  Importance of the Study
  Establishing the Program
  Statement of the Problem
  Hypothesis and/or Research Question(s)
  Definition of Terms

CHAPTER 2: REVIEW OF LITERATURE/RELATED RESEARCH

CHAPTER 3: RESEARCH DESIGN/METHODOLOGY
  Sample
  Materials
  Procedure
  Analysis of Data
  Results

CHAPTER 4: IMPLICATIONS FOR TEACHING/SUPERVISION AND RESEARCH
  Limitations of the Study
  Discussion/Conclusions

Implications for Teaching and Supervision
Implications for Further Research

REFERENCES

APPENDIXES

# Detailed Description of Steps for Quantitative and/or Qualitative Studies

## TITLE PAGE

[For example, "Implementation and Evaluation of a Gifted Program in P.S. XXX"]

## CONTENTS

## CHAPTER 1: INTRODUCTION

*Background* [1–2 pp.]

[Describes background information such as:

A) where study was conducted;

B) size of school, location, **population**, and other demographics;

C) performance levels and other relevant instructional information;

D) a description of who you are (I require my students to imagine they are a vice-principal, principal, superintendent, department chairperson, or are in any other leadership position in order to undertake the study from a leader's perspective.); and

E) any other information that sets the stage for your study.]

*Importance of the Study* [1–2 paragraphs]

[Describes why you are undertaking this study, why it is significant, and what you hope to ascertain.]

*Establishing Program* [2–4 pp.]

[Outlines in detail the steps you would take to establish or implement the program in your school/district. Be specific by using the steps outlined in

Chapter 4. Obviously, if your study doesn't involve program evaluation, then omit this section.]

*Statement of the Problem* [1 paragraph]

[States the purpose of the study and should begin as follows: "The purpose of this study was . . ." (Use past tense throughout to indicate this report was written after completion of the study.)]

*Hypothesis and/or Research Question(s)* [a list]

[If you triangulated, then hypothesis *and* research question(s) are likely. Refer to **hypothesis** and **research questions** in the Glossary for details on definitions and types.]

*Definition of Terms* [1–2 pp.]

[Defines relevant words either conceptually or operationally. See **conceptual definitions** and **operational definitions** in the Glossary.]

## CHAPTER 2: REVIEW OF LITERATURE/RELATED RESEARCH [4–8 pp.]

[Use the first term for quantitative studies and the latter term for qualitative studies. If you triangulate, either will do.]

[This chapter reviews relevant literature pertaining to your topic. What previous research, for instance, informs your study? Professional educational leaders should be aware of relevant and recent literature in the area they are investigating. One easy way of doing so is by consulting the *Education Literature Review,* which is discussed in the annotated reference section later in the book.

In action research, however, such a review of the literature need not be formalized, but for teaching research in graduate courses, students are encouraged to undertake a formal review of the literature.]

## CHAPTER 3: RESEARCH DESIGN/METHODOLOGY

[Use the first term for quantitative studies and the latter term for qualitative studies. If you triangulate, either will do.]

*Sample* [1 paragraph]

[Describe your **sample** in terms of:

A) who they are (including gender, ages, grade level data, ability levels, ethnicity, if relevant);

B) where they are from, how many are participating, how they were selected and assigned; and

C) any other relevant information the reader may need to know about the sample.

> Refer to **sampling** in the Glossary for definition and discussion of different types.]

*Materials* [2 paragraphs]

[List and briefly describe any relevant materials used in the study. For example, a researcher-developed survey should be described and a sample placed in an appendix. Reference appendix in this section by noting, for example, "See survey in Appendix B."

Also, include names and descriptions of any commercial tests, games, computers, children's literature, or other surveys.

Discussion of **validity** and **reliability** of testing instruments and/or surveys are discussed in this section.]

*Procedure* [1–2 pp.]

[Describes, step-by-step, how you conducted your study, including a timeline. Anyone reading your report should be able to explain or, at least, understand the steps you took in conducting your study. In other words, they should be able to replicate your study from the information provided in this section. Include a description of the **treatment** and precisely how it was administered.]

*Analysis of Data* [1 paragraph]

[Brief statement as to how you analyzed your data. See Chapter 6 for details.]

*Results* [1–2 pp.]

[State and describe the results of your study. Just provide the raw data. Reserve your conclusions and insights for the next chapter. Results should also be presented in table form using graphs, charts, or any other acceptable manner of presenting your findings.]

## CHAPTER 4: IMPLICATIONS FOR TEACHING/SUPERVISION AND RESEARCH

*Limitations of the Study* [a list]

[Every study is limited by factors beyond your control, such as mortality (see **internal validity**), **sample** size, time factor, etc. List and briefly explain each limitation. Refer to **confounding factors**, **internal validity**, and **external validity** in the Glossary.]

*Discussion/Conclusions* [2–4 pp.]

[Describe your observations, opinions, and conclusions based on the results reported in the previous chapter. Provide possible explanations and note interesting, significant, and/or curious findings.]

*Implications for Teaching and Supervision* [1–2 pp.]

[Describe the implications your study has for instructional improvement. Be specific about implications for supervision and school improvement.]

*Implications for Further Research* [1–2 paragraphs]

[Describe areas of further investigation that you might recommend others to undertake. Include areas of investigation you couldn't delve into, but were important nonetheless.]

## REFERENCES

[I recommend use of the American Psychological Association's (APA) *Publication Manual*, the most recent edition. All documentation throughout the paper should conform to APA style. See brief description of APA in Appendix E.]

## APPENDIXES

[APA prefers "appendixes" to "appendices." Any relevant materials such as copies of surveys, selected curriculum materials, photos, etc. should be placed in separate appendixes and labeled A, B, C, etc.]

See Appendix D for evaluation criteria for the report. Happy report/thesis writing!

# Chapter Summary

The following worksheets facilitate data interpretation and reporting. These worksheets are meant to allow you to brainstorm different ideas. Changes in your plan can always be made at a later date. These worksheets serve as a review of the ideas discussed in this chapter.

## Data Interpretation

*Refer to sample in Table 7.1. Here is a blank table of your own. Inputting data will aid data interpretation. Feel free to devise your own data interpretation table as well:*

### Using Prespecified Standards to Interpret Data

| Instrument | Standard | Percentage Meeting | Conclusion |
|---|---|---|---|
|  |  |  |  |
|  |  |  |  |
|  |  |  |  |

# Reporting Data

*Feel free to devise your own report based on your needs. Refer to excerpted suggestions in Table 7.2. The following format is one I suggest my students use in reporting their findings. Use this outline to jot down ideas or take notes as you begin to organize your thoughts and gather information:*

*TOPIC:*

*TITLE PAGE:*

*CHAPTER 1: INTRODUCTION*
 *BACKGROUND*
 *IMPORTANCE OF THE STUDY*
 *ESTABLISHING THE PROGRAM*
 *STATEMENT OF THE PROBLEM*
 *HYPOTHESIS*
 *RESEARCH QUESTION(S)*
 *DEFINITION OF TERMS*

*CHAPTER 2: REVIEW OF THE LITERATURE OR RELATED RESEARCH*

*CHAPTER 3: RESEARCH DESIGN OR METHODOLOGY*
 *SAMPLE*
 *MATERIALS*
 *PROCEDURE*
 *ANALYSIS OF RESULTS*
 *RESULTS*

*CHAPTER 4: IMPLICATIONS FOR TEACHING/SUPERVISION AND RESEARCH*
 *LIMITATIONS OF THE STUDY*
 *DISCUSSION/CONCLUSIONS*
 *IMPLICATIONS FOR TEACHING AND SUPERVISION*
 *IMPLICATIONS FOR FURTHER RESEARCH*

*REFERENCES*

*APPENDIXES*

*OTHER INFORMATION:* _____

_____

# References

[Note that the reference with an asterisk is annotated later in the book.]

Duckworth, E. (1986). Teaching as research. *Harvard Educational Review, 56*(4), 481–495.

Foshay, A. W. (1994). Action research: An early history in the United States. *Journal of Curriculum and Supervision, 9,* 317–325.

Gronlund, N. E., & Linn, R. L. (1990). *Measurement and evaluation in teaching* (6th ed.). New York: Macmillan.

*Herman, J. L., & Winters, L. (1992). *Tracking your school's success: A guide to sensible evaluation.* Newbury Park, CA: Corwin Press.

# Action Research in Action

CHAPTER 8

*"Research that produces nothing but books will not suffice."*
*(Lewin, 1948, p. 203)*

*"The process by which practitioners attempt to study their problems scientifically in order to guide, correct, and evaluate their decisions and actions is what a number of people have called action research."*
*(Corey, 1953, p. 6)*

*"We must find a way of bridging the traditional divide between educational theory and professional practice."*
*(Whitehead cited in McNiff, 1991, p. ix)*

*"[Action research] can take place anywhere: in one's office, in one's mind."*
*(Gauthier, 1992, p. 192)*

*"Action research is a powerful tool for simultaneously improving the practice and the health of an organization."*
*(Calhoun, 1993, p. 63)*

*"I fail, therefore I research."*

*(Mellor, 1994, n.p.)*

211

*"Think of action research as a huge meteor falling into the middle of the supervision ocean. As it hits, it causes a rippling of water . . . The rippling of water continues to increase in force until a giant wave gathers and crashes onto all instructional shores, sweeping away the old sand of past instructional failures and replacing it with the new sand of instructional improvement."*

*(Glickman, Gordon, & Ross-Gordon, 1998, p. 412)*

*"Action research is more of a commitment than a set of techniques—a commitment to exploring—exploring the meanings of, and hence, the practical possibilities for, our professional lives."*

*Editors of* Educational Action Research:
An International Journal, *1996, Vol. 4)*

# Action Planning and Implementation

Becoming reflective practitioners through action research is not so easy. Many organizational and individually imposed obstacles exist. Finding the time and support for action research undertakings are challenges that you are likely to encounter. Finding the time and support of action planning certainly warrants much discussion. Although a complete analysis of this urgent problem goes beyond the purpose of this volume, a few words are in order.

Given the current organizational framework of many schools, action research projects are not likely to be encouraged or supported. Too many schools and districts still administer programs, innovations, and interventions by administrative fiat or mandate. Change, however, is in the offing. The literature is replete with new visions and new realities. Schools that are framed as learner-centered communities where empowerment and collegiality are the norm are growing in number and quality. These schools, in which action research is possible, are energized with a mission that affirms that "quality learning for all students depends on quality learning for all educators" (Fullan, 1995, p. 5).

If educators are to make a difference in the academic and social lives of students, then educators themselves must be exposed to quality learning.

According to Fullan (1995), quality learning depends on the "development of the six interrelated domains of teaching and learning, collegiality, context expertise, continuous learning, change process, and moral purpose" (pp. 5–6). As Figure 8.1 demonstrates, all educators:

- understand that teaching is complex and contextual; that teachers are facilitators of learning; that learning occurs when learners construct meaning on their own (Cochran, DeRuiter, & King, 1993).

- value collegial relationships and participate as active members in a democratic learning community (Glickman, 1993; Goodlad, 1997; Guarasci, Cornwell, & Associates, 1997).

- demonstrate a commitment to specific knowledge, understanding, and skills needed for relating to and taking account of parents, communities, businesses, and social agencies and as such appreciate and consider all aspects of cultural diversity among students and community (Nieto, 1996).

- develop intellectual and emotional habits of critical reflection and action about one's professional work; and recognize that the mark of a professional is exhibited in a sustained effort of self-improvement (Goodlad, 1994).

- tolerate ambiguity, remain flexible, and are willing to take risks; and realize that in a complex, ever-changing world, they must not only cope with unpredictable events and trends, but must become agents of change in their own right (Fullan, 1993; Gunter, 1995).

- believe that they make a difference in the lives of all students; that they are driven by a moral purpose that affirms human dignity and a sense of caring for all people (Noddings, 1992).

Within such a framework, action research becomes part of a continuous improvement process, whereby leaders "take stock" within their organization (or "learning community") and collect data for the purpose of identifying problems. Also, action research can be used for benchmarking, for examining what other organizations are doing and assessing the applicability of certain interventions for their own organization. Therefore, educational leaders might first collect diagnostic or benchmarking data, then act, and evaluate the results. More importantly, however, many educational leaders would benefit from a greater understanding of the flexible planning process now recommended for creating meaningful organizational change. Parenthetically, if you would like to see how schools (sub-

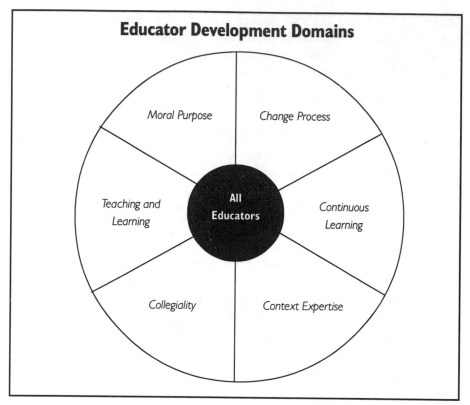

**Educator Development Domains**

Figure 8.1

urban and urban) are implementing these ideas, I highly recommend that you view the *Action Research* video series produced by the Association for Supervision and Curriculum Development (ASCD), and read and use the facilitator's guide (Glickman, 1995).

As educational leaders, you are the change agents to effectuate the kind of milieu in which action research is not only viable, but an integral part of a learning community (refer to Fullan's, 1993, discussion of the eight basic lessons of the "new paradigm" of change). The organizational framework of schools and districts were created by people and it stands to reason that people can change them. Educational leaders can and must create the readiness and willingness for changes that our schools need. Educational leaders are in pivotal positions in which to overcome inevitable resistances by articulating a vision of a school that supports a learning community. Vision leads to commitment and commitment leads to action planning and implementation. I think it was Margaret Mead who once said: "Never doubt that a small group of thoughtful, committed citizens can change the world; indeed, it is the only thing that ever has." And it was, to be sure, Michael Fullan and Andy Hargreaves (1996) who stated that we must "fight" for what we think is best for our schools. "It is individuals and small groups of teachers and principals who must create the school and professional culture they want" (p. 107).

What can *you* do tomorrow to make your school or district a learning community? What can *you* do tomorrow to make action research a viable and meaningful tool for school improvement? Can you think of some small steps you can take to make action research a reality in your school?

Finally, some practical guidelines for school improvement drawn, in part, from Fullan and Hargreaves (1996) are helpful.

- *Locate, Listen to, and Articulate Your Inner Voice.* Recall our discussion in Chapter 1 of the importance of finding time for reflection-on-action. Review the suggestions offered for finding the time to do so. Know that educational leaders must want to reflect deeply. As Fullan and Hargreaves (1996) underscore:

  Often, when we say we have no time for something, it's an evasion. What we mean is we have more immediate or convenient things to do with that time. Of course, bulletin boards and visual aids are important. But doing them doesn't make you feel personally uncomfortable. It isn't disquieting. It isn't a personal challenge. Listening to our inner voice is. It requires not just time, but courage and commitment too. Having the courage and commitment to reflect means putting other things aside to do it. (pp. 65–66)

- *Develop a Risk-Taking Mentality.* Change (that is, innovation and improvement) is accompanied by anxiety and stress. Whenever we take steps to change anything, we are undertaking a degree of risk. One concrete way, among many others, to minimize the risk is to start small, take a first-step. One of my mentors once quipped, "change occurs best by degree, not decree." Collect some data for the purpose of identifying any instructional problem you think may exist. Present the data you collected objectively to faculty, perhaps at a grade conference. Facilitate discussion that will include their reactions and suggestions for follow-up. Realize that no initial interest may be generated. "It is all right to fail, as long as you learn from it" (Fullan & Hargreaves, 1996, p. 73). But, continue by listening to your inner voice.

- *Balance Work and Life.* Change requires not only commitment, but priority-setting. As committed and enthusiastic educators, we sometimes try too hard. "More is not necessarily better" and sometimes "enough" is "too much." Stephen Covey (1989) described his last habit of a "highly effective" person as "sharpening the saw." We need to take the time to "sharpen our saws." We must realize that our effectiveness as educational leaders is dependent upon leading a fulfilled social and personal life, not only a professional one. Those who take the time to balance work and life and to "sharpen the saw" make the best action researchers.

- *Believe That You Can Make a Difference.* The importance of developing a learning community has been stressed. Commit to continuous improvement and perpetual learning as a foremost goal. Educational leaders must demonstrate the intestinal fortitude, if you will, to "push themselves to create the professional learning environments they want" (Fullan & Hargreaves, 1996, p. 82). More than that, educational leaders must believe that they can make a difference (Denham & Michael, 1981).

# Becoming Reflective Practitioners Through Action Research

Carl Glickman (1993) laments the tendency in American education to eschew reflective inquiry in favor of employing quick-fix approaches when addressing rather serious educational and instructional problems:

> Do not act unless you can study what you act. It is irresponsible for a school to mobilize, initiate, and act without any conscious way of determining whether such expenditure of time and energy is having a desirable effect. This sounds obvious, but most schools move from innovation to innovation, expending great amounts of time developing new curricula, learning new practices, and acquiring new materials and equipment. Then, after the ini-

tial enthusiasm has passed, they have no sense of whether
these efforts helped students. This is the American tendency in regard to education: grab the latest innovation,
get on with it as quickly as possible, and drop it just as
quickly when a new innovation appears. (pp. 54–55)

As foremost educational leaders, we must think critically about the plethora
of instructional challenges that confront us daily. We must first reflect on
what needs to be accomplished and then take purposeful actions to enhance school improvement. Action research may be the very means to
accomplish these objectives.

Formulating **research questions**, designing data-collection tools, analyzing data, drawing conclusions from data, and considering action plans
are part of the new professional repertoire of educators, as action researchers. As explained in Chapter 1, action research empowers educational leaders
by affording them the opportunity to reflect upon practices, programs,
and procedures for instructional improvement.

Educational leaders who are proactive and willing to apply research
strategies for instructional improvement know the value of "learning by
doing." As John Dewey (1899) said nearly a century ago, there's nothing
to compare with learning by doing. Educators are indeed lifelong learners
who appreciate new learning experiences and look for opportunities to
improve instructional programming. They realize that "learning" involves
"doing." They realize that to improve the school's programs, procedures,
and practices involves "doing"—taking action by proactively planning a
research agenda to accumulate information on ways to improve the school
organization. And that's what "action research" is all about—"learning by
doing."

Three stages of action research, then, become apparent:

## REFLECTION → ACTION → IMPROVEMENT

Every educational leader should keep in mind the premise that "reflection" must lead to "action" in order to "improve" our schools.

As was mentioned in Chapter 1, reflection involves time for "reflection-on-action." Problem identification and planning are integral in this
initial stage. Action involves observing, gathering data, analyzing and interpreting the data, and making a decision that will hopefully lead to some
degree of instructional improvement.

Still, as Illustration 8.1 shows, more stages are inevitable:

REFLECTION → ACTION → REFLECTION → ACTION

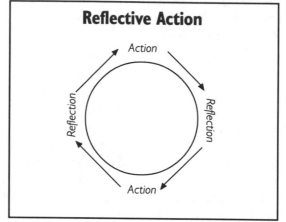

**Illustration 8.1**

Yes, indeed, action research is a cyclical process. A proactive, reflective practitioner understands that in order to maintain instructional improvement one must continually reflect and take appropriate, judicious action. School improvement can only be accomplished by sustained efforts at systematic, gradual, and ongoing attempts to find a better way.

This book has not merely advocated reflection that should lead to action, but has provided you with concrete strategies and tools to accomplish instructional improvement through action research. Now, it's up to you to apply these principles in your school. Begin slowly, as was mentioned in the previous section, by conducting a small action research study (use the worksheet at the end of Chapter 3). Learn from your experiences and build your confidence. In a short time, you will truly realize the efficacy of action research to enhance school improvement. You can and will become the catalyst for developing a learning community in your school or district.

## Action Research in Action

If you are using this book as part of a course on action research, then you will likely be involved in actually designing an action research project. Such simulated experiences are wonderful opportunities to apply action research skills without any of the possible harmful side-effects that we, as educators, inevitably experience as we seek to improve our schools. Instructional improvement involves, of course, risk-taking. The rewards, however, far outweigh any possible disadvantages. To minimize as many negative consequences as possible, experiencing simulated activities will likely build your confidence levels and raise your self-efficacy (Sullivan, 1996).

Begin by designing an action study on your own by applying these three steps: *PIE.*

## PLAN → IMPLEMENT → EVALUATE

The first step is to plan. As educational leaders, you may be interested in conducting studies involving some of the following broad areas of concern:

1. *classroom environment*—e.g., how does the physical and psychological environment affect student learning and attitudes?

2. *school climate*—e.g., how does the school climate affect parental involvement and teacher morale?

3. *instructional materials*—e.g., do the instructional materials reflect issues of diversity and multiculturalism?

4. *classroom management*—e.g., what new behavioral management strategies might be employed to encourage and support appropriate student behavior?

5. *teaching*—e.g., how might supervisors or lead-teachers encourage and support innovative teaching strategies and practices?

6. *communication*—e.g., how can communication linkages between parents and teachers be enhanced?

7. *supervision*—e.g., how might a developmental model of supervision be effectively implemented and evaluated?

8. *curriculum*—e.g., what changes are necessary to realign curricula in the state/district/school?

9. *evaluation*—e.g., how might a more collaborative and comprehensive plan be developed for evaluating teaching effectiveness?

10. *public relations*—e.g., how might supervisors engender community involvement and support for instructional practices?

11. *leadership*—e.g., which leadership style is most conducive to encouraging and supporting site-based management?

How might you initiate a research study to answer a question posed in one of the areas noted above? What evaluative measures will be taken to determine the impact of a particular approach?

To assist you in building your confidence levels, the remainder of this chapter presents eleven (11) *exercises* for you to practice planning, implementing, and evaluating various aspects of instructional improvement.

---

## Exercises

1. Evaluate, Interpret, and Apply Research Findings

   One of the important responsibilities of an educational leader is to read relevant educational research, interpret its findings, and apply them to practical situations in a school.

   Consider that you are an assistant principal in an elementary school of an urban school district. You are responsible for grades 4–6, consisting of approximately 500 students.

   A. Identify one major problem in any of the following areas: teacher-training, teacher-methods, curriculum, and school/community relations.

   B. Describe the problem in detail. Be creative, realistic, and specific.

   C. Conduct an Internet Web search for any information that will inform the problem you have highlighted above.

   D. Explain how the findings of the study can be applied to the problem you have identified in your school.

   E. Describe the course of action you would take based on your evaluation of the research findings in order to alleviate the problem. Describe the leadership (including supervisory) strategies you would employ.

   F. Be prepared to discuss your answers.


2. Evaluate a Program

   Situation:

   You are a District Office supervisor whose specialty is professional development. The superintendent has informed you that she wants you to evaluate the district's *teacher mentor/intern* program which is now completing its first year of operation. It is now April and she wants your completed evaluation report by August 1.

---

The district has 15 schools (five elementary, five intermediate, and five high schools) which are involved in the teacher mentor/intern program. Each school has two teacher mentors and four interns.

**Question:**    Assuming you have all the necessary resources at your disposal (the board of education's Office of Educational Assessment has provided sufficient funding), how would you conduct your evaluation of the teacher mentor/intern program? Be specific about research techniques and procedures employed, evaluation criteria, recommendations, etc.

_____

_____

_____

3. Evaluate a Program

Develop a written plan for evaluating a specific area of an instructional program with which you are familiar (for example, a K–6 math program, a senior high school Spanish program, or a remedial reading program). Discuss research design(s) utilized. Develop a questionnaire you would employ. Be specific, realistic, and practical.

_____

_____

_____

4. Needs Assessment

Your school has reorganized into a school-based management team. Committees have been formed and have met many times. Describe what site-based management and shared decision-making (SBM/SDM) is all about. Why is it so important (if it is)? What are some advantages/disadvantages of this strategy? Develop a questionnaire polling staff members' opinions about the concept, its effectiveness, suggestions, etc. Write a bibliography of ten books or articles that you as educational leader would distribute to faculty in order to familiarize them with site-based management. Describe the program (pros/cons). How would you evaluate its effectiveness?

_____

_____

_____

5. An Example of Action Research

   Consult Glickman, Gordon, and Ross-Gordon (1998). See pages 414–415 where an action research project is described: Classroom Research Using the Graphic Organizer in English. An excellent overview of an action research project is provided. Apply the principles of research design, data collection using both quantitative and qualitative measures, and data analysis and interpretation that you have learned in Chapters 4, 5, 6, and 7 in this book to the case study provided in the Glickman, Gordon, and Ross-Gordon book. Be as specific as possible and be prepared to share your strategies.

   _____

   _____

   _____

6. Miscellaneous Items

   Consider these questions:

   A. What are some ways that a supervisor or a lead-teacher might get teachers more interested in research?

   B. Explain two ways in which an educator might misuse test results.

   C. Create a self-evaluation instrument for supervisors and lead-teachers.

   D. Create an instrument by which teachers may evaluate supervisors' and lead-teachers' performance.

   E. Interview an educational leader and ask how he/she evaluates the instructional program. Describe and critique.

   _____

   _____

   _____

7. Research Applications: Directions and Case Stuudy 1

   These instructions should be followed for the remaining exercises:

   I. Purpose and tasks

      The purpose of these exercises is to apply the theories and principles of action research to practical school situations.

      Each group member is to carefully read each case study, noting the circumstances described and relevant information needed to adequately assess the situation. A brief discussion among group members should ensue in order to develop group strategies in dealing with the case study. Sufficient time should be allocated to complete research, analyze, and organize data; answer case-study questions; and prepare for group presentations in class. Format for presentation is at the sole discretion of the group.

II. Group Size

1.  Three to five people

III. Determining Factors in Formation of Groups

1.  Diversification

    A.  Different levels of schools: Elementary, Middle, and High School

    B.  Different levels of specialty in administration: Assistant Principal, District Office Supervisor/Coordinator, Principal, Lead-Teacher, and Special Education Supervisor, etc.

    C.  Compatible personalities

IV. Guiding Principles

1.  Cooperative group work

2.  Group strategy discussed

3.  Obligations of members defined

4.  Effective use of time

5.  Location of meeting places

6.  Preparation for group presentation

V. Suggested Strategies for Groups

1.  Thoroughly read and review case studies

2.  Group discussion of key points/strategies

3.  Assign each member a task or the group works as a unit

4.  Pitfalls to avoid

    A.  Excessive socializing

    B.  Postponing research

    C.  Arguing

    D.  Holding back information from other group members

5.  Rehearse for each oral group presentation

    A.  Develop strategies

B.  Individual/group discussions

C.  Techniques to enhance audience participation

### Developing a New Program

You are a principal of William Heard Kilpatrick Middle School, which has a population of 1200 pupils in grades 6 through 8. You are a conscientious administrator concerned about the welfare of the students and the quality of the curriculum. You are also an active participant in the meetings of the PTA, and you encourage parental interest in school affairs. You perform your duties effectively and serve your institution well.

At a recent PTA meeting, several parents complained that the school lacks a "gifted" program. They felt that such a program should be developed in order to meet the needs of a growing population of students in the school. You thanked them for their input and promised to consider the matter. You informed them that you would bring the matter to the attention of the superintendent at your next meeting with her.

Two weeks later, you meet with the superintendent. She is enthusiastic about the possibility of establishing a gifted program at the middle school level. Although there is no program for the gifted in the district, she informs you that a colleague of hers has developed and implemented a district-wide gifted program in a different township. "The program is very popular and successful."

The superintendent encourages you to develop a gifted program for your school, with the intent that the program you establish would serve as a model for other schools in the district. The superintendent requests that you address the following points:

A. definition of "gifted";

B. criteria used in selecting target population;

C. a curriculum based on the needs and interests of the identified target group;

D. teacher recruitment and training;

E. activities and approaches unique to the gifted;

F. integration of learning with highly realistic life experiences; and

G. administration, supervision, and organization of the program.

The superintendent requests that you submit a plan for the gifted program for her consideration.

NOTE: You are not at all knowledgeable about the gifted or talented.

*Your group should do the following:*

A. Develop a gifted program for your school.

B. Describe how you would utilize research in developing your program. Be specific.

C. Discuss steps that you would take to evaluate the program.

NOTE: Be creative in your approach. Assume that you have sufficient resources for materials, personnel, etc. at your disposal. Be certain to consider the seven (7) points the superintendent outlined above.

_____

_____

_____

8. Research Application Case Study 2

### Teacher Evaluation

You are a newly assigned Assistant Principal, in charge of grades 4, 5, and 6. In your new position, you discover low teacher morale, due in large part to the strict rating/observation methods used by the former AP. In your discussion with teachers, you find that the former AP used to observe teachers without notice and would write lengthy reports criticizing their teaching methods. Teachers did not find this supervisory approach to be worthwhile or constructive. Teachers were also anxious and disturbed about this method of teacher evaluation.

You are sympathetic toward the resentment felt by these teachers and you would like very much to allay their apprehensions by using alternative means of teacher improvement/evaluation. You were, however, trained to be a supervisor who uses the traditional methods of teacher observation. You have little, if any, knowledge about alternative approaches to supervisory observation.

However, you recently attended a convention for administrators sponsored by the Association for Supervision and Curriculum Development (ASCD), during which you heard about a unique approach to teacher observation. One of the speakers talked about Morris Cogan's "Clinical Supervision" and Carl Glickman's "Developmental Supervision." You were quite interested in these methods and would like to gain more information about "clinical and developmental supervision."

*Your group should do the following:*

A) Research these alternative approaches to traditional supervision. Describe these approaches and how you would implement them in your capacity as AP in the situation above. Be specific and be certain to mention the guiding principles or philosophy of the approach, the steps you would take to prepare for the observation, the criteria you would use for evaluating the lesson, and techniques you would employ during the post-observation conference. (See, for example, Morris Cogan, *Clinical Supervision*, 1973, pp. 10–12 for the eight-phase process for implementing clinical supervision. See Robert Goldhammer, *Clinical Supervision*, 1969, pp. 89–90 for eleven suggestions for using clinical supervision. See Glickman's model discussed in Glickman, Gordon, and Ross-Gordon, 1998.

B) Research at least one recent study showing the effects of these approaches to supervision (positive or negative). Present findings and interpret them.

C) Discuss how you would evaluate the effectiveness of this new supervisory approach.

9. Research Application Case Study 3

### The Problem of Change in Schools

You are a newly assigned principal in an elementary school of an urban school district. The school population is 900 pupils, with a staff of 35 teachers and 15 paraprofessionals. The former principal, who recently retired, had a reputation for running a "tight ship." He believed that a school should be academically oriented, traditional, teacher-centered, and administered closely.

You, on the other hand, although inexperienced (this is your first assignment as a principal), have a strong commitment to non-traditional education. You believe that alternatives to traditional teaching methods should be developed in order to offer choices not readily available to teachers or schools. Unfortunately, not many teachers in your school have experience or interest in alternatives to traditional education. In your observations of many teachers in the school, you find that instruction relies on the textbook and that many teachers do not even group for instruction in reading. You also observe that science instruction is neglected.

Your long-range goal as principal is to develop an alternative educational model school. Your reasons for interest in alternative education are based on the following assumptions:

A) existing programs are not meeting the needs of pupils, especially in reading and science;

B) advances in science and technology are rapidly changing the organization of instruction and the content of curriculum;

C) a whole-child approach is more beneficial than an intellectual aims approach; and

D) the educational theories of Dewey, Brunner, Trump, Goodlad, Oakes, Dunn, and Gardner are most intriguing.

Your short-range goal is to improve instruction in reading and science schoolwide.

## IMMEDIATE STRATEGIES

1. What would you do immediately to remedy weaknesses in reading and science instruction and justify recommendations in terms of benefits to learners?

2. How would you help teachers handle science equipment and improve their science instruction?

3. Which research design would you use to determine the effectiveness of the changes you incorporate. Describe, in general, the research methodology you would employ.

## LONG-TERM STRATEGIES

1. Describe how you would effect the changes you desire in each of the following areas: curriculum, instruction, and teacher attitudes.

2. Describe how you would use research in establishing and evaluating your new program.

In answering these questions, it may be helpful to consider the following points relating to any innovation:

I. Program Definition

A. Clarify the problems the program is designed to solve.

B. Identify objectives of the program.

C. Identify possible alternatives for reaching the objectives.

D. Establish priorities.

E. Anticipate criteria and strategies for evaluating the program.

II. Program Initiation

A. Create a climate of concern and interest in the new program—pupils, faculty, parents, school board members, community.

B. Planning and decision making.

III.  Program Implementation

A. Coordinate all activities needed to implement the program.

1.  arrange schedules

2.  provide for space needed

3.  assign staff

4.  order and distribute materials

B. Provide for necessary supervisory assistance.

1.  professional development for faculty

2.  school-wide pupil activities (fairs, poster contests, trips, assemblies, etc.)

3.  parent activities

IV.  Program Evaluation

A. Establish criteria.

B. Select instruments of evaluation.

C. Involve all participants.

D. Utilize results to modify the program.

10.  Research Application Case Study 4

### Test Evaluation in Mathematics and Science

You are one of the lead-teachers of mathematics and science in a high school. The principal is concerned about the lack of clarity and comprehensiveness of the school's testing program in math and science. The principal has asked you to set up a testing program for these two curriculum areas.

Describe, as specifically as you can, what you would do to establish a comprehensive testing program for the following areas:

A. In Relation to Pupils

1.  to determine student progress and achievement in math and science

2.  to assess potential abilities and special aptitudes

3.  to assess student difficulties and recommend remediation

B. In Relation to Teachers and Teaching
   1.  to increase teaching effectiveness
   2.  to assist teachers in self-evaluation
   3.  to determine necessary areas of emphasis in instruction

C. In Relation to Supervision and Administration
   1.  to specify responsibilities for planning, scheduling, administering, scoring, and recording test results
   2.  to interpret and analyze test results
   3.  to utilize test results

D. In Relation to Community
   1.  to report progress to parents

*Be sure to consider:*

1. The kinds of tests involved (achievement, criterion-reference, diagnostic, intelligence, formal/informal, **teacher-made tests,** etc.).
2. Guidelines for evaluating a test (**validity, reliability,** scales, norms, etc.).
3. Scheduling and dates.
4. Professional development (workshops, conferences, etc.).
5. Training of students in test-taking skills.
6. Arranging for locations, retesting, scoring, etc.
7. Statistical procedures for test interpretation.
8. Strengths and weaknesses in specific areas.
9. Workshop for parents to explore significance and limits of testing and to interpret test results.

_____

_____

_____

_____

_____

_____

_____

_____

11. Research Application Case Study 5

### School Improvement

You have been newly appointed as a principal of a pre-kindergarten through sixth-grade elementary school.

The school plant is forty-five years old and is in relatively good condition. Custodial care of the school is considered satisfactory.

The school is located in a community that has a low- to middle-income public housing project, a number of six-story apartment buildings, and a number of two- and three-family brownstone homes. There are several streets in the community that have a number of unoccupied, sealed, apartment buildings.

The school has on register 750 pupils. The ethnic background of the pupils is 45% African-American, 40% Hispanic-American, 10% Asian-American, and 5% others. Forty percent of the pupils are reading on grade level or above.

The school has a full complement of classroom teachers. Sixty-five percent of the teachers have been teaching fewer than 10 years.

The executive board members of the Parents Association work hard to support programs that will benefit the pupils in the school. There is limited participation in school programs and activities by the parent body, in general.

As the new principal you realize that much remains to be done to make this school into an "effective school." Your long-range goal is to establish strong instructional leadership, a safe environment, school-wide excellence in basic skills, and a disciplined student body. You are eager to apply the research findings on "effective schooling" to your school situation. Describe the steps you would take to improve your new school.

_____

_____

_____

_____

_____

_____

_____

_____

# References

[Note that references with an asterisk are annotated later in the book.]

Calhoun, E. F. (1993). Action research: Three approaches. *Educational Leadership 51*(2): 62–65.

Cochran, K. F., DeRuiter, J. A., & King, R. A. (1993). Pedagogical content knowing: An integrative model for teacher preparation. *Journal of Teacher Education, 44*(4), 263–272.

Cogan, M. L. (1973). *Clinical supervision.* Boston: Houghton Mifflin.

*Corey, S. M. (1953). *Action research to improve school practices.* New York: Teachers College Press.

Covey, S. (1989). *The seven habits of highly effective people.* New York: Simon & Schuster.

Denham, C., & Michael, J. (1981). Teacher sense of efficacy: An important factor in school improvement. *The Elementary School Journal, 86,* 173–184.

Dewey, J. (1899). *The school and society.* Chicago, IL: University of Chicago Press.

*Educational Action Research: An International Journal.* (1996).

Fullan, M. (1995). In M. J. O'Hair & S. J. Odell (Eds.), *Educating teachers for leadership and change* (pp. 1–10). Thousand Oaks, CA: Corwin Press.

Fullan, M. (1993). *Change forces: Probing the depths of educational reform.* Bristol, PA: Falmer.

Fullan, M., & Hargreaves, A. (1996). *What's worth fighting for in your school.* New York: Teachers College Press.

Gauthier, C. (1992). Between crystal and smoke: Or, how to miss the point in the debate about action research. In W. Pinar & W. Reynolds (Eds.), *Understanding curriculum as phenomenological and deconstructed test* (pp. 184–194). New York: Teachers College Press.

Glickman, C. D. (1993). *Renewing America's schools: A guide for school-based action.* San Francisco: Jossey-Bass Publishers.

*Glickman, C. D. (1995). Action research: Inquiry, reflection, and decision-making. (Video). ASCD.

Glickman, C. D., Gordon, S. P., & Ross-Gordon, J. M. (1998). *Supervision of instruction: A developmental approach* (4th ed.). Boston: Allyn and Bacon.

Goldhammer, R. (1969). *Clinical supervision: Special methods for the supervision of teachers.* New York: Holt, Rinehart, and Winston.

Goodlad, J. I. (1994). *Educational renewal.* San Francisco: Jossey-Bass.

Goodlad, J. I. (1997). *In praise of education.* New York: Teachers College Press.

Guarasci, R., Cornwell, G. H., & Associates. (1997). *Democratic education in an age of difference.* San Francisco: Jossey-Bass.

Gunter, H. (1995). Jurassic management: Chaos and management development in educational institutions. *Journal of Educational Administration, 33,* 5–20.

Lewin, K. (1948). *Resolving social conflicts.* New York: Harper and Brothers.

*McNiff, J. (1991). *Action research: Principles and practice.* London: Routledge.

Mellor, R. (1994). *Action Researcher, 1.*

Nieto, S. (1996). *Affirming diversity: The sociopolitical context of multicultural education.* White Plains, NY: Longman Publishers.

Noddings, N. (1992). *The challenge to care in schools: An alternative approach to education.* New York: Teachers College Press.

Sullivan, S. (1996). Creating leaders: Fostering self efficacy in aspiring educational administrators. *Focus on Education, 40,* 24–28.

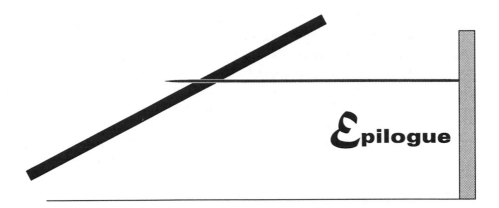

*"Through action research . . . changes in educational practice . . . [are] more likely to occur because teachers, supervisors, and administrators . . . [are] involved in inquiry and the application of findings."*
*(Oja & Smulyan, 1989, p. 4)*

Congratulations, you have completed *Action Research: An Educational Leader's Guide to School Improvement.* Allow me to offer seven suggestions for educational leaders who are interested in implementing action research to improve schools.

## Seven Suggestions for Action Researchers

Some of the following stories were called from *The Executive Speechwriter Newsletter* [(802)748-4472] and from Oracle Service Humor Mailing List (jokes@oraclehumor.com).

### 1. Expect the Unexpected

Implied in this common sense admonition is the notion that one must realize that research is a slippery, unpredictable process which, by the way, reminds me of a story:

> There was once a fellow who worked in an office in New York City and would leave the building for lunch at noon each day. He would pass the pretzel stand on the corner

and place a quarter on the cart, but would never take a pretzel. This would continue every day, week after week. Finally, the elderly woman running the stand spoke up as the fellow put his daily quarter down without, of course, taking a pretzel. "Sir, may I have a word with you?" she asked. The fellow said: "I know what you're going to say. You're going to ask me why I give you a quarter every day and don't take a pretzel." And the woman responded, "Not at all, I just wanted to tell you that the price is now 35 cents!"

Learning to expect the unexpected when conducting action research is highly recommended. Action research is not a neat, uncomplicated process of applying "four easy steps." Researchers too often undertake a project with preconceived notions. They sometimes *expect* certain situations to develop. Research is unpredictable. As action researchers who work in school settings, we must be ready for change at any moment. Of course, we cannot foresee everything that may happen, but once aware that endless possibilities exist, we're less likely to be surprised and caught off guard. Enjoy the thrill of being engaged in the exciting, yet unpredictable experience of action research. Not only will your school benefit by the process, but you'll also have lots of fun.

## 2. Be Receptive to Both Quantitative and Especially Qualitative Approaches

I cannot overemphasize the importance of a mixed methodology approach to action research. Too often researchers have a latent bias against **qualitative research** as being "unscientific," especially if a project doesn't incorporate meta-analyses or multivariate statistics. Similarly, many educators are skeptical of traditional research that doesn't have immediate utility. Both views are short-sighted. Action researchers should incorporate both methodologies, when warranted and reasonable.

Making a case, it seems to me, for **quantitative research** is not very difficult since it has had a long and cherished tradition in American educational research communities. Qualitative methods, however, are sometimes viewed less favorably. I'm reminded of a wonderful little story about Picasso that the makes the point quite well.

A story is told of a French railroad passenger who, upon hearing that his neighbor in the next seat was Picasso, began to grouse and grumble about modern art, saying that it was not a faithful representation of reality. Picasso demanded to know what was a faithful representation of reality. The man produced a wallet-sized photo and said, "There! That's a real picture—that's what my wife really looks like." Picasso looked at it carefully from several angles, turning it up and down and sideways, and said, "She's awfully small. And flat." (cited in Shagoury-Hubbard & Miller Power, 1993, p. xvi)

## 3.    Give It Your All

Good advice for life in general, "giving it your all" also has relevance for action research. Certainly, action research requires persistent efforts over time. Even though identifying problems, posing critical **research questions**, collecting and analyzing data, reporting initial results, monitoring progress, and offering solutions that are research-based are essential elements of action research, they are difficult to accomplish and sustain. Yet, reflective practitioners know that their efforts, in the long run, will pay off.

Persistence and hard work are critical, especially for reporting your research findings through written reports. The written final report is an important document for reporting your research findings. The report communicates your results and offers recommendations. Your diligent efforts in conducting the study are worthwhile only to the extent that you've taken the time to write the report carefully and accurately.

I once submitted a report to a superintendent based on an evaluation of the district's gifted program. My written report could have been more thorough and precise. To make a long and unfortunate story more concise, the superintendent wasn't a happy camper. Take my advice, "giving it your all" is especially important in writing final reports. Preparing reports that represent your best work is the point of this anecdote involving Henry Kissinger:

> During the Tonkin Gulf situation, Henry Kissinger asked an assistant to prepare an analysis. The assistant worked night and day for a week and put the document on Mr. Kissinger's desk only to receive it back within an hour. Affixed to the report was a note asking that it be redone. The assistant dutifully redid it; he slept a total of nine

hours for a week. The document again went to Mr. Kissinger's desk, and an hour later it was returned with a note from Mr. Kissinger asserting that he expected better and asking that the work be done again. And so the assistant went back to the drawing board once more. Another week of intense work, and then the assistant asked if he might present it personally to Mr. Kissinger. When he came face to face with Henry Kissinger, he said, "Mr. Kissinger, I've spent another sleepless week. This is the best I can do." Said Henry Kissinger, "In that case, now I'll read it."

Point well taken?

## 4.  Don't Make a Decision Too Quickly

Action researchers sometimes think that since "action" is required, one must hurry to make a decision. If you've learned anything from reading and studying this book, you've learned that the purpose of action research is to carefully deliberate prior to making any important decision. Decision making in educational administration and supervision is too often plagued by snap judgments. Not rushing a decision before all the information is in is the point of these two stories:

> One night at sea, the ship's captain saw what looked like the lights of another ship heading toward him. He had his signalman blink to the other ship: "Change *your* course 10 degrees south." The reply came back: "Change your course 10 degrees north." The ship's captain answered: "I am a captain. Change your course south." To which the reply was: "Well, I am a seaman first class. Change your course north." This infuriated the captain, so he signaled back: "Dammit, I say change your course south. I'm a battleship!" To which the reply came back: "And I say change your course north. I'm in a lighthouse."

This next story is told by British actor Jeremy Irons to illustrate the potential fatal effects of making a decision too quickly:

> Recently, a small aircraft was flying over the Nevada Desert carrying three passengers: the President of the United States, a priest, and a California hippy. Engine trouble

occurred and the pilot came back into the cabin to break the news to the passengers.

"You're going to have to jump," he told them, "and, unfortunately, we only have two parachutes for the three of you, so you must decide amongst yourselves who is left behind."

The President made a strong case about how he was a possible Saviour of the world, the man who singlehandedly is defending democracy on all fronts and the man who is the figure-head of the free world. There was, therefore, no doubt that he should be allowed to live. The priest and the hippy agreed, and, with that, the President strapped on a backpack and jumped out of the airplane.

Next, the priest began to say how, since he was an old man and had little more to give to the world, the last remaining parachute should be taken by the hippy. But the hippy disagreed, saying:

"Don't worry, man, the Saviour of the world just jumped out wearing my knapsack!"

Certainly make decisions, but do so thoughtfully only after conducting a well-planned action research project.

## 5.  Keep Lines of Communication Open and Clear

Throughout an action research project, especially when collecting and analyzing results, clear communication among participants is essential. The value of exact communications to prevent misunderstandings is the point of the next story:

When I was working my way through college, I got a job one summer as a delivery man. I had a small pick-up truck, and if anyone had an item they wanted delivered, I did it.

One day, I had a very unusual delivery. I was to pick up six penguins and deliver them to the local zoo before closing time.

I loaded the penguins into the truck and I was doing fine until I developed a flat tire on a major highway. I pulled over and surveyed the damage. I knew that I could fix the flat, but it was getting late, and I doubted that I could get my cargo to the zoo before it closed.

I was just wondering what it would be like to spend the night with six penguins when I saw a friend of mine driving down the highway in his own truck. I flagged him down and explained the situation to him.

"Look," I told him, "I have to get these penguins to the zoo before it closes. It's going to take at least a half-hour to fix this flat, so I wonder if you'll do me a favor. I'll give you ten dollars. Will you take them to the zoo?"

My friend said that he would, so we transferred the birds to his truck, and he took off down the highway.

By the time I had fixed the flat tire, it was rather late. I drove into town and decided that what I needed was a cup of coffee. I parked my truck and went into the local diner.

I was sipping my coffee and gazing absentmindedly out the front window of the diner, when all at once, my eyes went wide. There, coming down the main street of the town was my friend—followed by the six penguins, all in a row, looking like a procession of head waiters.

I rushed out of the diner and ran up to my friend.

"What is this?" I shouted. "I thought I gave you ten dollars to take them to the zoo!"

My friend was puzzled.

"I did take them to the zoo," he answered, "and they enjoyed it very much, but that only cost four dollars, so I figured that with what was left I'd take them to the movies."

## 6.  Yes, Appreciate Your Enlightened Eye

Most of us think that the reason we're known as "supervisors" is because we are presumed to have SUPERvision. The origins of supervision are, unfortunately, based on hierarchical and bureaucratic notions about supervisory practice (Glanz, 1991). Hence, the term "supervision" implies that supervisors are embued with superior status and, perhaps, even intelligence. No doubt many supervisors of the past relied on these hierarchical, and sometimes patriarchical, sources of authority to accomplish their supervisory tasks. Current thinking and practice of supervision, however, refrain from such outmoded conceptions.

Still, supervisors do have special knowledge and skills that allow them to influence instruction in positive ways. Supervisors do not gain legitimacy by virtue of their status or position in schools. Rather, their unique training and experience affords them *special*vision, *super*, if you must, regarding, for instance, observing classroom interaction during a lesson. Just as a connoisseur can distinguish tastes from a variety of wines that a novice to wine-tasting might overlook, so too educational leaders have special skills that allow them to *see* things during a lesson that might otherwise be overlooked by the untrained or *unenlightened* eye.

In *The Enlightened Eye*, Elliot Eisner brilliantly describes the unique contributions trained supervisors make while observing classroom interaction. Eisner distinguishes between "seeing" and merely "looking." He says, "Seeing, rather than mere looking, requires an enlightened eye" (Eisner, 1991, p. 58). So too, supervisors, while undertaking action research, "see" things that others miss. Do you see the image in Figure E.1 on the next page? (*There is an image; keep trying or ask someone for assistance.*) Hint: Turn illustration sideways with the words "Figure E.1" to the right way.

## 7.   Take Action

> There is a story about a geologist who was doing research in Alaska in 1964. That also happened to be the year the great earthquake hit. It seems that the geologist was at home when he felt the floor suddenly sway under him. Then the walls buckled and finally part of the roof collapsed. With the earthquake in full tilt, so to speak, Joe runs outside to see a street full of people shocked, confused, and helpless. At that point, his neighbor with her children under each arm, rushes up to him and says, "Joe, you're a geologist! For G-d's sake, do something!"

Like the geologist in the story, we, as educational leaders, are also being asked to respond to problems and "do something." To take action now and meet the challenges we face is our greatest task. Armed with action research, I believe we are in an optimal position to effectuate fundamental and positive changes in the school organization.

---

# Ethics of Action Research

---

*"The first rule of ethics in action research . . . is 'Do no harm.'"*
*(McLean, 1995, p. 45)*

## Do You See the Image?

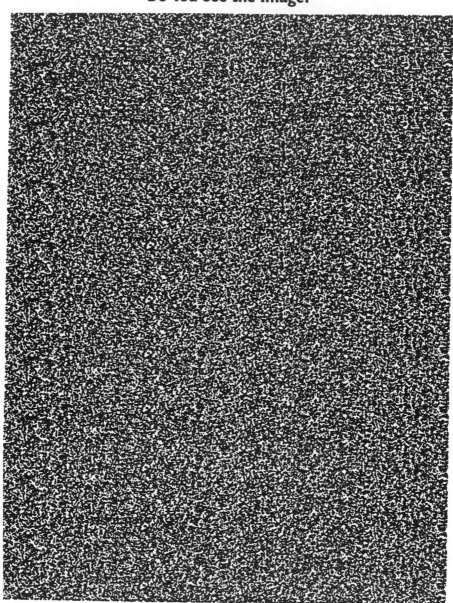

Figure E.1

Reprinted with permission, Kodesh, Inc.

The study of ethics focuses on moral issues involving right or wrong behaviors and actions. As professionals who utilize action research as a tool to achieve and maintain school improvement, we have a moral responsibility to conduct ourselves honestly and ethically. Conducting research may present us with challenging dilemmas. Do the ends justify the means? If our ultimate concern is school improvement, does that lofty goal allow us to pursue a research agenda that may border on unethical behavior? Should you inform survey respondents, for example, that their anonymity will be assured when, in fact, you have no intention of assuring such?

A complete treatment of this important issue is not our primary concern in this section. For a more complete discussion of a range of guiding principles when conducting research, see, for instance, Charles (1995, pp. 8–16) and Drew, Hardman, and Weaver Hart (1996). Also, the American Educational Research Association has developed six "ethical guiding standards." They have been reproduced by Crowl (1996, pp. 376–382) and warrant your attention. Also, consult Newman and Brown (1996) for ethics in program evaluation. In this section, I'd like to just point out some ethical principles that I consider to be of foremost concern to action researchers.

1. Principle of accurate disclosure—participants in a study should be informed of the general purposes of the research project and any unusual procedures or tasks in which they will be involved.

2. Principle of beneficence—research will not harm people in any way, but be conducted to benefit people educationally.

3. Principle of confidentiality—participants in your study should be assured that the information they share with you will not be made public knowledge AND THAT THEIR IDENTITIES WILL REMAIN ANONYMOUS. If you inform respondents or participants that they will remain anonymous, you should do everything to ensure that their identities are concealed.

4. Principle of honesty—as an action researcher you are obligated to report your findings in an honest fashion without embellishment or intentionally erroneous information. Report data, for example, exactly the way they were obtained.

5. Principle of privacy—whether conducting an interview or distributing a survey, questions of a personal nature should be avoided. Many researchers, for instance, ask for a respondents ethnicity or gender

when these factors have no relevance to the study. Should you wish to report private information such as demographics or opinions about sensitive issues, be certain to obtain *written* consent.

To support some of these principles, I have included Sample Consent Forms (reprinted with permission from Crowl, 1996)—See Appendix B.

In general, keep in mind the following question that I have posted on the bulletin board opposite my desk at home: "What ethical concerns should I, as an action researcher, consider when conducting research in order *not to violate anyone's individual rights?*"

# A Closing Statement

In September 1995, the National Council for the Accreditation of Teacher Education (NCATE) established curriculum guidelines for advanced programs in educational leadership for principals, superintendents, curriculum directors, and supervisors. As part of the first major area of "strategic leadership," NCATE outlined specific guidelines for preparing supervisors in what is termed "Information Management and Evaluation." Prospective supervisors, according to the guidelines, must demonstrate an understanding of, and the capability to:

1. conduct needs assessment by collecting information on students; on staff and the school environment; on family and community values, expectations and priorities; and on national and global conditions affecting schools.

2. use qualitative and quantitative data to make informed decisions, to plan and assess school programs, to design accountability systems, to plan for school improvement, and to develop and conduct research.

3. engage staff in an ongoing study of current best practices and relevant research and demographic data, and analyze their implications for school improvement.

4. analyze and interpret educational data, issues, and trends for boards, committees, and other groups, outlining possible actions and their implications. (*Guide to Folio Preparation for Advanced Programs in Educational Leadership*, 1995, p. 150)

*Action Research*, to a great extent, addresses these critical areas and guidelines. I have stressed our obligation as educational leaders-as-researchers. Educational leaders are thoughtful, reflective practitioners who question, reflect, and make sense of their situations. They are committed to inquiry and scholarship. They mediate ideas, construct meaning and knowledge, and act upon them (Atwell, 1991). *Action Research* has, hopefully, equipped you with necessary prerequisite knowledge, skills, and values (dispositions) that can be easily implemented in your school.

As a former teacher and administrator for twenty years in the New York City public schools, I appreciate the complex social, political, and technological challenges confronting practitioners. I truly believe that action research, as described in this volume, can assist you in confronting and solving many problems as you attempt to improve your classrooms and schools. Action research is an invaluable asset that will not only lead to schoolwide instructional improvement, but will serve to enhance your professional practice. Continued success to all!

# References

[Note that references with and asterisk are annotated later in the book.]

Atwell, N. (1991). *Side by side: Essays on teaching to learn*. Portsmouth, NH: Heinemann.

Charles, C. M. (1995). *Introduction to educational research*. New York: Longman.

Crowl, T. K. (1996). *Fundamentals of educational research* (2nd ed.). Madison, WI: WCB Brown & Benchmark Publishers.

Drew, C. J., Hardman, M. L., & Weaver Hart, A. (1996). *Designing and conducting research: Inquiry in education and social science*. Boston: Allyn and Bacon.

Eisner, E. W. (1991). *The enlightened eye*. New York: Macmillan.

Glanz, J. (1991). *Bureaucracy and professionalism: The evolution of public school supervision*. New Jersey: Fairleigh Dickinson University Press.

*Guide to folio preparation for advanced programs in educational leadership*. (1995). Alexandria, VA: Educational Leadership Constituent Council.

*McLean, J. E. (1995). *Improving education through action research: A guide for administrators and teachers*. Thousand Oaks, CA: Corwin Press.

Newman, D. L., & Brown, R. D. (1996). *Applied ethics for program evaluation.* Thousand Oaks, CA: Sage Publications.

Oja, S., & Smulyan, L. (1989). *Collaborative action research: A developmental approach.* London: The Falmer Press.

Shagoury-Hubbard, R., & Miller Power, B. (1993). *The art of classroom inquiry.* Portsmouth, NH: Heinemann.

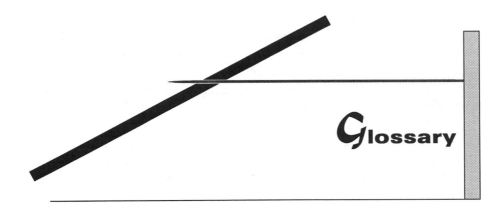

**Glossary**

**A-B; A-B-A; or A-B-A-B research designs**   types of single-subject designs. See **Single-Subject Research Designs**.

**Achievement tests**   commonly used measures or **assessment** tools in action research. An achievement test is a kind of **standardized test** in which an individual's knowledge or proficiency in a given content area is assessed. The Stanford Achievement Test and the Iowa Test of Basic Skills are examples of standardized achievement tests.

**Analysis of covariance (ANCOVA)**   a statistical technique used in group comparison research when equivalence between the groups (usually only two in action research) cannot be ascertained. To compute an analysis of covariance, you would use a computer program such as STATPAK, as was explained in Chapter 6.

**Analysis of variance (ANOVA,** sometimes called the F test)   a statistical technique for determining whether or not significant differences can be found among the means of *three* or more groups. To compute an analysis of variance, you would use a computer program such as STATPAK, as was explained in Chapter 6.

**Aptitude test**   a kind of **standardized test** used as a **data collection** instrument (or data source) designed to predict someone's ability to perform. The use of IQ tests is an example of an aptitude test. The SAT test taken by precollegiate students is another example of an aptitude test.

**Assessment**   a process of interpreting information to aid decision making. Assessments include all information an educator collects to help make an informed, thoughtful decision. Thus, assessment is a general term for interpreting data collected. As an educational leader, for example, you may collect data (by various **measurements**, e.g., **interviews**, observations, **portfolios**, and **surveys**, among others) about teachers in your school. Assessment occurs when you interpret the meaning of these data. Your interpretation of the data may lead you to conclude that a particular teacher is having trouble dealing with disruptive students. Your assessment leads you to believe, in other words, that this teacher needs classroom management training.

Since the terms assessment, measurement, and evaluation are often used synonymously, an attempt to clarify differences may be in order. Measurement refers to the process of gathering information and is often expressed numerically. In the case above, for instance, the number of times this teacher refers students to the dean or vice-principal is one form of measurement. Ordinarily, scores on tests are considered measurements. However, a measurement really refers to any way of collecting data, including **questionnaires**, **aptitude tests**, and other **surveys**.

Assessment is a broader term that includes measurements, but also includes interpreting measurements in order to make some sort of decision. Concluding that a student is reading on the 6th grade level or that a teacher is suffering from burnout are derived though assessment; i.e., interpreting various measurements.

**Evaluation**, in contrast, refers to the process of making a decision based on the assessment process. For example, referring a burnt out teacher to counseling might be a decision made as a result of interpreting the data collected. Placing a student in a remedial class is an evaluative measure taken after having interpreted or assessed various measurements or data collected.

Every competent leader is continually taking measurements, assessing them and, then, taking a course of action by making some decision or evaluation.

**Baseline**   a graphic record of measurements taken prior to introducing an **intervention** or **treatment** in **single-subject research designs** such as a time-series design. For a fuller treatment of baseline measurements see detailed discussion in Chapter 3.

**Case study research**    one of three methods of qualitative research, discussed in this book (see Figure 1.5 in Chapter 1). Case studies involve in-depth investigations of an individual or group of individuals. Findings are stated verbally, not numerically. Case studies are reported by describing in detail observations made of individuals, groups, or school settings.

**Chi square**    (often symbolized by $X^2$) a statistical technique for assessing the relationship between two or more **nominal variables**. "Chi" is pronounced "kiy (long i sound)." To compute chi square, you would use a computer program such as STATPAK, as was explained in Chapter 6.

**Closed-ended questions**    questions on a **questionnaire** that limit possible responses by providing specific choices or options (e.g., yes, no, uncertain) to a respondent. **Likert scales** are examples of close-ended questionnaires. See discussion of close-ended questions in Chapter 5.

**Collaborative action research** (and schoolwide action research, see Chapter 1)    forms of action research in which parents, teachers, and principals might be involved in an ongoing program of **assessment** and improvement. Each group member shares in the planning, implementation, and analysis of the research. A premise underlying this book is that educational leaders should develop their skills in *individual* action research projects before involving others in the process. However, if your school is interested in developing collaborative action research teams, consult the *Institute for Responsive Education* (see Annotated References) and other works that discuss collaborative and schoolwide action research.

**Conceptual definitions**    one of two ways to define terms in a research study. A conceptual definition is a typical dictionary-type definition of a term or concept. Sources for conceptual definitions usually are authorities in the field. The following is an example of a conceptual definition:

Cooperative Learning "involves positive interdependence among students, face to face interaction, individual accountability for mastery of material and the development of personal and small group skills." (Johnson & Johnson, [year]).

See **operational definitions** for a second way of defining terms.

**Confounding factors**    can cause erroneous conclusions to be drawn from a study. In group comparison studies, for example, changes in the **dependent variable** may not be caused by the **treatment** under study, but may, in fact, be influenced by some other intended or unforeseen factors. Two such confounding factors are the Hawthorne and John Henry Effects.

The Hawthorne Effect occurs when members in the **experimental group** know they are receiving "special" **treatment** and, thus, will improve no matter what treatment they are receiving. Members of such experimental groups consider themselves special or privileged. The original Hawthorne studies were conducted by Elton Mayo and his associates in the late 1920s and early 1930s at the Hawthorne Plant of Western Electric near Chicago.

The John Henry Effect, the opposite of the Hawthorne Effect, occurs when subjects in the **control group** know they are, in a sense, competing with some other group (experimental) and, consequently, expend extra effort to perform better than the **experimental group**.

Both the Hawthorne and John Henry Effects may cause erroneous conclusions to be drawn from your study and are, thus, called confounding factors. Obviously, every effort to make each group "feel" special would avert problems with the Hawthorne Effect, for example. In **group comparison** research (e.g., assessing the effect of computer-assisted instruction on computational skills between two groups) both groups should be exposed to some special **treatment** (computers, in this case) without letting the participants know what you are measuring. For example, the control group may use computers to enhance writing skills, while using traditional methods to learn computational skills. The experimental group is exposed to computers to enhance their mathematical computational skill development. Participants in this study do not know what you are measuring and, thus, the Hawthorne Effect is minimized.

Discussion of other confounding factors are included in the "limitations" section of your report (see Chapter 7). Although your study may be limited by several factors (see **internal validity**), confounding factors only refer to those factors or situations which may cause erroneous conclusions to be drawn.

**Content analysis**   a method of data analysis in which you analyze the content in a given document according to prescribed categories or criteria while following explicit rules of coding.

**Control group** (sometimes called comparison group)   the term used in **group comparison** studies to identify the group, sometimes assigned randomly, that remains untreated or receives a **treatment** other than the one received by the **experimental group**. Data collected from individuals in a control group are compared with data collected from members of an **experimental group**. These groups then serve as comparisons or controls for subjects who are receiving special treatments.

**Converted scores**   refer to **raw scores** that are converted into **grade equivalents, percentiles, stanines**, or other forms. Raw scores that are converted are more easily understood, compared, and interpreted.

**Correlation** (synonymous with the word "relationship")   a statistical technique for evaluating the degree to which two **variables** relate to one another.

Correlational analyses are most easily computed using STATPAK or any similar program (see Chapter 6).

**Correlation coefficient** (or coefficient of correlation)   a statistic ($r$) that indicates the degree of relationship between two or more **variables**, as explained above. Examples are provided in Chapter 6.

**Correlational research**   one of three methods of research that assume a quantitative approach (see Figure 1.6 in Chapter 1) in studying a given educational issue or problem.

**Criterion-referenced tests**   one of two major types of **testing** instruments that measure minimum levels of student performance. Teacher-made tests are one example of a criterion-referenced test. (In contrast, see **norm-referenced tests**).

**Data collection**   the process of collecting information to answer one's **research questions** and/or confirm or reject an **hypothesis**. One of the major steps of the **scientific method**, data collection should be comprehensive and multiple (as described in Chapter 2). Examples and applications of data collection methods was discussed in Chapter 5.

**Degrees of freedom** (usually abbreviated as "*df*")   a term used in statistical inference to connote the "degree of freedom" a researcher has in selecting a given **sample** for one's study. Degrees of freedom is one of the more difficult statistical terms to fully understand. All you have to know is that *df* always = N – 1; i.e., the number of subjects in your sample minus one subject.

Let's say I asked you to choose any 5 numbers you would like, as long as the **mean** was 10. You would have, theoretically, 4 "degrees of freedom" to choose any four numbers you wish. Try this: choose any number. Okay, say you chose 5. Now, choose another number and say you chose 9. Now choose a third number, 7, and still another number, say, 10. Stop. You have selected 4 numbers (5, 9, 7, 10). You have had complete "freedom" to choose any four numbers you wished. The mean of these four numbers, however, is . . . well, you figure it out. . . . Right, add them and divide by 4 to get a mean of 7.75. But, wait, I said the mean must be 10. So in selecting a fifth number, you have no "freedom." You must select the number 19. Right? Add, 5, 9, 7, 10, and 19 and divide by 5 to get a mean of 10. Therefore, *df* always equals $N - 1$; in this case, $5 - 1$.

This concept of degrees of freedom *(df)* will come into play when you interpret **statistical significance**, as you have seen in Chapter 6.

**Dependent variable** (see **variable**)   the term used for the "outcome" variable in **group comparison research**. In such research, the experimenter manipulates one variable (the **independent variable**) and measures its effect on a second variable. That second variable is known as the dependent variable; i.e., the variable that *depends* on the other variable (the independent one). In order to easily remember which variable is dependent, know that the dependent variable is synonymous with the word "outcome."

Consider this **research question**: How is math achievement affected by computer-assisted instruction? What is the desired outcome in this research question? Of course, it's math achievement. Math achievement is the dependent variable.

**Descriptive research**   one of three methods of research that assumes a quantitative approach (see Figure 1.6 in Chapter 1) in studying a given educational issue or problem. **Survey** and observational reports are *types* of descriptive research. Descriptive research may use statistics or numbers (usually percentages) to describe data.

**Descriptive statistics**   one category or type of statistics (the other is **inferential statistics**) that is used in **descriptive research** to describe and summarize data.

Two of the most common ways to describe data statistically are **mean** and **standard deviation**.

**Design**   See **research design**

**Empirical research**   refers to methods of investigation based on observations. In other words, any study you conduct that involves investigation by observation is considered empirical research. Action research may be thought of as a form of empirical research. Although, as defined and understood in this book and, as was previously explained, action research encompasses many other methods of investigation as well.

**Ethnography** (or **ethnographic research**)    one of three methods of **qualitative research** discussed in this book (see Figure 1.5 in Chapter 1). It is used to observe individuals or groups of individuals in natural settings. The ethnographic researcher takes many notes describing what was observed. Further information can be found in Chapter 3.

**Evaluation**    an ongoing decision-making process about the quality of a program, product, or procedure. Evaluation takes place only after measurements have been taken and **assessment** (interpretive) procedures completed. Once data are collected and interpreted, an educational leader can now make a better decision or judgment. Evaluations may occur informally or formally. For a more detailed explanation of evaluation, see Chapters 1 and 4.

**Evaluation research**    the most common use of action research. Evaluation research is *not* a separate research method, as is ethnographic or correlational research. Rather, as defined here, evaluation research is a common use of action research (see Figure 1.1 in Chapter 1) that may incorporate quantitative and/or qualitative approaches. For a more complete description of evaluation research see Chapters 1 and 4.

**Experimental group**    a group, assigned randomly in **experimental research**, that receives a special **treatment**. Data are then collected to determine the effect that this treatment has on the experimental group. The experimental group is contrasted with data collected from a **control group**. Chapter 3 provides examples and further discussion of experimental groups.

**Experimental research**    one of the three types of **group comparison** research that utilizes quantitative approaches. Experimental studies assign individuals to either experimental or control conditions. **Randomization** occurs in experimental studies. See Figure 1.7 in Chapter 1 and discussions of experimental research designs in Chapter 3.

**Ex post facto research**    one of the three types of **group comparison** research that utilizes quantitative approaches. Ex post facto studies involve intact classes which are assigned to either experimental or control conditions. No **randomization** occurs in these studies. See Figure 1.7 in Chapter 1 and discussions of ex post facto **research designs** in Chapter 3.

Briefly, ex post facto research studies involve groups already formed, such as intact classes (e.g., classes in periods 2 and 4 in a high school). In other words, the study is carried out after the fact (ex post facto); i.e., after classes or groups have been formed. You as the researcher have no control over the fact that these students are part of periods 2 and 4. That is a fact or condition beyond your control. Studies that use intact or ex post facto groups are called ex post facto research. A study involving self-concepts of mainstreamed and non-mainstreamed students is an example of ex post facto research because mainstreamed and non-mainstreamed groups already exist with varying degrees of self-concept. You are merely using these preexisting or intact classes as part of your study to compare self concepts.

Therefore, the major difference between ex post facto research and experimental studies is that in the former, neither groups nor individuals are randomized to form comparison groups. Comparisons are thus made with intact or pre-existing classes.

**External validity**   a form of **validity** that is synonymous with **generalizability**; i.e., the degree to which results can be generalized to other populations. Action research studies are rarely generalizable and, therefore, have weak external validity. This lack of external validity does *not*, in any way, diminish the significance of action research.

For further explanation, see **validity**.

**Focus groups**   groups of individuals who are selected by a researcher and consent voluntarily to share their views and opinions on specific topics related to an action research project. As a type of **survey**, a focus group is not unlike a group interview.

**Generalizability**   the degree to which findings derived from one context or under one set of conditions may be assumed to apply to other settings or conditions. Action research studies do not generally yield findings that are generalizable.

Studies, for example, with large numbers of subjects or participants are more likely generalizable than action research studies that involve a small group of individuals. Again, the lack of generalizability does not diminish the impact of action research as a viable tool, used by educational leaders, for school improvement.

**General semantics**   helps us use language more scientifically and accurately. General semantics is the study of the relationship among language, thought, and human behavior. Often errors occur when we begin to interpret collected data, for example, about a program in our school. To avoid possible errors and misinterpretations, the study of general semantics cautions us to incorporate multiple sources of data when undertaking any research project. Using a variety of approaches lessens the chance that we might reach an unwarranted conclusion. Relying on the weight of many sources of information is far better than making some sort of decision based only on one or two pieces of evidence. Examples of general semantics are provided in Chapter 2.

**Grade equivalents** converted scores that report how well or poorly a student has done on a **standardized test**. **Raw scores** on standardized tests are converted into grade equivalents by indicating grade levels and months. A grade equivalent of 5.3 in reading, for example, indicates that a student is reading at a fifth grade level in the third month. Grade equivalents are usually reported in **school profiles**. Although more revealing than **raw scores**, grade equivalents are not as accurate as **stanines** or **percentiles**.

**Group comparison research** one of three methods of quantitative research (see Figure 1.6 in Chapter 1) that can be used by action researchers. In these studies, the researcher administers different **treatments** to groups and then compares the groups on a **dependent variable**.

**Historical research** one of three methods of **qualitative research** discussed in this book (see Figure 1.5 in Chapter 1).

**Hypothesis (hypotheses)** a researcher's educated or informed guess about the relationship between two or more **variables**. An hypothesis is a statement of prediction, an anticipated outcome. Hypotheses are utilized only in quantitative studies.

There are three major types of hypotheses: *directional, non-directional,* and *null.*

*Directional* hypotheses indicate some direction between the variables under study, as in the following example: Teachers supervised by clinical supervision will have more favorable attitudes towards their supervisors than teachers supervised by traditional forms of supervision. Note that this hypothesis indicates that one group will demonstrate more favorable attitudes, thus, indicating that a particular variable will influence or *direct* the other. Can you construct your own directional hypothesis?

*Non-directional* hypotheses, in contrast, indicate, as in the previous example, that there will be a difference between teachers who are observed, but do not specify a direction between the two variables. "There will be a difference between self concept levels between mainstreamed and non-mainstreamed students" is an example of a non-directional hypothesis. Construct a non-directional hypothesis of your own.

*Null* hypotheses indicate that no relationship or difference between the two groups or variables is likely. "There will be no difference in self concept levels between mainstreamed and non-mainstreamed students" is an example of a null hypothesis. As was indicated in Chapter 6, null hypotheses are usually employed when statistical analyses are calculated.

In traditional educational research, hypotheses are generated only after an extensive review of the literature on a given topic. Since a literature review is *not* employed in action research, I advise my students to always frame their hypotheses in the null form, especially when some statistical work will be done.

**Independent variable** (see **variable**)   refers to the variable manipulated by the experimenter in group comparison research to determine its effect or influence on another variable (i.e., the dependent variable).

Let's say you're interested in researching the following question: How is teacher satisfaction (morale) influenced by leadership style of the principal? Leadership style is the independent variable that is manipulated by the researcher to determine its impact on the dependent variable (*outcome*, remember?), in this case *teacher morale*. The independent variable is considered *manipulated* because the researcher could have chosen any variable in order to study its effect on teacher morale. Also, it's manipulated in the sense that various leadership styles may be studied in a given context or situation. For example, democratic leaders may influence morale differently than autocratic styles, under various circumstances.

An easy way to remember which variable is dependent and which is independent is: Dependent variables always signify outcomes, whereas independent variables can be manipulated.

Consider this research question: How is math achievement affected by computer-assisted instruction? What is the desired outcome in this research question? Think. . . . Of course, it's math achievement. Math achievement is the dependent variable. The other variable, therefore, has to be independent. It's independent because you could have selected any variable to study its influence on math achievement. It's also independent because you can *independently* assign one group to computer-assisted instruction, while another group is exposed to some other **treatment**.

**Inferential statistics**   one category or type of statistics (the other is **descriptive statistics**) that tells us how much confidence we can have in generalizing from a **sample** to a **population**. Action research is not very concerned with inferential statistics (see definition of **Generalizability**).

**Instrument**    any device used to collect data such as a test, **questionnaire,** or portfolio. Use of the word *techniques* in Chapter 5, entitled "Data Collection *Techniques* That Work," should be considered synonymous with the term *instrument*. Although the terms are interchangeable, I prefer the word *techniques*, at times, because it conveys action.

**Internal validity**    a form of **validity** that assesses the degree to which data you collect are unbiased and undistorted. The following two measures, for instance, increase internal validity:

A) longer periods of **data collection.**
B) more subjects (e.g., more respondents to a survey).

While these aforementioned factors increase internal validity, the following factors are threats to internal validity:

A) mortality    refers to a situation in which respondents or subjects of a study drop out for one reason or another. A poor rate of return of a **questionnaire** is an example of the concept of mortality. Fewer returns of the questionnaire reduces the number of participants in your study, and, thus, becomes a threat to internal validity.

B) maturation    refers to students who do well due to natural maturation (physical or mental) and not necessarily due to the **treatment.**

C) history    refers to a situation unrelated to the study that may influence a change in behavior or achievement levels. Let's say you wanted to assess a particular workshop on teacher morale in your district. If at the same time of this study or in the recent past a budget crisis loomed that froze teacher wages, results from your study might be influenced by this budgetary situation and not be caused by the series of workshops offered.

D) reactivity    refers to the likelihood that a pretest administered will affect posttest results. Respondents to a **questionnaire**, for example, may figure out what "you are looking for" and respond accordingly on the posttest.

**Intervention**    See **treatment** because the two terms are synonymous.

**Interview**    one method of collecting data based on surveying the views of an individual or group of individuals. Although face-to-face interviews are the most common type, phone interviews are frequently employed in action research projects. See Chapter 5 for further discussion on interviews.

**Interview protocol** a predetermined set of questions used by an interviewer to conduct an interview.

If you were to interview your superintendent, you might want to prepare a set of interview questions in advance of the actual interview. These questions are known as the interview protocol. An interview protocol, especially for an inexperienced interviewer, will lessen anxiety and structure the interview positively. Sometimes the protocol may be shared with the interviewee to allow her/him to see the range of questions that may be asked.

**Level of significance** a term used in quantitative studies to refer to the probability that the difference between the **variables** studied occurred by chance and not due to your **treatment**. In most educational studies, the desired level of significance is 5% (.05). For some action research studies the level is less stringent (10% or .10) (see, for example, the **sign test** in Chapter 6). In other words, there's only a 5% or 10% chance that differences between the **experimental** and **control groups** could have occurred by pure chance without any **treatment**.

Levels of significance are represented by the "$p$" level or "alpha" level. You are likely to see a level of significance reported as follows: $p < .05$, meaning that the probability that differences between both groups were due to chance factors are less than 5 chances in 100 or 5%. Further explanation of levels of significance are discussed in Chapter 6.

**Likert scale** a type of **questionnaire**, developed by Rensis Likert, that utilizes the following categories of possible responses: strongly disagree, disagree, agree, and strongly agree. For a complete discussion on designing and interpreting Likert scales see Chapter 5.

**Mann-Whitney U-test** a statistical technique used to determine whether or not two *small* groups differ significantly from one another. This test is often used for **static-group comparison designs**. This test operates like a **t-test** and was discussed in Chapter 6.

**Matched pairs** a technique for equating groups on one or more **variables**, resulting in each member of one group having a direct counterpart in another group. Matched pairing is used to form equivalent or comparable groups when **randomization** is not possible. A teacher, for instance, may divide her intact class into two comparable groups for purposes of conducting a **group comparison** study. Matched pairs is a very useful technique used by action researchers.

**Mean**   the arithmetic average of a group of scores. The mean is calculated by the sum of the scores divided by the number of scores. (See discussion above—**descriptive statistics**, as well as applications of mean in Chapter 6).

**Multiordinality**   a concept from the study of **general semantics** that implies that language often inadequately describes what we see. What we all call a "chair," for example, is a "chair" only because we have agreed that the object should be called a "chair." There is nothing inherent in the object itself that necessitates that we call it by that name. Moreover, similar words may have multiple meanings or multiordinality. For example, the word "bridge" may have multiple meanings depending on the context in which it is used. "The bridge of your nose" is very different than the "bridge that you cross in your car." In sum, multiordinality refers to the fact that misunderstandings in the language we use are all too common. Therefore, as researchers, we must be aware that when we examine a given phenomenon limitations exist in our ability to accurately describe what is really happening. The point of Chapter 2, in which this concept is described, is to indicate that collecting data from a variety of sources and using a variety of approaches when conducting research helps us more adequately understand the problem we are investigating.

**Non-equivalent control group design**   a **research design** used in **ex post facto** studies involving at least two groups (see Figure 1.1 in Chapter 1). Both groups are pretested, while one group receives a **treatment**. Both groups are then posttested. Individuals are not randomly assigned to groups.

**Norm-referenced tests** (synonymous with **standardized tests**)   one of two major types of **testing** instruments that measure differences among individuals being tested. Norm-referenced tests are usually used as important **data collection** sources.

**One-group pretest-posttest design**   a **research design**, sometimes called preexperimental research design, involving one group that is pretested, exposed to a **treatment** and posttested. This design is considered weak because no comparison group is utilized. Yet, one-group pretest-posttest designs are commonly employed by educational leaders as part of action research projects (1) because often only one group is available and (2) because of its relative ease at administering and analyzing.

Although such a design is not usually one's first choice, one-group pretest-posttest designs can be used effectively by employing the sign test for analysis, as was demonstrated and explained in Chapters 3 and 6.

**Operational definitions**   one of two ways to define terms in a research study. Operational definitions involve observable, measurable, and quantifiable descriptions of key terms in a research study. Science achievement, for example, can be operationally defined as follows: a passing score of 70% on a teacher-made science test. A supervisor-made questionnaire could also be defined operationally by stating the nature of the survey (e.g., **Likert**), the design (e.g., designed by researcher, as opposed to using some commercially developed **instrument**), and how the questionnaire will be measured (e.g., a favorable attitudinal score would be 25 and above). Operational definitions do not merely define the terms conceptually (see **conceptual definitions**), but rather describe them and state how they will be measured.

**Percentile**   indicates the percentage of individuals who scored above or fell below a given score. For instance, if a third grader scored at the 76th percentile, her score exceeded 76% of the third graders who took that same test (see **norm-referenced tests**). Percentiles are **converted scores**.

**Raw scores**   are frequently converted into percentiles so that comparisons can be made among individual test or questionnaire scores. A raw score of 32 does not indicate how well or poorly a certain individual performed on a test. The score merely indicates the number of correct responses. Once the raw score is converted into percentiles (e.g., 89%), one might then ascertain how this particular individual performed in relation to the other test-takers. In this case, we may conclude that the individual scored higher than 89% of the test-takers.

Percentages, in contrast, denote the "percentage" of individuals who gave a particular response or achieved a particular score. Percentages are often used to describe and analyze data in action research projects (see Chapter 6).

**Performance-based assessment**   a type of measurement in which an individual is asked to perform a specific skill (e.g., write an essay on the causes of the Civil War or to perform a series of ballet movements). Students' performance is assessed against established criteria. Gymnastic performances at the Olympics are examples of performance-based assessments.

**Population**    refers to the large or total group from which a **sample** is derived. For example, all male college students, all principals in New Jersey, or all graduates under age 25 are considered populations. As a researcher, I want to draw a **sample** from a given population. Members of a sample are called **subjects** (Ss) or participants. Relationships between samples and populations were explored in Chapters 3 and 6.

**Portfolio**    a **data collection instrument** (or data source) that includes a great deal of information about a particular individual or group of individuals. Portfolios may include a student's achievement test scores, book reports, homework assignments, art projects, in-class tests, oral presentations, self-assessments, art work, etc. Portfolios are excellent ways of collecting data from a variety of perspectives.

**Posttest-only control group design**    a **research design** used in **experimental research** involving at least two randomly formed groups in which one group receives a **treatment** and then both groups are posttested for comparison. (See Figure 1.1 and a discussion of this design in Chapter 3).

**Pretest-posttest control group design**    a **research design** used in **experimental research** involving at least two randomly formed groups in which one group receives a **treatment** and then both groups are pretested and posttested. (See Figure 1.1 and a discussion of this design in Chapter 3).

**Program evaluation**    a very common type of **evaluation research** used by educational leaders who undertake action research projects. Program evaluation was discussed in Chapter 4.

**Qualitative research**    approaches examine questions that can best be answered by *verbally* describing how participants in a study perceive and interpret various aspects of their environment.

**Quantitative research**    approaches examine questions that can best be answered by collecting and statistically analyzing *numerical* data.

**Quasi-experimental research**    one of the three types of **group comparison** research that utilizes quantitative approaches. Quasi-experimental studies assign groups, not individuals, to either experimental or control conditions. No **randomization** occurs in quasi-experimental studies. See

Figure 1.7 in Chapter 1 and discussions of quasi-experimental **research designs** in Chapter 3.

Quasi-experimental studies are the most commonly used in education because teachers and supervisors rarely have the opportunity to truly randomize subjects into groups. Intact classes or groups are most common. For example, let's say you wanted to compare Method A to Method B. As a high school teacher you might have two equivalent or comparable groups of 10th graders during periods 4 and 7. These are, of course, intact classes because you didn't randomly assign them to these classes. You can, however, randomly assign the *methods*. Period 4 may be assigned Method B and period 7 may be assigned Method A. In other words, quasi-experimental studies randomly assign intact groups to different *methods* rather than randomly assigning *individuals*.

Note that quasi-experimental research, as used in this volume, also refers to studies that do not use control groups. Chapter 3 referred to single measurement, static, one-group pretest/posttest, interrupted time series, and single subject designs as examples of quasi-experimental studies.

**Questionnaire**   a type of **survey** that is distributed to a **sample** to ascertain attitudes about a particular issue or concern. A questionnaire, then, is a type of survey; the two terms are not necessarily synonymous. Chapter 5 discussed questionnaire construction and Chapter 6 discussed analysis of results derived from questionnaires. (Also, see **Likert scales**).

**Randomization** (or **sampling**)   See **sampling**

**Raw score**   (or number) a numeral that indicates a score obtained on a test or a **questionnaire** before the score is converted into a **percentile**, **grade equivalent**, **stanine**, or some other analogous form. A raw score of 56, for example, indicates the number of correct responses attained by an individual on a test or a questionnaire. Raw scores are considered **interval** data (see **scales of measurement**). Although raw scores are a preferable way of obtaining quantitative data (since data analysis is much easier using raw scores as opposed to using percentiles, grade equivalents, or stanines, as was indicated in Chapter 6), sometimes you might want to convert raw scores in some way in order to make them more easily understood and comparable (see **converted scores**).

**Reliability**   the degree to which an **instrument** yields consistent results under repeated administrations. When you hear the term "reliability" you should immediately think of "consistency."

Usually, if you want to know whether a particular **instrument** was reliable you would consult the test maker's manual. Reliability, whether reported by a manual or computed on one's own, is reported in terms of a **correlation coefficient**. The closer the coefficient of correlation, which is expressed in hundredths, comes to +1.00, the higher the reliability factor. Thus, for instance, a reliability coefficient of .80 would indicate that the **instrument** (e.g., a test) is reliable. Remember that no test is ever 100% reliable.

In qualitative approaches to research, two kinds of reliability are common:

A) *external reliability*    refers to the degree to which your study can be replicated by others. In other words, if someone followed your procedures and methods, they would likely report similar findings. Yet, the nature of qualitative research is so personal that external reliability is difficult to attain.

In a study I recently completed, I wanted to ascertain the kinds of images of principals that were depicted in film and television. After previewing dozens of sitcoms and movies, I identified, through **content analysis**, three categories of images. External reliability was confirmed, in this case, by having independent researchers view the same episodes to confirm my categories.

B) *internal reliability*    synonymous with *interrater reliability* (see below).

Common reliability tests include:

A) the *test-retest method*, in which the same test is repeated over a period of time. Two test administrations are required. **Correlations** are taken between the two sets of test results. The resultant **correlation coefficient** is the index of reliability. Note that **correlations** can be inflated if the time interval between tests is short. Why do you think this is so?

B) the *parallel (or equivalent) forms method*, similar to the previous method, in which you retest the same group with an equivalent form of the test. This method requires two administrations (Form A of the test administered, for instance in September, and then Form B administered to the same group in March). The two sets of scores are correlated as they were in the test-retest method.

C) the *split-half method*, in which the test is split into two parts (or halves), such as odd-numbered items and even-numbered items.

The test is administered to the same group. Two sets of scores are obtained for each person: a score based on the odd-numbered items and a score based on the even-numbered items. These two sets of scores are correlated to obtain a reliability coefficient. Note that the longer the test, the more reliable the test will be. Why do you think this is so?

Note that a split-half reliability quotient may be calculated by referring to Crowl's 1986 book titled *Fundamentals of research: A practical guide for educators and special educators*, published by Horizons, Inc., in which easy-to-follow, step-by-step procedures are provided in his appendixes.

D) *KR-21* (Kuder-Richardson Formula), used to measure the consistency of an **instrument** in which all items have the same characteristic or degree of difficulty. Tests that include diverse items or varied levels of difficulty should be subjected to split-half reliability assessments. KR-21 may be calculated by referring to Crowl's work cited above.

E) *Interrater reliability* (also known as *internal reliability*), used in **qualitative research** and **single subject research designs**, involves comparing ratings or rankings given by independent observers. The more similar the rankings, the higher the reliability. Interrater reliability, therefore, refers to the percentage of agreement among independent observers. Teachers use this form of reliability in grading standardized writing tests. Three teachers rate a given essay separately and an average score is then computed. In this way, no single rating is given preference.

Reliability is enhanced by use of multiple data sources (see Chapter 2). Why do you think this is so? Reliability of qualitative studies is enhanced through the use of multiple observers. Why do you think this is so?

**Research design**   was discussed in 3 ways:

(1) As an overall plan—The research design, explained in Chapter 3, is the overall plan for conducting systematic inquiry.

(2) As a quantitative plan—In quantitative approaches, various ways of designing a study may be employed. Chapter 3 discussed adequate research designs such as pretest-posttest control group designs and time series designs.

(3) As a qualitative evaluation plan—In qualitative approaches (see Chapter 4), a way of designing **program evaluations** was discussed.

**Research questions**   the questions posed by action researchers as they undertake qualitative studies. Research questions guide the research and are answered as a result of conducting the study.

Robert Slavin, in his 1992 volume titled *Research methods in education* published by Allyn and Bacon, tells a story of his two-year-old daughter who when asked by her older brother "what is fourteen minus seven?" immediately responds "seven." When asked, "eighty-eight minus 79" she responds "nine" and when asked the cube root of 125, she confidently answers "5." Someone listening to this apparent two-year-old genius would be amazed. In truth, she has only learned a trick that when asked those particular questions she should always respond by repeating the last number she heard. When asked "what's three plus zero?" She would incorrectly respond zero. Slavin explains that the message of the story is that "it's not only the answers you get but the questions you ask that determine the value of a study" (p. 1). Research is about finding answers to questions worth asking. Developing research questions is necessary in order to select an appropriate research design.

Simply ask yourself, "What do I want to learn from this investigation?" You might pose this question, for example: "What factors seem to account for differences among boys and girls in math and science achievement in my high school?" Your research would attempt to discover those critical factors that account for such presumed differences. Can you pose another research question?

**Research report**   a formal document that describes how a study was conducted, including results and conclusions. Formats for research reports will vary depending on the school district or agency. A format that I suggest my students follow is presented in Chapter 7.

**Response set**   the tendency to respond in a particular way to the content of a questionnaire. See Chapter 5 for a detailed explanation.

**Sample**   refers to the group of subjects or participants chosen from a larger group, known as the population. Relationships between samples and populations were explored in Chapters 3 and 6. On sample selection, see **sampling**.

**Sampling** (often synonymous with **randomization**)   a technique used to select participants for a study. Sampling involves a process by which members in the population have an equal chance of being selected. Note that as a general rule, the larger the **sample**, the greater the likelihood for obtaining significant results.

Types of sampling are:

A) *random sampling*   involves each member of the population having an equal chance of being selected. The Table of Random Numbers, which can be found in any book on statistics, can be used for studies involving many subjects. For smaller studies, simply shuffling cards with names of all the members of a population and then selecting a certain number of cards from the top of the deck (like pulling names out of a hat) could also be used as long as all members of the population have an equal chance of being selected.

B) *stratified sampling*   involves identifying two or more subsets (e.g., gender, ethnicity, geographic location, etc.) in a population and taking a random sampling of each subset. Identifying subsets in advance of obtaining a sample reduces the possibility that an important group is left out of the sample.

   Let's say you wanted a representative number of elementary, middle, and high school teachers for a survey you are conducting throughout a district on attitudes toward supervision. You would identify the numbers of elementary, middle, and high school teachers and then take a random sampling from each category, thus ensuring representation from all three groups of teachers.

C) *systematic sampling*   involves systematically selecting a fraction of the population (e.g., every tenth name on a list).

D) *cluster sampling*   used by identifying a site (e.g., schools, a district, or classes) and then taking a random sample from that cluster or site.

Qualitative sampling procedures may be quite different from techniques previously described. Obtaining a representative sample is less important in **qualitative research** studies because generalization is not a concern. Often, samples are chosen for qualitative studies based on convenience, individual preference, or happenstance.

**Scales of measurement**    are important in order to determine what types of statistical analyses are appropriate (see Chapter 6).

Four (4) scales of measurement are:

**nominal** (categorical)    the lowest scale of measurement. Nominal categories are not quantifiable; i.e., non-numerical, such as gender, ethnicity, and religious affiliation. An easy way to remember nominal **variables** is to know that nominal = naming. That is, a nominal variable just names things. For instance, gender (male or female), names of states (e.g., Texas or California), socioeconomic status (upper, middle, lower), and political party affiliations (Republican, Democratic, etc.) are nominal. Nominal variables have no order (from high to low), one category is not better than another; they are non-numerical. As was mentioned in Chapter 6, **chi square** analyses are conducted with nominal data.

**ordinal** (order)    a scale that puts subjects in order from high to low, but does not indicate how much higher or lower one subject is in relation to another. An example of an ordinal variable is: ranking height from tallest to shortest (e.g., Mary #1; Sue #2; Fran #3; Bill #4); or ranking three brands of cereal by consumer preference. Note that **Likert scales** are really ordinal, but in education they are treated statistically as **interval**.

**interval**    a scale of measurement that tells us how much subjects differ from one another. For example, **raw scores** are interval scales. Subject 1 (S1) with a raw score of 100 (out of 100) has 50 points more than subject 2 (S2) with a score of 50. Although we can say that S1 scored 50 points higher than S2, we can't say that S1 is twice as smart as S2 because interval scales have no absolute zero point (as do **ratio** scales). Differences between categories in interval data are considered real differences in that the difference between a raw score of 4 and a raw score of 2 is the same difference between raw scores of 6 and 8.

**ratio**    the highest and most precise scale or level of measurement. The ratio scale is the same as the interval scale, except for the fact that it has an absolute zero point. Weight, for example, is based on a ratio scale. Someone who weighs 140 lbs. is twice as heavy as someone who weighs 70 lbs.

Here's a mnemonic to help you recall the 4 **scales of measurement**: No One Is Ready (**N** = nominal; **O** = ordinal; **I** = interval; **R** = ratio).

Summary:

> **N** = Shaquelle O'Neil is tall, and I am short
> **O** = Shaquelle O'Neil is taller than I
> **I** = Shaquelle O'Neil is 7' tall and I am 5' tall
> **R** = Shaquelle O'Neil is 7\5ths as tall as I am

**School profile**   a document that summarizes quantitative data about a given school. Usually published annually by the district office or board of education, a school profile includes demographic data and detailed summaries of student achievement levels. A school profile summarizes important data from a variety of **instruments** and, as such, is an invaluable means of **data collection**. Obtain a recent profile of your school to see the kinds of useful data provided.

**Scientific method**   a 4-step approach to disciplined inquiry. The scientific method is most usually applied to quantitative studies. As an educational leader who wishes to examine the impact of a new literature series on reading comprehension achievement of two equivalent groups of students, you would apply the scientific method as follows:

(1) define the problem to be investigated;
(2) state the **hypothesis**;
(3) collect and analyze the data; and
(4) confirm or reject the hypothesis.

Let's analyze each step in the **scientific method**.

(1) *define the problem*   Let's say you wanted to determine the impact of invented spelling on kindergartners' ability to spell. The first step would be to express the problem as specifically as possible. Problems need to be expressed behaviorally. Problems that are not defined precisely cannot be investigated scientifically. To ask "Is invented spelling good for kindergarten students?" is imprecise because of our inability to measure "good." Defining the problem more accurately one might ask: "What is the impact of invented spelling on kindergartners' ability to spell?"

(2) *state the hypothesis*   Action research does not require an extensive review of the literature. Rather, one makes an educated guess about a specific situation. In the case above, one might hypothesize as follows: "Kindergarten students taught spelling by invented spelling will score significantly higher on a spelling test than students

taught by another method." When some statistical work will be done, hypotheses should be framed in the null form. Can you restate the directional hypothesis above in null form? . . . Right, "there will be no difference in spelling achievement between kindergarten students taught by invented spelling and students taught by another method."

(3) *collect and analyze data* We collect data in order to test our hypothesis. How might we collect data in order to determine the impact of invented spelling on kindergartners' ability to spell? Yes, we might administer some sort of spelling test. This test would be our primary means of collecting data. We might also, of course, collect data by noting the amount of words spelled correctly during classwork.

After collecting the data, we analyze the data, statistically, to confirm or reject our hypothesis. (See Chapters 5 and 6).

(4) *accept or reject the hypothesis* At this point in the scientific method, analysis of collected data will provide evidence to either reject or accept the hypothesis. If the evidence supports the hypothesis, then the hypothesis is accepted. If the evidence is contrary to the hypothesis, then the hypothesis is rejected. Students often think that a rejected hypothesis means a less worthy study. Such a conclusion could not be farther from the truth. As long as you have applied the steps of the scientific method properly, your study is valid regardless of findings contrary to existing literature in the field.

**Sign test** a simple statistical technique or test to determine if the posttest scores are different from the pretest scores in **one-group pretest-posttest designs**. See Chapter 6 for a complete explanation of the **sign test**.

**Single-subject design** (a type of **time series design**) a **research design** used in **quasi-experimental research** that can involve only one individual and sometimes up to four or five individuals. **Single-subject designs** allow a researcher to investigate one or just a few individuals with respect to a given **variable** (e.g., changes in behavior). Subjects are exposed to a **treatment** and then multiple measurements are taken over a period of time. The objective of this sort of research is to determine if the treatment had any effect on the behavior of the subject(s).

This design is frequently used in special education. Applicability for action researchers is significant as well.

**Standard deviation**   a **descriptive statistic** that measures the variability of a group of scores. The higher the value of the standard deviation, the wider the spread of scores. (See applications of standard deviation in Chapter 6.)

**Standardized tests**   See **norm-referenced tests** because the two terms are synonymous. It should be noted that some authorities don't equate norm-referenced tests with standardized tests since some **criterion-referenced tests** may also be standardized.

**Stanines**   converted scores that are frequently reported in **school profiles**. Stanines convert individual scores into bands of scores. Stanines are divided into nine bands; hence, the term is derived from *standard nine*. In other words, the range of scores is divided into nine bands. A student scoring in the first stanine scores the lowest, while a band of nine represents the highest score. The average or **mean** score is found in the fifth band. Although test results are usually reported in more easily understood ways (e.g., **grade equivalents** or **percentiles**), a basic understanding of stanines may come in handy to show the relative position within which all scores are distributed.

**Static-group comparison design**   a **research design** used in **quasi-experimental research** involving two groups in which only one group, the **experimental group**, receives a **treatment**. Although a posttest is administered to each group (experimental and control), no pretest is administered. Individuals are not randomly assigned to groups.

**Statistical significance**   a term used in **quantitative research** to refer to results when the probability of their occurrence by chance is less than .05 in educational research in general, and less than .10 in action research projects. Significant findings do *not* mean that your study is necessarily important or meaningful (see distinction between statistical significance and educational significance in Chapter 7). Significant findings mean that the probability that your research findings would have occurred by chance, without the **treatment**, is low (see **level of significance**).

Let's say you were conducting a study by comparing two groups (e.g., period 4 and period 7 classes) as regards their achievement levels in science. You set up a **non-equivalent control group design** and after a period of 4 months you posttest both groups on science achievement. You employ a statistical technique (e.g., the **t-Test**) to determine whether or not one group (class) scored *significantly* higher than the other group. Let's say the t-Test analysis indicates the following finding: $p < .01$ (for an explanation on how to arrive at this statistically significant finding, see Chapter 6). This means that the probability ($p$) that the difference in achievement levels occurred by mere chance is less than 1% (less than one chance in a hundred), which is a statistically significant finding.

How do you know that this finding is statistically significant? Recall, as noted above, that in order to assert a statistically significant finding you must achieve a $p$ (probability factor) of less than .05 in educational research in general, and less than .10 in action research projects. Since $p < .01$, your findings are statistically significant.

A caveat: many people think that arriving at a statistically significant finding is, by itself, sufficient to incorporate a particular practice or program, for example. This may not be necessarily true. See discussions in Chapters 2, 3, and 7 to determine whether or not it makes sense to rely only on a statistically significant result.

**Subjects** (*Ss*)    individuals who have been selected or have volunteered to participate in a study. Sometimes researchers like to refer to people who participate in their study as "participants," rather than using the more manipulative word *subjects*. Subject is often abbreviated simply as "S". *S1* would connote subject one. In survey research, the "subject" is often called the "respondent."

**Survey**    a general term for any **instrument** used to assess attitudes or views of respondents. **Questionnaires, interviews,** and **focus groups** are types of surveys. Surveys are, perhaps, the most common methods for **data collection** used in action research.

**t-Test**    a popular and common statistical technique that determines the degree of significance between the **means** of two groups. In other words, the purpose of a t-Test is to determine whether the difference between two means is statistically significant. See Chapter 6 for a complete explanation and application.

**Teacher-made tests**    **testing** or **assessment** procedures created by classroom teachers for purposes of measuring growth in a particular content area. Three types of teacher-made tests are common: **norm-referenced, criterion-referenced,** or **performance-based.** In action research projects, teacher-made tests are quite commonly used.

**Testing**   refers to any form of measurement that yields clear, consistent, meaningful data about a person's knowledge, aptitudes, intelligence, or other traits. **Standardized** and **norm-referenced tests** are examples.

**Theory**   a statement of interrelated sets of assumptions and propositions which help us to explain our world. Theories are like mental road maps, guiding the way we perceive the world. Action research contributes very little, if at all, to theory development. Still, one may conduct an action research project to assess a particular theory.

**Time series design**   See **single-subject design** because the two terms are related.

**Treatment**   (synonymous with **intervention**) any specific instructional practice, program, or procedure that is implemented by a researcher in order to investigate its effect on the behavior or achievement of an individual or a group.

   Examples of treatments or interventions are behavioral management strategies, various textbook series, different methods of teaching, use of instructional technology as well as a host of other instructional methods, and many other programs, procedures, and practices. As an educational leader, you'll need to evaluate such treatments in order to decide whether they should be retained, modified, or discarded.

**Triangulation**   refers to multiple research approaches, data sources, **data collection** procedures, and analytic procedures. Triangulation strengthens the credibility of data collection and analysis as well as findings. Action researchers should appreciate that the inclusion of both qualitative and quantitative methods is desirable. Triangulation can also be used within each approach to research, especially in qualitative studies. Qualitative researchers emphasize the importance of triangulating on the basis of data sources, data collection methods, researcher perspectives, and theoretical frameworks. To the extent to which you can *triangulate*, you will make more effective decisions. For further explanation see Chapters 2 and 5.

**Unobtrusive measures**   refer to **data collection** methods that are obtained without directly involving subjects or participants. An educational leader who determines, for example, staff morale by examining the quantity and pattern of staff attendance by collecting written reports and documents utilizes an *unobtrusive measure* in the sense that data can be obtained without conferring with the staff directly.

**Validity**   refers to the extent to which a test, survey, or some other **instrument** measures what it is intended to measure.

At the outset of *Action Research* you were asked to complete a pretest (Appendix A) on your knowledge of some aspects of research. If the pretest was comprised of mathematical questions only, then the test would *not* be valid as it did not measure your knowledge of research, but rather your ability to compute and solve mathematical problems.

There are four (4) general types of validity: *concurrent, construct, content,* and *predictive*. Descriptions of each type of validity are not necessary since for action research projects you will unlikely ever need to use any of these four types of validity.

Perhaps the only exception would be use of *content* validity, to some extent. In the previous example, a **content analysis** of the curriculum or knowledge base of action research would be undertaken and then the test items on the pretest would be compared to the *content* base to ascertain that the questions on the pretest reflect the content.

Have you ever taken a test in which you said, "we never covered this stuff?!" If you were to administer, for example, a test to a group of 12th graders based on Chapter 12 in their social studies textbook, you would check for *content* validity after writing the test to see whether or not answers to each question can be found in the chapter. If each question is, in fact, derived from the content of Chapter 12, then your test may be said to have *content* validity. By the way, determining content validity for standardized tests involves more sophisticated procedures.

Two other types of validity, although not thought of highly by many experts in the field, are useful for action research purposes: *consensual* and *face* validity.

*Consensual* validity would be ascertained by asking people who will not be administered the test or survey (e.g., a colleague or a student in another class) whether or not the questions selected for inclusion are appropriate given the purpose of the assessment.

*Face* validity would be ascertained by asking participants or subjects to share their views about how valid a test or survey appears. Ever take an examination that was fair because it accurately reflected the content of the course? Such an exam might have high face validity. The converse could, of course, also be true if the content of the course didn't match the questions asked on the exam.

Know that, like **reliability**, the coefficient of validity is determined. The validity coefficient is likewise expressed in hundredths and the closer the coefficient comes to +1.00, the more valid the **instrument** is considered.

See explanation of **internal validity** and **external validity** above.

**Variable**   any factor having two or more values or distinguishably different properties or characteristics. Two examples of variables are:

*Sex* or *gender*—two distinct properties are maleness and femaleness,

*Mathematics achievement*—multiple properties are represented by different student test scores.

There are two (2) types of variables: dependent and independent:

A **dependent variable** is one that represents a desired instructional *outcome*, such as student achievement or high school attendance.

An **independent variable** is one whose relationship to the dependent variable is being investigated. In a study that attempts to correlate gender and science achievement, gender is the independent variable and reading achievement is the desired outcome or dependent variable.

Some independent variables cannot be manipulated by the researcher to determine their effect on a particular dependent variable. For example, if you were to investigate the years of experience of a group of teachers on morale levels, the independent variable in this case (the number of years of experience) cannot be manipulated because you have no control over a teacher's experience. In other words, years of experience is a characteristic of a particular teacher that you, as researcher, cannot manipulate or control. You can't say, for instance, "for purposes of my study subject 1 (S1) will be assigned ten years of experience." In this case, the independent variable is non-manipulable.

Examples of manipulable variables are: type of textbook series, exposure to computer-assisted instruction, or a particular method of teaching (e.g., cooperative learning). Can you name one example of a non-manipulable variable and one example of a manipulable variable?

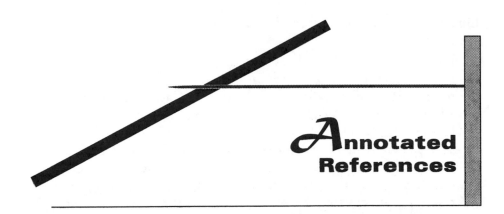

**Annotated References**

The literature on action research pertaining to teachers-as-researchers is extensive. For an annotated list of selected sources related to teachers, consult *Teaching Education*, Volume 8, Number 1, Spring/Summer, 1996.

The selected titles below represent a small portion of the literature in the field of action research. No attempt has been made to annotate every reference on the topic. I've selected some of the excellent works that should be part of your reference library.

Corey, S. M. (1953). *Action research to improve school practices*. New York: Teachers College Press.

The classic work in the field, this book represents the first systematic attempt to apply action research in education. Corey, a professor at Teachers College, Columbia University, encouraged teachers and supervisors to use action research to improve their own practice. Corey, a man ahead of his time, advocated that fundamental change could not occur without direct involvement of teachers *and* supervisors. Not a "how-to" volume, Corey's work lays the groundwork for systematic inquiry into practical problems in schools. His advocacy for supervisors to play an active role in action research makes this book unique.

Elliott, J. (1991). *Action research for educational change*. Bristol, PA: Falmer Press.

Providing case study analyses to demonstrate the impact that action research can have on educational reform, this volume presents various collaborative research projects. Case studies focus on a variety of issues such as curriculum reform for average and below-average students, the Ford Teachers Project, and TSIQL (Teacher Student Interaction and Quality of Learning Project). Thus, Elliott, a well-known authority in the field of action research, provides concrete examples of direct applications of action research. Emphasizing the role of teachers, this well-organized and clearly written book indicates the benefits that action research has on teaching and learning. Elliott's book has been published in Spanish under the title *El cambio educativo, desde la investigacion-accion*, 1993.

Fink, A., & Kosecoff, J. (1985). *How to conduct surveys: A step-by-step guide*. Newbury Park, CA: Sage Publications.

This book is one of the most useful of the texts that discuss survey construction and design. Any action researcher will benefit from this well-organized, easy-to-read guide to survey construction. Various types of surveys are discussed and many practical examples provided.

Glickman, C. D. (1995). *Action research: Inquiry, reflection, and decision-making* (video). ASCD.

This video series describes the basic steps of action research. Three case studies are presented showing how action research has guided an elementary school, a junior high school, and an entire school district. Interviews with Carl Glickman and Emily Calhoun explain why action research ensures sound decision making because decisions are developed from concrete data, rather than from snap judgments. Teachers and administrators also relate how action research helps them pinpoint problems and develop solutions that work. The video includes a 5-step approach to action research: selecting a focus; collecting data; organizing data; analyzing and interpreting data; and taking action.

Herman, J. L., & Winters, L. (1992). *Tracking your school's success: A guide to sensible evaluation*. Newbury Park, CA: Corwin Press.

A highly readable and informative guide to evaluation, this book enumerates practical evaluation strategies to match your school's needs, priorities, and goals to action research projects. The steps included in this text were used as a basis for discussing evaluation research in this book. Highly recommended!

McLean, J. E. (1995). *Improving education through action research: A guide for administrators and teachers*. Thousand Oaks, CA: Corwin Press.

One of the few, if not only, works written on action research for administrators, this brief handbook provides a cogent rationale for using action research to enhance school improvement. One of the book's contributions is to illustrate how computer applications can easily be used by practitioners to conduct action research.

McNiff, J. (1991). *Action research: Principles and practice*. London: Routledge.

Advocating that educational research be taken out of the confines of academia, McNiff makes an impassioned plea for action research by practitioners. McNiff provides a cogent rationale and reviews some of the major philosophical tenets of action research. She provides some practical strategies for starting an action research project and provides interesting case studies of attempts at applying action research. This work is an important contribution to the literature in the field and serves as an introduction to action research.

Sagor, R. (1992). *How to conduct collaborative action research*. Alexandria, VA: Association for Supervision and Curriculum Development.

A brief book that describes how teachers can use collaborative action research to improve teaching. After defining and providing a rationale for collaborative action research, this booklet presents a practical 5-step approach, which includes a particularly useful chapter on data collection.

Sanders, J. R. (1992). *Evaluating school programs: An educator's guide.* Newbury Park, CA: Corwin Press.

This work is a practical general guide to help you plan and conduct evaluations of any school program. The five-step approach adopted by the author is easy to follow and one which I have personally used to evaluate many programs. Highly recommended!

Seidman, I. E. (1991). *Interviewing as qualitative research: A guide for researchers in education and the social sciences.* New York: Teachers College Press.

In my estimation, this book is the most useful guide to in-depth interviewing as a research approach. This work demonstrates that interviewing, as a qualitative approach, is applicable to a wide variety of educational situations. Practical methods for conducting interview research are discussed and guidelines are provided for easy adoption. The steps to follow when conducting an interview are outlined clearly.

Stringer, E. T. (1996). *Action research: A handbook for practitioners.* Thousand Oaks, CA: Sage Publications.

Introducing the teacher practitioner to some basics of research, this volume describes a community-based action research model. Framing a "look, think, act" rationale or methodology for action research, this well-organized book provides a convincing rationale for the legitimacy of action research.

# Resources

*Education Literature Review*

Demands made on supervisors and teachers are tremendous. Consequently, many educational leaders who would love to "keep up with the educational literature" simply can't find the time. *The Education Literature Review* summarizes articles in ten selected journals, including *Educational Leadership, Phi Delta Kappan, Harvard Educational Review, American School Board Journal, Principal,* and *NASSP Bulletin.* This resource will keep you abreast of the latest research in the field.

*Institute for Responsive Education*

The Institute is a national non-profit research and development organization committed to community-based approaches to systemic educational change. One of the major projects sponsored by this organization is to encourage schools and districts to collaborate with their community to find ways of improving teaching and learning. The central mission is to conduct research, evaluations, policy analyses, and dissemination to produce new and useful knowledge about how families, schools, and communities influence student motivation, learning, and development. The Institute has published several reports outlining action research projects on varied topics. If your school or district is interested in large-scale collaborative or schoolwide action research, the Institute is perhaps the best source of information. Write:

Institute for Responsive Education and the Center on Families, Communities, Schools, and Children's Learning
605 Commonwealth Avenue, 6th floor
Boston, MA 02215
(617) 353-3309.

# Additional Non-annotated Resources

*Action Researcher: The Magazine for Action Researchers Everywhere*
Hyde Publications
57 Exeter Road
Bournemouth, BH2 5AF, U.K.
(01202) 292621

The Gold File
NASSP
Information Services
1904 Association Drive
Reston, VA 22091-1537
1-800-253-PRIN

NOTE: The Gold File is particularly useful because for a nominal fee you can order dozens of some of the most recent articles on a specific topic. The Gold File index lists more than 650 topics, including technology, professional growth, diversity issues, inclusion, learning theories, school restructuring, and much more. The time and resources expended in usual research efforts are worth the expense of obtaining information from the Gold File. Educational leaders with limited time are urged to consider reviewing the literature on a given topic by referring to this valuable resource.

*Management Development Associates, Inc.*
PO Box 9328 - Drawer U
Winter Haven, Florida 33883-9328

*National Center for Restructuring Schools, Education, and Teaching*
Box 110
Teachers College, Columbia University
New York, NY 10027
(212) 678-3432

*National Center for Accelerated Schools*
School of Education
Stanford University
Stanford, CA 94305-3084
(415) 926-3300

*Participatory Research Group*
720 Bathurst Street, Suite 500
Toronto, Ontario, Canada M5S 2R4
416-588-6989

# Resources on the Web

1.  Simple and complex directories:
    *   http://www.yahoo.com
    *   http://www.infoseek.com
    *   http://www.altavista.com
    *   http://www.webcrawler.com
    *   http://www.lycos.com
    *   http://www.excite.com
    *   http://www.dogpile.com

2.  ERIC (Educational Resources Information Center)—1-800-USE-ERIC
    - e-mail address: askeric@ericir.syr.edu

      NOTE: You can simply e-mail your request for a series of references on a specific topic and within 48 hours one of the ERIC researchers will e-mail you back the citations (not the actual articles) you requested. For instance, if I wanted to know what articles ERIC held for Howard Gardner I would simply write to the address above and request this information. Are there limits to using this approach? Why not try to write a message and find out how you can best use this resource?

    - Web: http://www.edrs.com

      This Web address links you with ERIC directly. Browse ERIC as you would have had you gone to your local college/university library and used the ERIC CD-ROM.

    - Web: http:// www.ericsp.org

      This Web address links you with the ERIC Clearinghouse on Teaching and Teacher Education.

    - Web: http://ericir.syr.edu/

      This Web address links you with the ERIC Clearinghouse on Assessment and Evaluation and provides you with sample attitude scales and much more.

3.  Surf the NET (or WEB) to locate other valuable educational resources. Here are only some of the many resources I have personally found useful:
    - http://www.education-world.com
    - http://www.ed.gov
    - http://www.ascd.org/
    - http://aera.net/
    - http://www.care.panam.edu/
    - http://mel.lib.mi.us/education/edu-research.html
    - http://www.coh.modlang.arizona.edu/inst/eda663/links.html
    - http://www.eval.org/

4.  A wonderful reference list for Web resources can be found in the October 1996 issue of *Technology & Learning*. Also, consult a fine resource titled *The Best Web Sites for Teachers* by Sharp, Levine and Sharp, 1996, published by the International Society for Technology in Education, Eugene, Oregon.

# Appendix A
## Pretest

---

## Part I

---

Choose the answer that is correct or most nearly correct.

1. You are an Assistant Principal in an elementary school and you want to raise student attendance rates in grade 5 by fostering school spirit. You initiate a program that fosters school spirit by involving students in school-wide projects, elections, and competitive academic contests. Which of the following methods of data collection would most accurately allow you to conclude that, indeed, school spirit affects higher rates of student attendance?

    a. descriptive data that includes pretest/posttest attendance rates
    b. attitudinal surveys distributed to students
    c. informal observations
    d. analysis of standardized test scores

2. Janice Barnett, Supervisor of Curriculum, wanted to evaluate a new reading series that her district was considering. She decided to study fifth graders in a particular school. She selected one class of fifth grade students who were introduced to the new reading series. Another comparable fifth grade class would use the "old" reading series. At the end of the year, Ms. Barnett tested all students in reading comprehension. What type of study is this?

   a.   pretest-posttest control group
   b.   non-equivalent
   c.   case study
   d.   historical

3. The major purpose of using an interview protocol is to

   a.   offer respondents a way to participate in the interview without having the interviewer present.
   b.   increase the chances that the respondent will respond honestly.
   c.   be able to conduct the interview in case the interviewer is not present.
   d.   provide the interviewer with a set of guidelines for conducting the interview.

4. Classify the following study:

   RESEARCH HYPOTHESIS: Achievement in Spanish is affected by class size

   PROCEDURE: At the beginning of the school year the students in Highpoint High School are randomly assigned to one of two types of Spanish classes: a class with 20 students or less and a class of 40 or more. The two groups are compared at the end of the year on Spanish achievement.

   a.   historical
   b.   descriptive
   c.   correlational
   d.   experimental

5.  As an educational leader you will have to evaluate many programs in order to ascertain their effectiveness. Let's say you are experimenting with a new supervisory technique known as "clinical supervision." After five months of its implementation, you wish to evaluate its usefulness. You therefore prepare a number of evaluative tools in order to determine whether or not to continue its use,

Clinical supervision in the example above is known as the
    a.  dependent variable.
    b.  independent variable.
    c.  treatment.
    d.  status dependent.
    e.  coefficient.

6.  You are a principal in an intermediate school with a population of 750 students. As indicated by recent district-wide tests, student reading achievement has increased. You are interested in discovering how well the students in your school perform in reading compared to students in other schools throughout the country. Which of the following instruments of measurement would you use?
    a.  a classroom achievement test
    b.  observation
    c.  examination of school records
    d.  a questionnaire
    e.  a standardized test

7.  As an AP in an inner-city elementary school with a population of 650 students, you have recently addressed the 5th grade assembly about their behavior in the lunchroom. You explained a number of behavioral procedures for them to follow. Before you decide to take more drastic measures, which of the following instruments of measurement would you use?
    a.  a written essay test
    b.  a questionnaire
    c.  an interview
    d.  examine records
    e.  observation

8. Which of the following is the best example of an "unobtrusive instrument?"
   a.  supervisor walks into class for an on-the-spot observation
   b.  supervisor peeks into window of classroom without letting the teacher see him/her
   c.  supervisor determines staff morale by examining the quantity and pattern of staff attendance
   d.  interviewing teachers
   e.  anonymous questionnaire

9. A quasi-experimental design involving one group which is repeatedly pretested, exposed to an experimental treatment, and repeatedly posttested is known as a
   a.  pretest/posttest design.
   b.  posttest only design.
   c.  time-series design.
   d.  revolving series design.
   e.  none of these.

10. Sampling where every tenth name is picked from an alphabetical list of students would be an example of which type of sampling?
   a.  cluster.
   b.  stratified.
   c.  random.
   d.  systematic.
   e.  none of these.

11. In qualitative data analysis the goal is to
   a.  discover patterns among the data.
   b.  uncover errors in data interpretation.
   c.  compare findings to quantitative studies.
   d.  all of the above.

12. A "good" sample is one that is
    a.  free of random errors.
    b.  large.
    c.  representative.
    d.  small.
    e.  systematic.

13. You take fifty 4th grade students, assign 25 randomly to one class and 25 randomly to the other class. Both groups are measured beforehand. Two different treatments are presented, then a follow-up measurement is given. Which type of design is this?
    a.  pretest-posttest control group design
    b.  pretest-posttest only design
    c.  one-shot case study
    d.  non-equivalent control group design
    e.  one-group pretest-posttest design

14. Mrs. James teaches computers at P. S. 999. She has a new programmed instruction textbook which she wishes to use with her classes. She decides to test the effectiveness of the new textbook. She chooses two classes that rank similar in ability on a pretest in computer literacy. She gives her programmed text to group A but with group B she continues her normal instruction. At the end of the semester, she gives a test on computer knowledge and discovers that the class using the new text outperformed the other group (B). She concludes that the new text should be incorporated in all the classes. What research design did Mrs. James use?
    a.  non-equivalent design
    b.  interrupted time series design
    c.  pretest-posttest design
    d.  pretest-posttest control group design
    e.  control group only design

15. Mr. Solomon is a supervisor in an elementary school. Mr. Jones, a 6th grade teacher, complains that one student, Billy, is disruptive and recalcitrant. Mr. Solomon tells the teacher to record Billy's behavior in anecdotal form for two weeks before scheduling a conference with the guidance counselor. During the first week, Mr. Jones discovers that Billy acts out 26 times. During the second week, he acts out 22 times. During the third week, Mr. Jones meets with the guidance counselor to work out Billy's problems. The counselor sets up a special reward system for Billy. During the fourth week, Billy acts out 18 times. During the fifth week, the disturbances decrease to only 5 times. Mr. Jones and the counselor conclude that the technique used with Billy is successful. What research design was employed?

    a. pretest-posttest control group design
    b. control group only design
    c. interrupted time series design
    d. single measurement design
    e. non-equivalent control group design

16. As an educational leader who wishes to establish a new science program in your school what is the first step that should generally be taken?

    a. consult with parents
    b. hand out new textbooks and get feedback from teachers
    c. establish summative evaluative criteria
    d. disseminate goals and objectives to all staff
    e. needs assessment

17. The greatest obstacle an educational leader faces in undertaking evaluative research is that he/she

    a. is deluged with other administrative and instructional tasks.
    b. doesn't really care to go to the trouble of undertaking extensive research.
    c. is not knowledgeable about how to conduct research in schools.
    d. is not given sufficient leeway from the building principal.
    e. has no support from the district office or central board of education.

18. The purpose of giving a pretest to both the experimental and control groups is to
    a.   ensure equivalence of posttest results.
    b.   define parameters of sampling techniques.
    c.   ensure group comparability.
    d.   develop reliability of assessments.
    e.   all of these.

19. When would you employ a Mann-Whitney U-Test?
    a.   in collaborative planning
    b.   assessing posttest results in a quasi-experimental study
    c.   assessing posttest results in a single measurement design
    d.   when randomization is impossible

20. A researcher wished to test the effectiveness of a new reading program as compared to an older one. If the difference between the two programs was statistically significant at the $p<.05$ level, this means that
    a.   the new program made meaningful changes in the student's reading skills.
    b.   the results are probably due to the researcher's program and not a chance occurrence.
    c.   the probability of being incorrect is 95 chances out of 100.
    d.   the new program should be introduced to all grades.
    e.   the statistical analysis used was the correct one and the program has educational significance.

21. Which is not an accurate statement regarding the four steps in action research?
    a.   Defining a problem can be teacher or supervisor initiated.
    b.   Always state the hypothesis, when applicable.
    c.   In the research design you must state how the sample was formed and what statistical measures will be employed.
    d.   The final stage is to collect and analyze the data.

22. Likert scales usually have half the items worded positively and half negatively in order to
    a.   ensure validity.
    b.   control for intervening variables.
    c.   avoid response sets.
    d.   calculate statistical regression.
    e.   ensure a mathematical balance among the questions.

23. A study entitled "pupil attitude toward mainstreaming" would most likely be
    a.   historical.
    b.   descriptive.
    c.   experimental.
    d.   correlational.

24. To determine if a particular textbook is appropriate for a 5th grade class, your analysis would entail which type of research?
    a.   content analysis
    b.   ethnography
    c.   case study
    d.   naturalism
    e.   simulation

25. A test of significance used to determine whether there is significant difference between two means at a selected probability level is known as
    a.   ANOVA.
    b.   self-report research.
    c.   chi square.
    d.   t-Test.
    e.   analysis of covariance.

26. The degree to which a test consistently measures whatever it measures is
    a.   reliability.
    b.   validity.
    c.   coefficient.
    d.   statistical analysis.
    e.   none of these.

27. An instrument which asks respondents to strongly agree, agree, disagree, or strongly disagree to a particular statement is called the
    a.  Likert scale.
    b.  Chi Square scale distribution.
    c.  Null Hypothesis.
    d.  Flander's Interaction Analysis.
    e.  Eisner's Continuum.

28. When a group of subjects sense that they are part of an experiment and react in a special way it is known as the
    a.  John Henry effect.
    b.  Norton's Law.
    c.  Halo effect.
    d.  Hawthorne effect.
    e.  Pearson r.

29. Which of the following is an identifying characteristic of a well-formulated research hypothesis?
    a.  it is stated in question form
    b.  it includes a detailed description of the population under study
    c.  it includes references to educational theory
    d.  it is always short
    e.  it specifies the variables to be studied and the nature of the expected relationship between these variables

30. "The correlation between the amount of time spent playing video games and scores on a science exam is .12." What does this mean?
    a.  there is a strong relationship between the variables but no causal statements can be made
    b.  there is practically no relationship between the 2 variables
    c.  there is a strong negative relationship between the variables
    d.  there is a cause and effect relationship between the 2 variables
    e.  not enough information is given to assess this study

Answers to Part I: 1. b; 2. b; 3. d; 4. d; 5. c; 6. e; 7. e; 8. c; 9. c; 10. d; 11. a; 12. c; 13. a; 14. a; 15. c; 16. e; 17. c; 18. c; 19. b; 20. b; 21. d; 22. c; 23. b; 24. a; 25. d; 26. a; 27. a; 28. d; 29. e; 30. b.

# Part II

Here is a question asked on the Board of Examiner's principal examination in New York City some years ago when I took my license:

"Assume that one of the teachers assigned to an elementary school of which you are the principal tells you in June that she has seen demonstrated at a recent convention a set of reading materials consisting of packets, each containing a coordinated filmstrip, a long playing record, and a colorful illustrated book. She says that these materials have not been evaluated as to their usefulness. She is eager to undertake such an evaluation and asks permission to use these packets during the next school year as supplementary reading materials in the second grade class which she will teach that year. An evaluation of their usefulness would be undertaken at the end of the school year, she explains, solely by judging through careful observation whether the children have grown a year in reading, more than a year, or less than a year.

Of the five 2nd grade classes scheduled for the coming school year, her class is to be the middle one in ability. The children programmed for it have reading grade levels, at present, which range from reading readiness to 1.5.

QUESTION: Evaluate, justifying each of your conclusions, the research plan proposed by the teacher referred to above. Be certain, in your answer, to cover each of the important considerations which should go into the construction of a meaningful and useful research design."

## Appendix B
## Sample Consent Forms

Reprinted with permission, Brown and Benchmark Publishers.

### Example of a Research Participant Consent Form

I, _____ (Printed Name of Participant), agree to participate in the research project, "Title of Project," being carried out by "Name of Researcher(s)." I have been informed by the researchers of the general nature of the project and of any foreseeable potential risks.

I understand that I may withdraw from this project at any time, and that even if I do not withdraw, I have the right to withhold permission for the researcher(s) to use any data based on my participation.

I also understand that upon my request, the researcher(s) will provide me with a written summary of the project's findings.

_____
(Participant's signature) (Date)

## Example of a Parental Consent Form

I, _____ (Printed Name of Parent or Guardian), agree to permit _____ (Printed Name of Child), to participate in the research project, "Title of Project," being carried out by "Name of Researcher(s)." I have been informed by the researchers of the general nature of the project and of any foreseeable potential risks. I understand the following:

1.  My child may withdraw from this project at any time.

2.  I may withdraw permission for my child to participate in the project at any time.

3.  Even if my child completes the project, I have the right to withhold permission for the researcher(s) to use any data based on my child's participation.

4.  Upon my request, the researcher(s) will provide me with a written summary of the project's findings.

_____
(Signature of Parent or Guardian)

_____
(Date)

_____
(Relationship to Child)

# Appendix C
# Are You a Good Writer?

Good writing is an art and a craft. You can achieve clear communication by presenting ideas in an orderly manner and by expressing yourself smoothly and precisely. Are you a good writer?

Good writing takes practice. Three approaches to achieving effective communication are: (1) compose an outline and just write without regard to style, punctuation, and grammar; (2) put aside the first draft, then reread it after a delay; and (3) ask a colleague to critique the draft for you.

I suggest you consult some of the many excellent publications available on writing style (see below). Some of you might benefit from taking a course on writing style as well. I suggest you carefully assess your writing ability and take the necessary steps for improvement. Good writing skills are necessary for continued success in your professional endeavors. Good luck *and* good writing!

NOTE: These questions refer to writing for research purposes, not necessarily for general writing.

Circle the correct/acceptable/better sentence for each of the following pairs of examples:

1.   a. Glanz (1994) designed the experiment.
     b. The experiment was designed by Glanz (1994).

2.   a. Participants sat in comfortable chairs equipped with speakers that delivered the tone stimuli.
     b. The participants were sitting in comfortable chairs equipped with speakers that delivered the tone stimuli.

3.   a. Glanz (1994) presented the same results.
     b. Glanz (1994) presents the same results.

4.   a. Since that time investigators from several studies have used this method.
     b. Since that time investigators from several studies used this method.

5.   a. The data are complete.
     b. The data is complete.

6.   a. The percentage of correct responses as well as the speed of the responses increases with practice.
     b. The percentage of correct responses as well as the speed of the responses increase with practice.

7.   a. The phenomena occur every 100 years.
     b. The phenomena occurs every 100 years.

8.   a. Neither the participants nor the confederate was in the room.
     b. Neither the participants nor the confederate were in the room.

9.   a. The positions in the sequence were changed, and the test was re-run.
     b. The positions in the sequence were changed, and the test rerun.

10.  a. The group improved its scores 30 percent.
     b. The group improved their scores 30 percent.

11.  a. The rats that completed the task successfully were rewarded.
     b. The rats who completed the task successfully were rewarded.

12.  a. Name the participant who you found scored above the median.
     b. Name the participant whom you found scored above the median.

13.  a. We had nothing to do with their being the winners.
     b. We had nothing to do with them being the winners.

14.  a. Using this procedure, the investigator tested the subjects.
     b. The investigator tested the subjects using this procedure.

15.  a. I hope this is not the case.
     b. Hopefully, this is not the case.

16.  a. Brag (1989) found that participants performed well, whereas Bohr (1990) found that participants did poorly.
     b. Brag (1989) found that participants performed well, while Bohr (1990) found that participants did poorly.

17.  a. The names were difficult both to pronounce and to spell.
     b. The names were difficult both to pronounce and spell.

18.  a. In regard to this matter, . . .
     b. In regards to this matter, . . .

19.  a. Charles's friend
     b. Charles' friend

20.  a. None of us is perfect.
     b. None of us are perfect.

Answers: choice "a" for all questions

## Suggested book list:

1.    Consult the classic—Strunk, W., Jr., & White, E. B. (1979). *The elements of style* (3rd ed.). New York: Macmillan.

2.    Bates, J. D. (1980). *Writing with precision: How to write so that you cannot be misunderstood* (3rd ed.). Washington, D.C.: Acropolis Books.

3.    Consult the latest edition of the American Psychological Association (APA) manual for other relevant books.

# Appendix D
# Evaluation Criteria
# for Report

Students need to be informed in advance how their projects will be evaluated. Below is a list of criteria students have found useful:

The research project will be graded based on the following criteria (serious deficiency in any one of these criteria can affect your grade):

(1) *Content:* Does your paper reflect a knowledge and understanding of the content/topic/problem? Is the problem stated clearly and precisely? Is the author aware of critical issues that relate to the problem?

Comments: _____

_____

_____

(2) *Citations:* Are appropriate and sufficient authorities cited? Does the research include at least 6 articles and 1 book (7 references)? Are the references timely (within the last 5 years)?

Comments: _____

_____

_____

(3)   *Coherence:* Is the paper well organized so that ideas "hang together"? Are ideas developed clearly? Are all sections of the research project included?

Comments: _____

_____

_____

(4)   *Clarity:* Is the paper clear and easy to read? Is it aesthetically pleasing?

Comments: _____

_____

_____

(5)   *Control:* Does the writing reflect good "technical control," i.e., complete sentences, spelling, correct punctuation, grammar, paragraph development, etc.?

Comments: _____

_____

_____

# Appendix E
# Brief Description of APA

The *Publication Manual* of the American Psychological Association (APA) (1994) is the accepted manual of style for writing reports in the social sciences. I recommend that my students adhere to this manual of style for several reasons:

(1)  APA is relatively easy to learn and use;

(2)  APA is widely used and known; and

(3)  APA enhances the professional appearance of reports.

Although you may have to refer to the *Publication Manual* for details about specific guidelines for documenting sources, here are eleven (11) basic rules and sample references that should, at least, get you started:

(1)  APA uses no footnotes.

(2)  All references are placed in the main body of the text as follows: Jones (1995) stated that . . .

> To find the Jones reference you would consult the list of *references* placed at the end of the report that lists alphabetically, by author's last name, all works referred to in the report. In this example, you merely paraphrase what Jones stated, rather than quoting directly from the source. Since paraphrasing is used, no mention of page numbers is necessary.

If you quote an author in the text of your report without mentioning her/his name, you might reference the work as follows: It is maintained that cooperative learning is an effective means of . . . (Johnson & Johnson, 1990). Note the use of the ampersand (&). The ampersand is always used, instead of *and*, when referenced with parentheses (for more explanation see below). To find the reference in which "cooperative learning" is explained, consult the list of *references* placed at the end of the report. Note that since paraphrasing is again employed, no mention of page numbers is necessary.

A direct quote within the text is referenced as follows: Moreover, Tanner and Tanner (1987) were correct when they stated that "the development of public education and the field of supervision are so completely intertwined that they defy separation, even for purposes of analysis" (p. 4).

Note that a page number is cited because a direct quote is used. Page is abbreviated as "*p.*" Notice the placement of the period after the closed parenthesis. Also, notice that *and* is used in "Tanner and Tanner" because you mention the names of the authors within the text, instead of just in parentheses.

Offset a lengthy quote as follows:
Spears (1953) stated:

> Thirty or forty years ago, when supervision was first settling down in the organizational scheme of things as a service to the classroom teacher, a supervisor was a supervisor. Today, when supervision is attaching itself to almost anything that has to do with furthering learning, a supervisor masquerades under a miscellaneous array of titles. Supervision today often travels incognito. (p. 84)

Note the page number placement at the end of the quote with parentheses, but without a period afterwards.

(3)  In general, APA recommends use of past tense when reporting research findings: Smith (1996) reported, not reports.

(4)  Use of "and" or "&". In reference list at the end of the report, always use "&". In text, the "&" is used within any parentheses, but when noting authors within text, without use of parentheses, the "and" is used. For example, in text you write Flinders and Bellack (1993) reported that . . .

(5)   Document a book in references as follows:

Glanz, J. (1991). *Bureaucracy and professionalism: The evolution of public school supervision.* New Jersey: Fairleigh Dickinson University Press.

Note several unique aspects of APA when referencing a book:

(A) Title of book is italicized (or underlined), including period.

(B) Always use initials for first and middle names.

(C) Only first letter of first word in title is capitalized as well as first letter in any word appearing after a colon. Always capitalize first letter of proper nouns wherever one appears in title.

(D) Year is placed in parentheses followed by a period.

(E) Usually two spaces placed after:

(a) name before year
(b) year before title
(c) title before place of publication

(F) When only state or country for place of publication is referenced, type complete spelling as in "New Jersey." However, when more specific information about place of publication is presented, reference as follows: "Cranford, NJ". Note that abbreviation for state is used with no periods as might usually be found in "N.J.".

---

## Exercise

1. APA REFERENCE FOR A BOOK TITLE

Which book is referenced correctly according to APA?

a. Waite, D. (1995). *Rethinking instructional supervision: Notes on its language and culture.* London: The Falmer Press.
b. Waite, Duncan. (1995). *Rethinking instructional supervision: Notes on its language and culture.* London: The Falmer Press.
c. Waite, D. 1995. *Rethinking instructional supervision: Notes on its Language and Culture.* London: The Falmer Press.
d. Waite, Duncan. (1995). *Rethinking Instructional Supervision: Notes on its language and culture.* London: The Falmer Press.
e. Waite, Duncan. (1995). *Rethinking Instructional Supervision: Notes On Its Language and Culture.* London: The Falmer Press.

Answer: choice "a"

---

(6) Document an article in references as follows:

> Glanz, J. (1994). Dilemmas of assistant principals in their supervisory role: Reflections of an assistant principal. *Journal of School Leadership, 4,* 577–593.

Note several unique aspects of APA when referencing an article:

(A)   Title of journal name is italicized (or underlined), including period, volume number, and comma following volume number.

(B)   As with a book, always use initials for first and middle names.

(C)   Only first letter of first word in title of article is capitalized as well as first letter in any word appearing after a colon. Always capitalize first letter of proper nouns.

(D)   As with a book, year is placed in parentheses followed by a period.

(E)   Usually two spaces placed after:
(a) name before year
(b) year before title
(c) title before name of journal.

(F)   Volume number is referenced by simply placing the number after name of journal preceded by a comma. Sometimes, an issue number is referenced as follows: "76(3)", which refers to volume number 76, issue number 3. An issue number is only referenced for journals that begin new pagination with each issue. For example, the *NASSP Bulletin,* a prominent journal in the field, begins each issue with page 1. Therefore, referencing any article published in this journal would include an issue number:

> Glanz, J. (1994). Where did the assistant principalship begin? Where is it headed? *NASSP Bulletin, 78*(564), 35–41.

> Notice that only the volume number is italicized along with journal name, but not issue number, which is always placed in parentheses.

(G)   Page numbers follow without designations of "p." or "pp.". Don't abbreviate numbers, such as "14–7", but rather state as "14–17". Note comma before page numbers to separate from volume number.

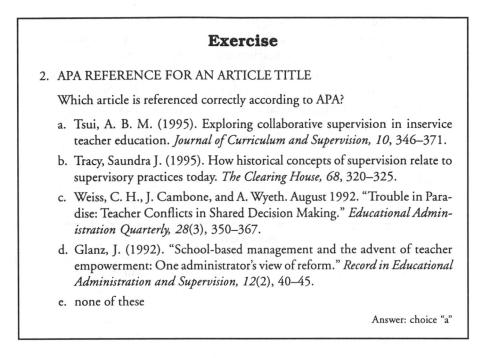

**Exercise**

2. APA REFERENCE FOR AN ARTICLE TITLE

Which article is referenced correctly according to APA?

a. Tsui, A. B. M. (1995). Exploring collaborative supervision in inservice teacher education. *Journal of Curriculum and Supervision, 10*, 346–371.

b. Tracy, Saundra J. (1995). How historical concepts of supervision relate to supervisory practices today. *The Clearing House, 68*, 320–325.

c. Weiss, C. H., J. Cambone, and A. Wyeth. August 1992. "Trouble in Paradise: Teacher Conflicts in Shared Decision Making." *Educational Administration Quarterly, 28*(3), 350–367.

d. Glanz, J. (1992). "School-based management and the advent of teacher empowerment: One administrator's view of reform." *Record in Educational Administration and Supervision, 12*(2), 40–45.

e. none of these

Answer: choice "a"

(7) Document a chapter or article in an edited volume as follows:

Garman, N. B. (1996). Is clinical supervision a viable model for use in the public schools? No. In J. Glanz & R. F. Neville (Eds.), *Educational supervision: Perspectives, issues, and controversies* (pp. 143–178). Norwood, MA: Christopher-Gordon Publishers.

Note several unique aspects of APA when referencing a chapter or article in an edited volume:

(A) Title of book is italicized (or underlined), including period.
(B) Always use initials for first and middle names.
(C) Only first letter of first word in title is capitalized as well as first letter in any word appearing after a colon. Always capitalize first letter of proper nouns.
(D) Year is placed in parentheses followed by a period.
(E) Usually two spaces placed after:
  (a) name before year
  (b) year before title of chapter or article
  (c) title before place of publication

(F)   When only state or country for place of publication is refer-enced, type complete spelling as in "New Jersey". However, when more specific information about place of publication is pre-sented, reference as follows: "Cranford, NJ". Note that abbre-viation for state is used with no periods as in "N.J.".

(G)   Names of editors (first initials, then last names). Editors' names separated by an ampersand. When only two editors', no comma between names. For three or more editors, comma is placed before ampersand.

(H)   Page numbers of chapter or article appear in parentheses as noted.

---

### Exercise

3.   APA REFERENCE FOR A CHAPTER OR ARTICLE in an edited volume

Which is correctly referenced according to APA?

a.   Pajak, E. (1993). Change and continuity in supervision and leadership. In Cawelti, G. (Ed.), *Challenges and achievements of American education* (pp. 158–186). Alexandria, VA: ASCD.

b.   Bolin, F., & Panaritis, P. (1992). Searching for a common purpose: A perspective on the history of supervision. In C. D. Glickman (Ed.), *Supervision in transition* (pp. 30–43). Alexandria, VA: ASCD.

c.   Firth, G. R. & Eiken, K. P. (1982). Impact of the schools' bureaucratic structure on supervision. In T. J. Sergiovanni (Ed.), <u>Supervision of teaching</u> (pp. 153–169). Washington, D. C.: ASCD.

d.   Glickman, C. D., Gordon, S. P., & Ross-Gordon, J. M. (1998). *Supervision of Instruction: A developmental approach.* Boston: Allyn and Bacon.

e.   none of these

Answer: choice "b"

---

(8)   Document a magazine article as follows:

Henry, W. A. (1990, April, 9). Beyond the melting pot. *Time, 135,* 28–31.

Note several unique aspects of APA when referencing a magazine article:

(A)   Title of journal name is italicized (or underlined), including pe-riod, volume number, and comma following volume number.

(B)  As with a book, always use initials for first and middle names.
(C)  Only first letter of first word in title of magazine article is capitalized as well as first letter in any word appearing after a colon. Always capitalize first letter of proper nouns.
(D)  As with a book, year is placed in parentheses followed by a period. However, include month and day magazine was published along with year of publication, as noted above.
(E)  Usually two spaces placed after:
     (a) name before year
     (b) year before title
     (c) title before name of magazine.
(F)  Volume number is referenced by simply placing the number after name of journal preceded by a comma.
(G)  Page numbers follow without designations of "p." or "pp.".

(9) Document a newspaper article as follows:

Schwartz, J. (1993, September 30). Obesity affects economic, social status. *The Washington Post*, pp. A1, A4.

(A)  Same documentation is used as with a magazine article except abbreviation "pp." for pages is used. "A1, A4" indicates that article appears on discontinuous pages.

(10) Document an edited book as follows:

Glanz, J., & Neville, R. F. (Eds.). (1996). *Educational supervision: Perspectives, issues, and controversies.* Norwood, MA: Christopher-Gordon Publishers.

(A)  Same documentation is used as with a regular book except abbreviation "Eds." is used to note the "editors".

---

### Exercise

4. APA REFERENCES

Which is referenced incorrectly according to APA?

a. Glanz, J., & Neville, R. F. (Eds.). (1996). *Educational supervision: Perspectives, issues, and controversies.* Norwood, MA: Christopher-Gordon Publishers.

b. Tracy, S. J. (1995). How historical concepts of supervision relate to supervisory practices today. *The Clearing House, 68,* 320–325.

c. Cooper, M. K. (1990, August 12). Crime in the cities. *The New York Times,* 44, 67.

d. Daresh, J. C. (1989). *Supervision as a proactive process.* New York: Longman.

e. none of these

Answer: choice "c"

---

(11) Document an electronic source as follows:

Glanz, J. (1997). Supervision news. [Online] Available: Http://www.kean.edu/~jglanz/

To obtain more information on electronic sources for APA citations, consult: Http://www.uvm.edu/~xli/reference/apa.html

## Sample Portion of a Paper in APA Style

The study of history is a struggle to understand the "unending dialogue between the present and the past" (Carr & Smith, 1961, p. 8). As such, the notion of temporality is relevant to understanding the flow of historical events. People and events cannot be explained only in terms of the present, but must be understood in terms of a past and a future as well. The past, present, and future, according to Cassirer, form an "undifferentiated unity and an indiscriminate whole" (Cassirer, 1953, p. 219). Kummel and Barnes (1966) explained this notion of temporality as a historical process "in which the past never assumes a final shape nor the future ever shuts its doors. Their essential interdependence also means, however, that there can be no progress without a retreat into the past in search of a deeper foundation" (p. 50).

The experience of reflective consciousness through historical inquiry implies an awareness of the past and its interconnectedness to present conditions and future possibilities. History, then, can be understood as an attempt to study the events and ideas of the past that have shaped human experience over time in order to inform current practice as well as to make more intelligent decisions for the future (Marsak, 1970).

History is more than simply recording all past experiences and events. Historians are interested in those aspects of the past that have historical significance. Since what may be historically significant to one may be irrelevant to another, the reconstruction of the past must be undertaken from different perspectives by different people. Moreover, significance is granted only when a sufficient amount of time has lapsed in order to ensure that contemporary demands alone do not dictate what is considered historically important (see e.g., Davis, 1992). Seen in this way, history is the retelling and interpretation of significant events of the past (Kliebard, 1995; Stephens, 1974).

The value of history is its concreteness, its placing of events, people, and theories within context (see e.g., Goodson, 1985; Kliebard, 1987). History supplies the context with which to view current proposals. More fundamentally, understanding how the field has come to take the shape it has is a compelling reason to undertake historical inquiry of supervision. History can also explore antecedents of current innovations or theories. Thus, having a supervision history will deepen and strengthen identity as a field of scholarship and provide a collective consciousness (cf., Garrett, 1994).

## References

Carr, E. H., & Smith, J. (1961). *What is history?* New York: Alfred A. Knopf Publisher.

Cassirer, E. (1953). *An essay on man: An introduction to a philosophy of human culture.* New York: Doubleday & Co.

Davis Jr., O. L. (1992). Memory, our educational practice, and history. *The Educational Forum, 56,* 375–379.

Garrett, A. W. (1994). Curriculum history's connections to the present: Necessary lessons for informed practice and theory. *Journal of Curriculum and Supervision, 9,* 390–395.

Goodson, F. (1985). History, context, and qualitative methods in the study of the curriculum. In R. G. Burgess (Ed.), *Strategies of educational research: Qualitative methods* (pp. 121–152). London: Falmer Press.

Kliebard, H. M. (1987). *The struggle for the American curriculum: 1893–1958.* New York: Routledge & Kegan Paul.

Kliebard, H. M. (1995). Why history of education? *The Journal of Educational Research, 88,* 194–199.

Kummel, F., & Barnes, M. N. (1966). Time as succession and the problem of duration. In J. T. Fraser (Ed.), *The voices of time* (pp. 31–55). New York: George Braziller.

Marsak, L. M. (1970). *The nature of historical inquiry.* New York: Holt, Rinehart, and Winston.

Stephens, L. D. (1974). *Probing the past: A guide to the study and teaching of history.* Boston: Allyn and Bacon.

Note two additional items:

(1) In text, when two or more references are noted within one set of parentheses, alphabetize according to author's last name. For example, as noted above: (see e.g., Goodson, 1985; Kliebard, 1987). Note: "e.g." is the abbreviation for "for example."

(2) In references list, if one author has two or more works cited, the earlier one is referenced first, as in:

> Kliebard, H. M. (1987). *The struggle for the American curriculum: 1893–1958.* New York: Routledge & Kegan Paul.
>
> Kliebard, H. M. (1995). Why history of education? *The Journal of Educational Research, 88,* 194–199.

# A Final Word

You will notice that the form and format for APA is a bit awkward, with its use of capitalization, no mentioning of author's first name, etc. You should consult the APA manual in order to accurately apply other rules for documentation. My purpose is only to introduce the style briefly and to indicate its importance. Investment in the *Publication Manual* is suggested. Knowledge of APA will serve you well in other courses and in writing any reports during your professional career. Happy referencing.

# Reference

American Psychological Association. (1994). *Publication manual of the American Psychological Association* (4th ed.). Washington, DC: Author.

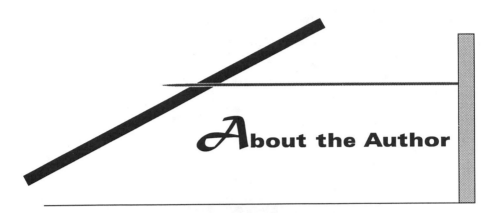

# About the Author

**Jeffrey Glanz** is an associate professor in the Department of Instruction, Curriculum, and Administration at Kean University located in Union, New Jersey. He is NCATE Coordinator and Associate Director of the Holocaust Foundation. He teaches graduate courses in supervision, curriculum, Holocaust studies, prejudice reduction, and action research. He served for four years on the editorial board of the *Journal of Curriculum and Supervision* and is currently an editorial board member of the *Journal of Educational Studies* and the *Record in Educational Leadership*. He also served as editor of *Focus on Education*, the New Jersey journal for ASCD. He is Director of the Instructional Supervision Network for ASCD. Dr. Glanz has authored *Bureaucracy and Professionalism: The Evolution of Public School Supervision*, co-edited *Educational Supervision: Perspectives, Issues, and Controversies*, is co-authoring *Supervision That Aims to Improve Teaching: Strategies and Techniques* to be published by Corwin Press, and is co-editing *Paradigm Debates in Curriculum and Supervision: Modern and Postmodern Perspectives* to be published by Greenwood Publishing Group.

# Author and Title Index

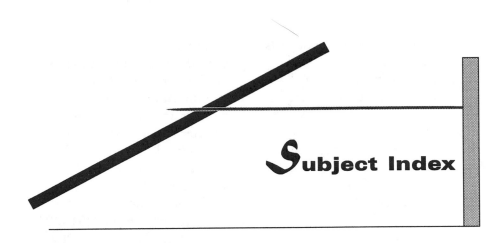

# $\mathcal{S}$ubject Index

## A

A-B-A-B single subject, 77–78
A-B-A single subject, 77
A-B single subject, 73, 76–77
Accuracy factors, 75–76
Achievement tests, 68, 145–146
Action research, 8–26. *See also*
  Research; Research design
  benefits, 21
  cyclical, 26–27
  defined, 2–3, 19–21
  evaluation, 12–17
  evolution, 17–19
  purposes, 19
  steps, 24–27
  types of, 8–12
Activity codes, 185
Administration
development, 115
evaluation, 126–127
AERA (American Educational
  Research Association), 19,
  241
Agents, change, 213–214

Allness principle, 42
Alternating treatment, 78
American Educational Research
  Association (AERA), 19, 241
American Psychological Associa-
  tion (APA), 299–308
Analysis. *See* Data analysis
Analysis of variance, 180–181
Analytic procedures, 184–187
ANCOVA (Analysis of covari-
  ance), 181
Annotated references, 273–280
ANOVA (Analysis of variance),
  180–181
APA (American Psychological
  Association), 299–308
Applied research, 8–9
Approaches to research, 10
Aptitude tests, 146
Arbitrary language, 37–38
Aristotelian thinking, 37–38
ASCD (Association for Supervi-
  sion and Curriculum Devel-
  opment), 5, 214

315